FROM WEDDED WIFE
TO LESBIAN LIFE

Stories of Transformation

Edited by Deborah Abbott and Ellen Farmer

The Crossing Press
Freedom, CA 95019

Photo Credits

Blake C. Aarens by Jen Willman, Deborah Abbott by Rebecca Tavish, Tina Buttry and Gale Edeawo by Coleen Douglas, Ellen Farmer by Todd Tsukushi and Coleen Douglas, Dr. Zandra Johnson-Rolón by Karen Borchers, Joan Larkin by Diane Edington, Stella Lopez-Armijo by Cathy Cade, Esther O'Donald © by Jude Keith, Ekua Omosupe by Maria Dávila, Sharon 'Joh' Paloma by Helga Motley, Juana Maria Gonzalez Paz © by Paz Press, Minnie Bruce Pratt © by Joan E. Biren, Margaret Randall © by Colleen McKay

Copyright © 1995 by Deborah Abbott and Ellen Farmer

Cover design by Bruce Lee/ Book design by Victoria May

Printed in the U.S.A.

3rd printing, 1997

Our thanks to the following authors for granting us permission to reprint their work in this anthology. Copyright for all works published in this anthology, unless otherwise stated, belong to the authors, and the works cannot be copied, reprinted, or excerpted without their written consent.

"Change" by Ellen Bass first appeared in *The Courage to Heal*, New York: Perenniel Library, 1988. Reprinted by permission. Copyright © 1988 by Ellen Bass.

"The Bridge Builder," Kathleen Boatwright, from *Making History: The Struggle for Gay and Lesbian Rights 1945-1990* by Eric Marcus. Copyright © 1992 by Eric Marcus. Reprinted by permission of HarperCollins Publishers, Inc.

Excerpts from *Serving in Silence* by Margarethe Cammermeyer. Copyright © 1994 by Margarethe Cammermeyer. Used by permission of Viking Penguin, a division of Penguin Books USA, Inc.

Bowen, Angela: author passage from *Lesbians at Midlife: The Creative Transition*, edited by B. Sang, J. Warshow, and A. Smith. Minneapolis: Spinsters Ink, 1991. Available from Spinsters Ink, 32 E. First St. #330, Duluth, MN 55802. Reprinted by permission.

Kadi, Joanna, "A Lesbian Love Letter" first appeared in a slightly different form in *Piece of my Heart: A Lesbian of Colour Anthology*. Anthologized by Makeda Silvera, Sister Vision Black Women and Women of Colour Press, Toronto, Ontario, Canada. Reprinted by permission of the author. Copyright © 1991 by Joanna Kadi.

Knight-López, Shirley, "Haciendo un lugar seguro para todos," first came to our attention through an article written by Leslie Smith for "Lavender Reader, News and Reviews for Santa Cruz County's Gay and Lesbian Community," Fall, 1994.

Larkin, Joan, "Want" first appeared in somewhat different form in *Hanging Loose 63* (1993). Copyright © 1993 by Joan Larkin; reprinted by permission. "Robert" first appeared in *Outweek*, June 5, 1991. Copyright © 1991 by Joan Larkin; reprinted by permission.

Lopez-Armijo, Stella, "For the Softness of a Woman" was first published in a slightly different form in *A Lesbian Photo Album: The Lives of Seven Lesbian Feminists* by Cathy Cade, Waterwoman Press, 1987.

Paz, Juana Maria Gonzalez, "From Battered Wife to Lesbian Land," was first published in a different form in "Sin Fronteras: A Gay Latino Journal" in 1984. It was a prize winner in the 1983 Gay and Lesbian Latino/a Essay Contest sponsored by Gay and Lesbian Latinos Unidos de Los Angeles. It also appeared in *Out of the Class Closet, Lesbians Speak*, a 1994 book published by The Crossing Press.

Pratt, Minnie Bruce, "The Laughing Place" first appeared in *Crime Against Nature*, Firebrand Books, Ithaca, New York. Copyright © 1989 by Minnie Bruce Pratt. Reprinted by permission of the author and publisher.

Excerpt from "Anger and Tenderness" is reprinted from *Of Woman Born: Motherhood as Experience and Institution* by Adrienne Rich, by permission of the author and W. W. Norton & Company, Inc. Copyright © 1986, 1976 by W. W. Norton & Company, Inc.

Excerpt from "A communal poetry" is reprinted from *What Is Found There: Notebooks on Poetry and Politics* by Adrienne Rich, by permission of the author and W. W. Norton & Company, Inc. Copyright © 1993 by Adrienne Rich.

Library of Congress Cataloging-in-Publication Data

From wedded wife to lesbian life: stories of transformation / [edited by] Ellen Farmer and Deborah Abbott.

    p. cm.

    Includes bibliographical references.

    ISBN 0-89594-766-8 (paper)

    1. Lesbians—United States—Social conditions. 2. Lesbians—United States—Psychology. 3. Lesbians—United States—Family relationships. 4. Married women—United States—Psychology. 5. Coming out (Sexual orientation)—United States. I. Farmer, Ellen. II. Abbott, Deborah.

HQ75.6.U5F76 1995

305.48'9664--dc20

                                         95-20301

                                           CIP

Acknowledgments

I give thanks to my mother Nettie Batinovich Abbott, who listened with infinite patience to the hundreds of poems I began cranking out at age six and whose indomitable strength gave me the courage to take pride in all of who I am. Even as she may be cringing to have my 'lifestyle' made so public, I hope she may let herself take some credit for my forthright spirit. To my father, Charles Abbott, whose affection and steady acceptance have made it possible to not only produce a book, but one in which the "L" word is mentioned at least once on every page. To my sons, Matthew and Forrest Abbotmoore, who are becoming fine young men in spite of all the grilled cheese sandwiches they had to endure in order to let this book come into being. To my ex-husband and co-parent, for doing his share so that there was time to write and edit, and for respecting my sexual nature even as it contradicts his religious beliefs.

I give deep appreciation to my friend and colleague, Amber Coverdale Sumrall, without whose unflagging support and unfailing advice on literary and related matters, I may have never even envisioned this book.

Thanks to Sue Greene, my partner in the beginning stages of this anthology, for her steadfast belief in me that surpassed my own at times, and for her fine, methodical mind which made the enormity of this project—threatening to engulf me on more than one occasion—manageable. To my current partner, Rebecca Tavish, who came into my life just when I needed her, for her proofreading, photographic and other essential talents, which have made late but lasting contributions to both the coeditor and the book. Thanks also to Sue Wanenmacher, Gypsy Powis, Marsha Isaacson, Kim Tyler, and Katie Elliot-McCrea for their keen editorial insights, late-night brainstorming, honest appraisals, and general sustenance through different and sometimes difficult phases of this three-year endeavor.

And most of all, enormous gratitude to my longtime friend, Gail Brenner, who served as an intimate witness to my transition from wedded wife to lesbian life, and whose love and friendship are more valuable to me than just about anything.

Deborah Abbott
March 1995
Santa Cruz, California

First, thanks to the authors for their generosity of spirit and patience with the editing process. For references, ideas, encouragement, and discussion I want to thank Jacqueline Marie, Arlyn Osborne, Bettina Aptheker, Cathy Cade, Adrienne Rich, Lauren Suhd, Nancy Bereano, Beatriz Lopez-Flores, Crystal Jang, Paula Gunn Allen, Cristina Case, Kamari Clarke, Trinity Ordona, Sharon Lim-Hing, Irene Reti, Valerie Chase, Eric Lane, Ellen Bass, Sarah Rabkin, Carol Howard, Robin Drury, Yael Lachman, and Jude Todd. My gratitude goes out to Zane Smith, Steve Turner of the Santa Cruz/Monterey local of the National Writer's Union, and Stephen Camber of the California Lawyers for the Arts for sound advice. I especially wish to thank my co-worker, Alexa Keihl-Valles, for the endless hours she spent keeping our office together when I was distracted. I am forever in her debt for her cheerful willingness to listen to my wild schemes while at the same time reminding me to meet our deadlines. Laura Davis gave generously of her time, helping us reel in our ideas and commit them to paper. Karen Narita, of The Crossing Press, devoted herself to this project in a way that guaranteed its quality.

Without the reliable, sensitve co-parenting partnership I've shared for 12 years with Steve Farmer, I would have had no time to coordinate an anthology. Not only does he listen to the children when they have concerns, but he talks it all over with me so we can come to consensus about what to do, even though we've lived in separate homes for many years. And he has unlearned homophobia in order to help his kids cope. I've watched him go from being fearful and cynical to being open-minded and appreciative of the challenges facing some very valuable human beings—the dykes in his life. I'm also glad I got out of his way so he could find a wonderful partner. I'm extremely proud of our children, Scott and Janna, who bring home interesting friends from great families, proving to me that people are not all from "Leave it to Beaver's" neighborhood and no one wants or expects them to be.

I gratefully acknowledge my open-minded parents for their enthusiasm for this project, the love they show my children and my partner, and the gracious way they retreat to their motor home when I have to work.

And to my partner, Coleen, I offer my sincerest gratitude, for the depth of her intuition and perception, her meticulous editing skills and considerable talent as a photographer, the sweetness of her love, and the way she leads lively dinner table discussions and keeps the kids happy on long car trips. Together we are making our contribution to gay and lesbian rights.

Ellen Farmer
March 1995
Santa Cruz, California

Table of Contents

Preface

Welcome to the world of formerly married lesbians—a world where seemingly ordinary women go about their lives in the wake of an extraordinary transformation. At one time these women stood before the priest, the rabbi, the preacher, the judge—repeated vows and clutched bouquets. As wives, they did their best to fulfill a host of expectations. But their marriages didn't ring true. Now each of these women is a lesbian—the quintessential gay divorcée.

From Wedded Wife to Lesbian Life is a collection of stories compiled by two of us who've been there. In spite of our attempts to note patterns and draw conclusions about the motivations of our authors, we've learned that their stories are as different as their birthplaces and family backgrounds. And while many described the coming out experience as a coming home of sorts, each creates a unique place for herself in the lesbian community.

You may be picking up this book for a number of reasons. Maybe you're curious, intrigued by the contradiction. Opening these pages, you're asking *Don't all lesbians get crushes on their high school gym teachers? Don't they all know?* Not necessarily. You'll discover a housewife, well into her 40's, who falls head-over-heels for the new gal in town. You'll also meet women who *did* know early on, and married to "straighten out," then took decades finding the courage to resume their lesbian lives.

You may be picturing lurid scenes here, wondering *Aren't innocent wives being spirited out of their marriages by seductive lesbians?* If so, you'll be surprised to meet more than one wife whose husband arranged a ménage à trois, only to find himself the odd man out. You'll also enjoy the story of the pregnant young wife making a pass at a thoroughly unnerved lesbian.

Some of you may expect to find horror stories, asking *Did these wives have terrible husbands who drove them into the arms of other women?* There *are* some shocking accounts here. You will read of an abusive husband who wins custody of his kids, and witness a Mormon woman leave her husband when she discovers he has turned their rumpus room into a meeting place for members of the Aryan Nations. Yet there are even more writers describing perfectly nice husbands... and perfectly miserable marriages.

Some of you may be drawn to this book with the question *Why on earth would a woman trade in all the benefits of marriage for such a controversial lifestyle?* Ask the sansei mother who finally decided honesty was the most important example for her children, rather than trying to fulfill the expectations of her Japanese culture. Other women who "had it all," felt something was missing or wrong, though they couldn't say what. And once they found it—in the form of a woman—were willing to take enormous risks and make tremendous sacrifices, proclaiming "In spite of it all, it's worth it."

Naturally, many of you may be reading to find out about sex. *Do women leave their husbands because lesbian sex is so much better?* While we're not going to give that answer away just yet, JoAnn Loulan and several other writers will fill you in on the before-and-after between the sheets.

For those of you who are formerly married lesbians yourselves, you may be holding this book in your hands exclaiming *It's about time!* We agree. When we began researching this project in 1992 we were amazed to discover that, in spite of numerous books and articles describing the coming out process, there was rare mention of an ex-husband. It was a challenge finding our writers. We found formerly married lesbians who were too afraid of repercussions from employers or landlords to write or use their real names. Some felt protective of loved ones. We found some who'd had bad experiences revealing their personal histories to lifelong lesbians. We spoke to many women who found it too painful to conjure up their marriages for publication.

But along with all the women who had to say no, we were delighted to find lesbians with a wealth of experience from a wide range of classes and ages, offering their stories for this volume. You'll hear from Ekua Omosupe, who as a child discovered her passion for girls, only to have her love forced underground by prying relatives. And from Mardi Richmond, who drank to keep her feelings for women at bay. You will read about Reva Talleygrone, who had to remodel her entire house before she understood what really needed fixing. And you'll hear Ann Kwong's uplifting account of sitting with her ex-husband watching her daughter and lover sing together in the church choir. There is also the story of Stella Lopez-Armijo, a retired grandmother and community volunteer, who has lived happily with her partner, Ina, for fifteen years.

We guarantee that *From Wedded Wife to Lesbian Life* will amuse, arouse, unsettle, and astonish you. This is a book full of heart. It's about women finding and loving other women, and in doing so, coming to fully honor themselves. It's about resilient and ingenious women who have weathered ostracism and rallied against homophobia in its myriad forms. It's about ordinary women who, in the face of challenges from without and within, have prospered, and in these pages share their extraordinary, passionate lives.

Marge Frantz, 1934 and today.

Introduction

MARGE FRANTZ

From Wedded Wife to Lesbian Life is full of rich and complex stories, told in each writer's unique voice. I've noticed a pattern, discernible in many of them, one that helped me understand my own personal history more clearly. It is this: Most of us experienced crushes on women or inklings, intimations, inchoate feelings somewhere along our various paths—some early, some late—that the object of our desire was a woman.

At the same time, all of us heard nonstop social messages, overt and covert, both positive and negative. The first: marry, and you'll get a bundle of heterosexual privileges; the second: you'd better forget those inklings, that was just a stage, a schoolgirl crush, you'll get over it but watch your step or you'll pay a very heavy price. These bribes, warnings, prohibitions, constraints, sanctions, assumptions pressed upon all of us from all sides with extraordinary power and did the work they were intended to do: they sent many of us into denial, causing us to hide our own feelings from ourselves, leaving us afraid, confused or uncomprehending, or trapped, or full of internalized homophobia. We wanted to believe we were "normal" or at least that we would live "normal" lives; we wanted to belong; we were fearful of social opprobrium and penalties; especially, we feared loss of economic support or jobs or children. We married.

Despite all of the cultural conditioning, however, there came that revelatory moment, that crucial awakening, like sunshine cutting through the fog—or was it burning desire and passion that caused the fog to lift? At some point, sometimes many years later, we somehow overcame the denial that had been caused by all those social expectations and demands, we managed to step outside and defy the whole heterosexual imperative, and we realized that lesbianism was a genuine, live option for us. It was never easy to renounce our heterosexual privilege, but we did come into possession of our real feelings and desires and found the courage and the clarity to claim and act on them.

Because much lesbian life, however defined, has been an underground affair, it is easier for a historian to locate and trace changes in social prescriptions and expectations than to trace the responses of women to them.

Evidence, the historians' standby, is in short supply, especially about the lives of working-class women and women of color who most lack time for journal writing and other ways of recording their lives. Even when we discover revealing private journals and letters from long ago, they tend to be self-censoring about the intimate details that would illuminate the nature of the relationships fully. Much lesbian history includes guesswork, is full of open questions, and will certainly have to be rethought and rewritten as we learn more.

And sometimes, when we do find fascinating tidbits of evidence, it isn't easy to interpret them without imposing contemporary, anachronistic and distorted readings on them. Here's a quote, for example, from an essay of William Cullen Bryant in 1843, about two women he had met in Vermont:

> In their youthful days, they took each other as companions for life, and this union, no less sacred to them than the tie of marriage, has subsisted, in uninterrupted harmony, for 40 years, during which they have shared each others' occupations and pleasures and works of charity while in health, and watched over each other tenderly in sickness...They slept on the same pillow and had a common purse, and adopted each others' relatives and...I would tell you of their dwelling, encircled with roses...and I would speak of the friendly attentions which their neighbors, people of kind hearts and simple manners, seem to take pleasure in bestowing upon them.[1]

We possess many nineteenth-century accounts, as well, of intimate, long-term relations between married women who did not live together but wrote constantly and visited often. They were considered perfectly "normal," and referred to as "romantic friendships." With or without the shared pillows, they were assumed to be asexual, chaste and innocent, and in many cases, they may have been. It would be a mistake to try to "fit" past relationships into modern polarized categories of homosexual/heterosexual.

We do know that the reigning Victorian ideology held that "proper" women simply weren't sexual creatures. Sex was about procreation; romantic love had no connection with sexual desire; it was on a higher plane. In the middle- and upper-class worlds, marriage was de rigueur, virtually the only avenue for economic survival as well as for status and respect; spinsterhood was considered degrading. But women and men, husband and wife, had little in common, inhabited separate spheres in the economic and social world. Woman spent their lives largely with other women, and close emotional bonds between them were expected and encouraged. Their letters reveal intensity and passion. Here is Emily Dickinson, writing to Sue Gilbert, her future sister-in-law:

> Susie, will you indeed come home next Saturday, and be my own again, and kiss me as you used to?...I hope for you so much and feel so eager for you, feel that I cannot wait, feel that Now I must have you, that the expectation to see your face again makes me feel hot and feverish, and my heart beats so fast...[2]

But it is necessary to read these words with a nineteenth-century cast of mind, not a twentieth-century one. Margaret Fuller, for example, writing in the 1840's, spoke of the superior love between women as a love "purely intellectual and spiritual, unprofaned by any mixture of lower instincts."[3] She was reflecting a widely, but probably not universally held, attitude of the period, a primary ingredient of the social climate of the time.

This climate began to change after the Civil War. As industrialization and urbanization grew apace, factories continued to pay working-class women barely enough for survival. But new jobs opened up for young, middle-class women in rapidly expanding offices (previously, all male establishments), and the possibility arose that some women might be able to live independently, rather than be forced into marriage, home and domesticity.

At the same time, the nineteenth-century "woman movement," as it called itself, had begun to make gains in its longstanding campaign to open higher education to women. By 1880, there were over 40,000 women attending colleges. By the turn of the century, these "New Women" were a much remarked-upon media phenomenon, and the word "feminism" first appeared. Not so coincidentally, the word "lesbian" also came into use for the first time.

It wasn't too clear what these newly-educated and newly-liberated-from-marriage women were going to do with their lives. They wanted to use their newly-freed talents for useful purposes but the society offered no clear professional path for women. A handful, Jane Addams and Lillian Wald the best known of them, founded inner-city settlement houses—what we would probably call community centers today. These were centers where women and sometimes a few men actually lived and worked together on an amazing range of social reform causes, attempting to ameliorate poverty and all its attendant ills for new immigrants and factory workers and their children. The settlement house movement took off and before long there were 400 around the country, full of young women college graduates and trade union organizers and pioneers in what would become the social work profession.

The all-female societies of women's colleges and settlement houses were important in creating opportunities for lesbian relationships among middle-class women. Between 1880 and 1900, 10 percent of American women did not marry; of those with college educations, 50 percent remained single.

Many of the women who met in these female enclaves and in reform activities became couples who lived together lifelong, and it seems likely that if women's friendships of an earlier generation were characterized by the Victorian asexuality, the social climate at the turn of the century changed the attitudes and behavior of many of them.

These women did not take pains to conceal the intimacy of their relationships. For example, Jane Addams, who was famous for her work in creating a more humane society, a Nobel Peace Prize winner, and voted America's outstanding woman in poll after poll, made no secret of her 40 year relationship with Mary Rozet Smith. In their travels, Addams wired ahead to reserve a large double bed.[4] Willa Cather and Edith Lewis, Mt. Holyoke College president

Mary Woolley and Jeannette Marks, novelist Sarah Orne Jewett and Annie Fields are other famous examples. There was even a name for these relationships: Boston marriages.

But the public acceptance of romantic friendships was about to change. In earlier circumstances, these relationships had not challenged the norms of traditional marriage. Now, U.S. society was already uneasy on many fronts. The 1890's had been a decade of economic depression and much social turbulence. The Progressive movement of the early twentieth century spawned a social activism of epic proportions, with women as major initiators and participants. A growing feminist movement was agitating for birth control, a few of its most radical members were even advocating "free love," and this pressure was undermining the strictures of Victorian morality and the idea of asexual women. With the possibility of increasing economic independence, women's love for each other appeared threatening to social stability.

It seems to have struck "sex o'clock in America," the magazine *Current Opinion* lamented in 1913. Was it coincidental that at this juncture, studies by British and German sexologists began to be widely published (Krafft-Ebing, Ellis, Freud) describing women's love for each other as sick, morbid, an anomaly of nature, pathological and deviant? "Sexual inversion" became the diagnostic label.

For the first time, lesbianism was used not to describe acts, but a category of person, an identity. The new public discussion of a previously taboo subject introduced many women to the phenomenon of women-loving women. Lesbians gained a name and for some, a recognition that their feelings were real and shared by others. The faint beginnings of a subculture, closeted to be sure, formed in bars and social gathering places in a few cities. Some lesbians became conscious of themselves as a group and conscious of their oppression. But, given the nature of the sexology discourse, it would have been almost impossible for these women not to internalize the stigma of abnormality the "experts" were writing about so voluminously.

Nevertheless, especially in Greenwich Village and Harlem, tiny oases from "straight" society did emerge. For African American lesbians, the black bohemian world and the show business life offered a relatively safe refuge. Such famous blues singers as Ma Rainey, Bessie Smith, Jackie "Moms" Mabley, Josephine Baker and Gladys Bentley did not have to sacrifice their sexuality to be successful and their often-explicit lyrics did not appear to be a serious liability.

A few women in the late nineteenth and early twentieth centuries chose to escape the earlier Victorian ideology in another way: to pass as men, sometimes taking brides of their own.

But back in the straight world, with the twist in social attitudes resulting from the sexologists' derogatory diagnoses, nineteenth-century homosocial relationships were now regarded in a new light. Many letters and journals were no doubt destroyed. One of many examples we happen to know about: in the

1920's when Emily Dickinson's letters were edited for publication, Sue Gilbert's daughter expunged the loving references. The feminist movement was lesbian-baited for the first but not the last time.

Along with the attack on lesbianism came a new heterosexual norm—sexual pleasure, romantic love and companionship characterized the new "companionate" marriage hailed in the 1920's (premarital and extramarital sex were still taboo). A new consumerism rode rampant; greatly expanded advertising exploited female sexuality; sales of cosmetics and the new fashion industry boomed. Charm schools, dance crazes, the automobile, and changing dating patterns marked the flapper scene.

The feminist movement of 1890-1920 helped set in motion the "new morality." Not really a "sexual revolution," as it was often called, it was more like a few liberal reforms. Despite the recognition of women as sexual beings, male domination and compulsory heterosexuality continued, and would remain largely unchallenged until the next feminist movement of the late 1960's.

Of course, women's emotional and erotic life continued, though for many years it was completely ignored by historians. This denial was well illustrated in the recent response to revelations about Eleanor Roosevelt's relationship with Lorena Hickok and other lesbians in the 1920s and '30s. There are available no less than 3,000 letters between Roosevelt and Hickok, 2,336 written by Roosevelt. They leave no ambiguity about their love for each other. "I remember...the feeling of that soft spot just north-east of the corner of your mouth against my lips..." or "Hick, darling, all day I've thought of you. Oh! I want to put my arms around you. I ache to hold you close..." [5] But a biography of Hickok in 1980 by Doris Faber called it "unthinkable" to label the correspondence "lesbian."[6] It was only a schoolgirl crush, she insisted, and to call their attachment anything else would be "immoral." Faber wanted to "save" Roosevelt's reputation and pleaded unsuccessfully with the archivist to lock up the papers until the year 2000. Blanche Weisen Cook's 1992 biography of Eleanor Roosevelt finally does the subject justice.[7]

The 1930's depression years meant terrible unemployment problems for millions of people, and women became the scapegoat of choice. Many argued that if working women would just leave their jobs, there would be enough for men. Hard times can fall especially hard on lesbians, since they have only themselves to rely on for support. Some got married because they saw no viable alternatives. Unfavorable images of lesbians, by now common in books and plays, made women too fearful to do otherwise. Some lesbians married gay men as covers to protect themselves in a period when the stigma of lesbianism was so powerful. Some women, realizing their lesbianism while married, stayed in their marriages and led lesbian lives simultaneously. Akasha (Gloria) Hull's biographical introduction to the diary of the African American poet and writer Alice Dunbar Nelson[8] reveals her secret lesbian liaisons in the 1930's while she was married. She was part of a network of bisexual friends, all of whom were prominent in the middle-class black community.

World War II ushered in four years of greater social and economic freedom for women. Suddenly a wide variety of skilled jobs, never before open to them, became available. In 1943, I myself was able to leave clerical work for the first time when I was hired for a coveted union organizing job. During this period, pants became acceptable garb for women, a major personal liberation. And the Women's Army Corps, with equivalents in the other branches of the service, created new all-female worlds. The need for military personnel was so great that, with minimal discretion, lesbians were fairly safe. Orders forbade witch hunts, and leniency was often the rule. The problem of lesbians finding other lesbians was quickly solved.

An interview with World War II WAC sergeant Johnnie Phelps is instructive. In response to a request from Gen. Eisenhower that she ferret out the lesbians in her battalion, she wrote:

> Yessir. If the General pleases, I will be happy to do this investigation...But, sir, it would be unfair of me not to tell you, my name is going to head the list...You should also be aware that you're going to have to replace all the file clerks, the section heads, most of the commanders, and the motor pool...I think you should also take into consideration that there have been no illegal pregnancies, no cases of venereal disease, and the General himself has been the one to award good conduct commendation and service commendations to these members of the WAC detachment.[9]

General Eisenhower's response: Cancel the order.

The end of the war, however, produced a far chillier climate. The military, needing the women no longer, conducted "lesbian hunts" and sent thousands of homosexual personnel home with dishonorable and undesirable discharges. Port cities became home to lesbian subcultures, now large enough to enable bars catering to lesbians to survive and flourish. In the bars, working-class and young lesbians found the only public places where they did not have to hide their identity; here, a culture and a community came to life. But the bars were dangerous spots, often raided by police.[10] Middle-class lesbians, more fearful of arrest and sometimes uncomfortable in the erotically-charged bar scene, turned instead to women's professional organizations and friendship networks.

The war was hardly over when the cold war began, soon followed by what we now call McCarthyism—more than a dozen years of fierce repression of political dissidents and their friends and allies—years of fear, suspicion, conformity and persecution of leftists in the name of protecting national security. Few people realize that gay men and lesbians, regardless of their political proclivities, were victims along with those accused of communist sympathies. President Eisenhower issued an executive order declaring homosexuality grounds for dismissal from a government job and many private employers followed suit; legislative bodies around the country held hearings on suspected homosexuals in government. The FBI conducted spying, mail opening, and general harassment of sexual "deviants" as threats to national security. Newspapers printed names and addresses of those arrested in bar raids; there were scare headlines like "Perverts Called Government Peril."[11] The American Civil Liberties Union refused to defend homosexuals.

The military now went after lesbians in the service with sexual surveillance, encouraging Navy WAVES to inform on each other. A WAVE who confided in her commanding officer could unknowingly initiate an anti-lesbian purge. A 1952 WAVE lecture program, in stark contrast to wartime orientations, branded lesbians as sexual vampires—manipulative, dominant perverts who greedily seduced innocent women, leading them down a path of addiction, degeneracy, loneliness and even murder and suicide. In fact, the purges themselves led to two documented suicides. Military discharges, on grounds of homosexuality, represented a lifelong stigma, precluding civilian employment with the government and elsewhere.

While the 1950's were a scary time, historian John D'Emilio, in his study of this period, comes up with a silver lining of sorts: "The tightening web of oppression in McCarthy's America helped to create the minority it was meant to isolate."[12] That minority, and the organizing set in motion by repression, led to fundamental changes in the social climate that make our lives so much more livable today.

The first formal lesbian organization in the U.S., the Daughters of Bilitis (D.O.B.), was very quietly founded in 1955 by Del Martin, Phyllis Lyon, and six other lesbians as a social club for lesbians who wanted a safe place to dance. Isolated and few in number, they nevertheless educated themselves and the public, created dialogue with sympathetic church leaders and medical personnel, and informed bar patrons about their legal rights. Despite few resources, the hostile climate, and police harassment, the group survived, published *The Ladder* from 1956 to 1970, established chapters in a few cities, and at least on a very small scale, challenged the public image of lesbians as "sinful perverts." For many women, D.O.B. or *The Ladder* was their only connection to a lesbian culture.

In "A Portrait of the Older Lesbian," Monika Kehoe says: "Anyone over 60 in 1985 grew up in an era when homosexuality was unmentionable, unthinkable, a sin, a crime, a disease, and for the great majority of the population, unheard of."[13] I was 63 in 1985 and I know all too well what Kehoe means. I fell in love with a woman in 1961 in Berkeley. Does that sound like a liberated time and place? Not so. I was 39, married, with four children between the ages of 4 and 11. I knew exactly one other lesbian couple willing to mention the "L" word. I had heard there were lesbian bars, but I didn't go to bars of any kind. I had never heard of D.O.B. or any other such groups. It was a long time before I could face giving up my marriage and the safety it bestowed on me; all I could imagine was to live a life of subterfuge. It is hard for lesbians today to know just how lonely it was. I will always be grateful beyond measure to the young lesbians in the early 1970s who courageously opened new paths.

The '70s were the years that saw the emergence of a newly energized, militant gay liberation movement, building, of course, on the struggles and experience of the civil rights movement, the anti-war movement and the women's movement. Charlotte Bunch, a pioneer during those years, who left her marriage to become one of the most eloquent voices of the gay movement, looks back on the accomplishments of the lesbians of that decade:

> We brought gayness out of the closet; we forced an acknowledgement of lesbian existence. We put lesbian and gay rights on the human rights agenda; it can at least be said openly. We've created a thriving subculture for women that has been fueled by lesbian energy. We've developed an analysis of our oppression adding to the understanding of sexism, an analysis of heterosexism and homophobia. And we've begun to build positive self-images so that as lesbians we can now see ourselves as people with joys and problems like anybody else...In the last decade we have made very powerful changes in our own lives and in other people's lives.[14]

The momentum of the '70s has continued until now. That's not to say the job is done, of course. Homophobia is alive and well and threatening in new and ominous ways. Despite the 1990s backlash, however, women's option of leaving a marriage is now a visible reality; increasing numbers of us are out there for all to see. But the pressures that keep women in marriages have not lost their power. Adrienne Rich summarizes them:

> Women have married because it was necessary, in order to survive economically, in order to have children who would not suffer economic deprivation or social ostracism, in order to remain respectable, in order to do what was expected of women, because coming out of 'abnormal' childhoods they wanted to feel 'normal' and because heterosexual romance has been represented as the great female adventure, duty and fulfillment.

She adds, "We may faithfully or ambivalently have obeyed the institution, but our feelings—and our sensuality—have not been tamed or contained within it."[15]

It is easier to leave a marriage now, but it's never easy. It's easier because in many places there are now networks of supporting institutions and grassroots groups ready to help.

Those of us who have led the way, the *marriage resisters*, as Adrienne Rich has called us, by our openness, by our witness, have changed social attitudes and created new social possibilities; and as more and more of us act on our feelings, it becomes even more possible for those who follow.

Notes:
1   Lillian Faderman, *Odd Girls and Twilight Lovers, A History of Lesbian Life in Twentieth Century America* (New York: Columbia University Press, 1991), p. 1.

2   Lillian Faderman, *Surpassing the Love Of Men: Romantic Friendship and Love Between Women from the Renaissance to the Present* (New York: Wm. Morrow & Co., 1981), p. 176.

3   Ibid., p. 160.

4   Blanche Weisen Cook, "Female Support Networks and Political Activism," in Nancy Cott and Elizabeth Pleck, eds., *A Heritage of Their Own* (New York: Touchstone, 1979), p. 419.

5   Blanche Weisen Cook, *Eleanor Roosevelt, 1884-1933* Vol. One (New York: Viking, 1992), pp. 479, 488.

6   Blanche Weisen Cook, "Review Essay, The Life of Lorena Hickok: ER's Friend by Doris Faber," *Feminist Studies 6*, No. 3 (Fall 1980), p. 514.

7   Blanche Weisen Cook, *Eleanor Roosevelt*, Vol. One.

8   Gloria T. (Akasha) Hull, ed., *Give Us This Day, The Diary of Alice Dunbar Nelson* (New York: W. W. Norton & Co., 1984), pp. 24-25.

9   Faderman, *Odd Girls*, p. 119.

10 See Elizabeth Lapovsky Kennedy and Madeline D. Davis, *Boots of Leather, Slippers of Gold, The History of a Lesbian Community* (New York: Routledge, 1993).

11 Andrea Weiss and Greta Schiller, *Before Stonewall: The Making of a Gay and Lesbian Community* (Tallahassee, Fl: Naiad Press, 1988), p. 42.

12 John D'Emilio, "Gay Politics and Community in San Francisco Since Word War II," in Martin Duberman, Martha Vicinus and George Chauncy, Jr., eds., *Hidden from History, Reclaiming the Gay and Lesbian Past* (New York: New American Library, 1980), p. 459.

13 Monika Kehoe, ed., *Historical, Literary and Erotic Aspects of Lesbianism* (New York: Harrington Park Press, 1986), p. 157.

14 Charlotte Bunch, *Lesbianism in the '80s* (Denver, Co.: Inkling Press, 1981), p. 1.

15 Adrienne Rich, "Compulsory Heterosexuality and Lesbian Existence," in *Blood, Bread and Poetry, Selected Prose 1979-1985* (New York: W.W. Norton & Co., 1986), p. 59.

"I have a very clear, keen memory of myself the day after I was married: I was sweeping a floor. Probably the floor did not really need to be swept; probably I simply did not know what else to do with myself. But as I swept that floor I thought: "Now I am a woman. This is an age-old action, this is what women have always done." I felt I was bending to some ancient form, too ancient to question. *This is what women have always done.*"

—Adrienne Rich
Of Woman Born, 1976

Stella Lopez-Armijo, 1956 and left, with her partner.

For the Softness of a Woman

STELLA LOPEZ-ARMIJO

I was born in Albuquerque in 1934. We moved to the San Francisco Bay Area when I was about eight and I grew up not a quarter of a mile from where Ina and I lived for fourteen years. Part of my family is still in Albuquerque and small towns of New Mexico, part of it is here. There's always been a lot of traveling back and forth.

I do not have too many memories of my childhood. I do vividly remember leaving right after school, going to the fields and orchards to harvest the fruit and tomatoes. We changed clothes in the car and worked until dark. When we got home we just fell out on the front lawn together, we were so tired.

I was so naïve when I was a child. We were brought up in a very, very Catholic family. Never eat meat on Fridays, go to confession on Saturday, always go to church on Sunday. All my friends were in the church choir.

At first when I was growing up I thought I was Spanish. My mother has always believed she's Spanish. I didn't know I was a Mexican until I started seeing pictures of my ancestors. In New Mexico, when I was growing up, if you were Mexican you weren't treated all too well, but if you were Spanish they really thought you were something. My father's mother is from Spain, the rest are Mexican Indians. I remember having to make a fuss in Albuquerque once to get served at a Woolworth's. I remember too as a senior in high school my Home Ec teacher having us write down everything we'd had to eat for a week. She looked at my list full of hamburgers and Mexican food, not a vegetable on it, and said, "You ought to get a carrot and wrap a chile around it." That really hurt. I talked back to her, told her, "You hate me because I'm a Mexican, don't you!" I got sent to the dean. About three days later me and my friends got together and stole her apple off her desk. She knew it was me, but, of course, I denied it.

I was a tomboy when I was growing up, but I always figured I'd outgrow it. Even in high school I always wanted to show my girlfriends how tough I was. At the same time, I wasn't doing so well in school and I wanted to drop out and adopt a baby. I played shortstop for the Oakland Recreational Industrial Association team for three years, 1953-56. Some of the women were gay and yet I didn't even know there was any such thing as a gay life. The team partied together a lot because we used to win all the time. Still, it never entered my mind; I was programmed not to know these things existed.

I went to work at Owens-Illinois glass container factory at eighteen. I was just going to work a few months while I was waiting to enter the convent. I had my papers all filled out, but when my friend who was going in with me got married, I backed out.

It was just like family at the "Glass House." We worked in rotating shifts of about three hundred people. We worked five days and got two off, but your days off rotated and might be Tuesday and Wednesday, or your shift might be working nights. So your friends were the people on your shift; that's all you had. We got really, really close.

I had to fight for every promotion I got at O-I, never knowing there were women, feminists, who could have helped me. They made you punch a card to go pee and you had to ask permission of the crew leader, which I eventually was. I used to tell the women, don't ask me, don't punch a card; if you get in trouble, I'll answer for it. It was like a prison.

Since I wasn't going to go into the convent and I was already twenty, I figured it was time I got married. I was very much in love with the man, and I was very happy for seven years. But after a while we lost communication; we didn't know what to say to each other. Helping out around the house didn't bother him. The only thing that did bother him was that I used to beat him in bowling. We're still friends. He's met a lot of my woman lovers and takes us out to dinner. He's close to the kids.

I had four children in less than four years. That's a lot of kids pretty fast, but being a Catholic like I was, I just kept shooting them out like bullets.

The divorce was terribly hard on me. I still thought we could patch things up; we didn't have divorces in my family. And then with four kids we had so many noodles and spaghetti I couldn't swallow them anymore. I'm just now getting back to where I can eat spaghetti a little bit. After the divorce this gay boy came to live with us. I met him through my gay brother. He needed a place to stay and I needed somebody to take care of my kids. He didn't want to work out and I didn't want to work in. It turned out just fine for both of us, and he stayed six years.

I got into the gay life when I was thirty-two. There was this one girl from work who was after me all the time: "Let's go for a ride." I'd say no. Then one time at the bowling alley she touched my knee and it sent chills up my leg. I told my husband, "Let's go home because I don't like what's going on here." But then I would be in bed with my husband and I would be thinking of my woman neighbor across the street. I'd be all turned on and really enjoying what I was doing. I thought there was something wrong with me, that I was the only one who had these feelings, because who do you ask? If I'd had a book or something, I probably wouldn't have gotten married.

A couple of years later, when I got divorced, this same woman said she wanted to introduce me to someone now that I didn't have to worry about my husband. I went over and it was a woman! This woman kissed me and the next thing you know we got to drinking and dancing. We went out a couple of times and then ended up going to bed. I didn't even know what to do. I was scared because I had heard about queers who attack little kids. So the whole sex scene was very scary. When she went to sleep I lay awake the whole night wondering what she was going to do to me if I fell asleep. We laughed about it later. We were together for about six months. With her I don't think it was really love, it was coming out and enjoying the softness of a woman.

Coming out at work was easy. Everyone knew me since I was eighteen. Besides, I had to tell someone, and once one person knows, everyone knows. One gay woman there told me she knew I'd been gay all the time.

I used to hit every gay bar there was. I didn't know there was any place else you could meet women, and I wanted to meet somebody. I would start drinking, and drinking, and drinking. I thought drinking was the gay life, I really did.

I used to hang out at the Carnation Club, a lesbian bar in East Oakland. I didn't play with the Carnation Club softball team, I was too fat by then, but they made me honorary cheerleader. I used to roll up my pants, roll up my shirt, jump up and down and yell. We used to have more damn fun.

It was a very hard decision, but after twenty-six years and with only ten years to retirement, I decided to quit O-I. I was as high as I could get, backup unit foreman, yet I felt like *anyone* could do my job. The pay was lousy, I was commuting fifty miles a day, and I no longer needed the security of seniority for my kids. I had a job lined up at General Motors where my oldest two kids were working, took a two-month's vacation to go to Albuquerque and play around with a lover over there, but when I came back, GM didn't want me. I never thought I'd find myself without a job. Finally, a friend got me into Peterbilt doing truck assembly. I like the work because I like working with tools. When my probation was ending they tried to fire me so I wouldn't get union protection. My best friend at Peterbilt is a gay man; we spotted each other the first day I went to work. He helped me when I was new, showed me how to do things, not like the other men who laughed at me or who were always eyeballing every girl that walked by. I had a run-in with one of the men on the line who kept nude pictures of women on the top of his tool box where everyone had to see them. I had to threaten the foreman that I'd bring pictures of men with great big ding-dongs hanging down for my tool box.

I don't go to church as much as I would like to, but I still follow my religion. I still believe. The first time I told the priest I was a lesbian he told me I couldn't receive the sacraments. I said, I'm happy, I hurt no one, I go out of my way to be good to people. I felt guilty, yet I didn't think I was really doing anything wrong. And I knew the priest wasn't going to change me, *that I knew.* I said to the priest, "O.K., but you can't keep me from the Church." But going to Mass without communion was like going to somebody's house for dinner and you can't sit at the dinner table. I left the Church for a while, but that was even worse.

Then I went to my gay brother who is very, very close to the Church. He showed me a place in the Bible where it didn't say only a woman and a man can be together. It was just a little thread, but we were hanging by that. I went back to confession and I didn't confess the fact that I was a lesbian. I didn't have the priest's absolution, but I figured I had God's. Well, the host caught in my throat! I thought, Oh my God, I have sinned taking this host! I went back to my brother. He said just keep receiving it, it will get easier for you. And it did.

Ina and I were introduced at a Gay Pride Parade and then she called me to find out if I wanted to go to this rally and that political meeting. I said, I don't do that stuff. I asked her if she went to bars. She said no. We didn't think we had anything in common. We went to a movie, she dragged me to a Slightly Older Lesbians meeting, and the next thing I knew I was at an Equal Rights Amendment rally.

Well, she believes in God, but I never dreamed I'd be with a *Mormon*—no drinking, no smoking. She's very active with Mormons for the Equal Rights Amendment and Gay Mormons. I go with her to meetings and rallies around that. I was looking for someone who can speak Spanish and appreciate Spanish music. She had everything but that. I thought, I'll teach her. She remembers what the words mean, but she can't pronounce them. She's found studying Spanish the hardest thing she's ever tried. She's learned to like country and Spanish music though.

A lot of things have changed since I've been with Ina, and I think I'm a better person for it. The first time we were going to the West Coast Women's Music Festival I told Ina I was not going to bare my body and I didn't want her to either. I said, "I'm not sharing you with anybody." But, my goodness, after you go and see all these bare-chested women, you see you're not the only one with a God-given body. I guess I was there three or four hours when I ended up taking my shirt off, too.

I never officially came out to my kids till Ina. I couldn't hide it, I was so happy. I told my gay brother and my nieces and nephews, "If my brothers ever ask you anything, tell them, 'Yes, she is.'" My older brothers are very Mexican in thinking they always have to protect their little sister, even though I'm sixty-one years old! But Ina's accepted now. We've gone on vacation to my brother's in Albuquerque. My mother loves Ina, is always getting Ina to hug her and hold her hand. She doesn't know such things as lesbians exist.

Ina has been encouraging me to go into some kind of community service work. A couple of times I was called over to the hospital where she worked to help as a Spanish translator. My gay brother got me started with a volunteer group, Concilia de la Raza. They need more bilinguals and someone to help run a yard sale and give away free cheese. It's been a long time since I've been around that many Mexicans who weren't relatives. It was very, very refreshing and great to be able to help.

The second obstacle to coming out [in Japan] is the strength of the institution of marriage, and the unchallenged assumption that all people will marry...those who do not marry are considered abnormal or mentally ill (i.e., homosexual), unless they forfeit marriage to care for elderly parents. Also, the institution of arranged marriage and its accompanying concept of marrying for economic or social reasons rather than for romance tends to downplay the importance of sexuality within a marriage and reinforces itself as a social institution.

—A. Kaweah Lemeshewsky,
from "Facing Both Ways: Japanese Lesbians in Japan
and in the U.S.," in *Between the Lines*

Ellen Symons, right, with her partner.

...on her wedding day.

Parallel Universes

ELLEN SYMONS

One story I tell myself each year is how we came together, Marjorie and me. Our husbands introduced us, but they wouldn't thank you for reminding them of it. We were married women, a little afraid of everything, relying on our husbands to get us through, and on our marriages for a sense of identity. When we talked later about how we were then, each of us knew she'd felt unfinished, hurting, and waiting. Waiting for the rest of life to come along.

A sense of duty kept me attentive to my husband, Max, and fear made me believe what he told me about the rules of life. Fear and duty weren't the first things you'd notice about me, though. I was fun and agreeable and a bit spunky. I was smart, something of a social critic, and I thought I was a feminist. Maybe that's how I explained it to myself when I agreed to go along with Max and his buddy Brian's plan for an evening of drinking, strip poker and maybe a group thing, Max, Brian, me, and Marjorie. It was feminist to like women, wasn't it, I asked myself? I didn't necessarily mean that in a sexual sense, but it followed. It was feminist to break down the male barriers of poker and drinking. It was feminist to be gutsy and daring. It also offered an answer to my secret question: what would it be like to touch a woman, to make love?

Marjorie and I were both giggly and nervous and drank too much too fast in order to get through the first awkward hour of conversation. Then the card games started. There was a civilized regression: Crazy Eights...euchre... poker...strip poker. Interspersed with drinking and joking, we all slowly got close to naked. And then what was there left to do? We'd gotten together for a specific reason, after all, though everyone pretended not to know what this was. But it was in all our eyes as we sat around the kitchen table and looked sloppily at each other. Truth-dare-double dare.

Our husbands weren't slow in daring Marjorie and me to touch each other, kiss, take off each other's remaining clothes, lick and bite. We arched in pleasure, showing off our physical compatibility for their reward. They joined in later, and I tried to concentrate on them, but my thoughts and eyes were still on Marjorie. Every time Marjorie's body and mine met, the meanings of sex and pleasure were redefined for me. For the first time, I learned how powerful an orgasm could really be. Later, I learned about being in love.

After that poker night, I spent fuzzy days feeling the aftershocks of an earthquake passing through my life. I would find myself on Marjorie's doorstep, but leave without ringing the bell. I would phone her and hang up before the last digit. Sometimes I would let it ring, have a cautious conversation, suggest shopping or coffee...She never said no.

One afternoon I realized I had been thinking about her every day and night for three weeks. She was in every daydream and fantasy. I understood I needed to tell her that since the poker night—the night we never talked about—every time I saw her, I tasted her on my lips, wanted to taste her again, could remember how her skin felt, could imagine holding her at night, in the morning, in the park in the middle of the afternoon.

Getting the words out was harder than knowing they were true. It took me another week of awkward starts and flushed retreats. One Friday night as we sat in her den watching Bette Davis and Olivia de Haviland while the boys bowled and drank for the umpteenth time that month, I managed to say, "Do you remember...I just wonder if you remember when we played poker...how did you feel, well, the next day? I had a vicious hangover. I just wondered how you felt."

"I had a good time that night," she said, but very softly and looking at her lap. "I was kind of surprised by how...comfortable I felt. At the time, I...wish I remembered better...I was pretty drunk. I'm embarrassed about that. About what you think of me, being drunk and being...passionate. Embarrassed about wanting to try it again."

We were quiet after she said that. I felt paralyzed by knowing that I wouldn't be able to unsay the words once I had let them out. Inside, I was screaming, "I want to kiss you. I need to touch you. I love you." But I felt as if lead weights had been clamped on my tongue, and my mouth had been riveted shut. My fear was so great that eventually my brain forgot what it wanted to shout and I sat in a vacant trance. Ridiculous, that I feared being rejected by this woman who had just told me she wanted to make love to me. But what if I had misinterpreted her or imagined she'd said it just because I wanted so badly for it to have been said? What if I was crazy or dreaming or the biggest fool alive? What if I had slipped into a parallel universe and would slip back again only in time to say the wrong thing to the real Marjorie whose eyes would fill with shock and disgust?

Finally, in slow motion, I turned to look at her again. "Don't miss your chance, don't miss your chance," the frantic flapping bird in my head beat over and over against my skull. "Don't miss it."

"Yes?" I said to her. "Yes," Marjorie echoed. "Yes." Me. "Yes." Her. "Yes." Stronger. Louder. Again. "Yes." "Yes, Marjorie, I want to."

Our first kiss was awkward, facing each other on the couch, our crossed knees between us, fingers gripping the pillows for support. Standing was better. When we turned the TV off and moved to the bedroom, I had a moment of fear again as we started to undress; this made it seem serious, the real thing.

This was not just drunk experimentation or an accidental rumpus room romp. This was grown-up women making love, on purpose, *in bed*, the conjugal monster. What travesty. What rebellion. What freedom.

Ekua Omosupe, as mother, as professor.

The Journey

EKUA OMOSUPE

As a child
I began this journey
to myself
looking for safe harbors
full moons
and a bosom
on which to rest my head

At twelve
I met Annie
a girl
who was also searching
for warmth   comfort   and arms
to hold her tight
we wrestled belly to belly
on the living room sofa
after Momma fell asleep
our eager kisses
and hungry fingers
tasted warm secrets
and sealed a pact between us
girl friends
who swore not to tell
what we found between each other
in the middle of that hot
North Carolina summer

We kissed and licked each others'
disappointments and hurts
to an innocent ecstasy
until
prying eyes and an univited guest

discovered us naked
without excuse
in the middle of the afternoon
on my mother's day bed
we were scared   angry   mute
in the face of accusation and whispers
"funny   funny"
"you girls are not normal"
"normal"
"normal"
we ran from ourselves
and from each other
enemies
who avoided each other's gazes
forgot our pact of sisterhood
and girlfriends
rumors spread
and we used them like stones
against each other
the distance between us grew into a gulf
and we each set sail
in different directions
looking for safe harbors
full moons
a bosom to rest our heads

At twelve
we did not know
that there were others like us
women
who kissed   held hands   made love
to each other in secret
our risk was theirs also

I do not know where
this first lover of mine
has gone to
I do not know what harbors she found
I hope she is safe
in woman arms
and is lulled to sleep with deep heart kisses

I too have traveled far
and battle against my own fears
of being caught naked
again
by prying eyes
and shamed by some one else's fears
on this journey
to myself
at every chance
I anchor at harbors
that feel safe
where
women stand guard
on the shore
and lull me to rest

I learn that safety is where we
make it
and I too
stand guard
at the shores
of women's lives
protecting
nurturing
loving
lulling them to rest

Robin Teresa Santos, 1970, and right, 1994.

Não pica daloroso, não saber sabroso
—As Marias

ROBIN TERESA SANTOS

I did what I did, [went to Vietnam] because I thought if I didn't, I'd lose the love of my family and my community. I am amazed at what I have done for love.
— Tim O'Brien,
author and veteran of the Mei Lei massacre

My great-grandmother was named Maria Helena. My grandmother, Maria Aldora, was the oldest of four sisters—Maria Alicia, Maria Agnes, and Maria Gloria. My family called this powerful coalition of Portuguese women, *As Marias*. This tradition of naming all the girls Maria, of course had to do with the Blessed Virgin.

My great-grandmother's bedroom looked like a side altar at Lourdes. Among the flickering votive lights was a parade of porcelain Saints—Rita, Bernadette, Clara, two different Teresas, Veronica, and many variations of the Blessed Virgin herself. I mimicked *As Marias'* adoration of these icons and relied upon the Blessed Virgin for favors—especially forgiveness.

As Marias, who filled their houses with images of the Blessed Virgin, loved the saints, but did not themselves exhibit qualities of sainthood. Their power was more practical than pious, as they immersed their hands in bowls of oily codfish, onions and garlic, or busied them with the labyrinth crocheting of doilies that covered the arms of sofas and easy chairs. *As Marias* practiced the art of *fofoca* (gossip) and *culpa* (guilt); I admired their common sense and stealthy cunning, and I basked in the fervor of their high emotionality. Since I was the only girl among the young ones in the family, they took a special interest in me. Allied with *As Marias*, I felt protected and right, but the thought of being judged unfavorably by them was intolerable.

From the time I was a young girl, I wanted to be Maria "Something." I wanted a name that evoked images of miracles and apparitions. But between *As Marias* and me, stood my parents, first-generation Portuguese-Americans, for whom the path of assimilation was a non-negotiable way of life.

I grew up in two different worlds; two worlds that often clashed and refused to respect the differences of the other. While my parents had moved into San Leandro—away from Jingle Town, the Portuguese "ghetto" in Oakland, California where my father had been raised—*As Marias* stayed on, sitting on their raised wooden porches at twilight, looking out over their neatly groomed rose bushes and gathering grist for their next gab session.

As Marias held fast to the culture of the old country, while my parents, intent on making those ways invisible, used shame and humiliation as powerful tools to force me to "act American." While *As Marias* taught me Portuguese and encouraged me to march in the Holy Ghost festival processions, my parents warned that the neighbors would think less of me if they found out I was Portuguese.

Something both cultures shared was Catholicism, and by the time I received my First Holy Communion at age seven, I was completely motivated by guilt. I judged myself harshly, carefully applying the Catholic hierarchy of sins to all of my thoughts and feelings.

After my fifteenth birthday, *As Marias* assumed—even though they never talked openly about sex, but only alluded to it in risqué or nervous innuendos—that I would begin to show an interest in boys. The truth was, I disliked boys. My family was infested with them, and I'd spent every family holiday since I could remember being aggravated to tears by their relentless teasing. In high school, I watched as the other girls suddenly became boy crazy; afraid of being labeled a misfit, I kept my aversion to boys to myself.

At the age of sixteen I first realized that I was sexually attracted to girls. My family had taught me that love was always conditional, and I was afraid that if they, or anyone else, knew about my interest in girls, they would humiliate and reject me. So, I said nothing to betray my feelings, but set out, quite successfully, to fit in. I pretended to be interested in the stories of other girls' crushes and sympathetic to their heartbreaks. I made sure I always had a boyfriend and never missed a single prom. Meanwhile, I suffered tremendous self-loathing and emotional isolation.

By the time I was sixteen, I was so terrified of being queer, and so isolated with my fear, that I tried to kill myself by eating a dozen aspirin. I did this in the afternoon while my mother was at work. Lying on my bed, never really believing that twelve aspirin would actually kill me, I felt an odd mixture of relief and disappointment when the only thing that happened was a loud ringing in my ears.

According to my parents, an important part of fitting in was to go to college. After being accepted at nearby Cal State Hayward, I began agonizing over what to major in. My secret desire was to be a physical education teacher. But, I was afraid to major in P.E. because that was where all the queers hung out; so, I chose psychology instead. Like a lot of other psych majors I knew, I hoped that by studying the science of the mind, I'd gain a better understanding of my own confusion.

During my freshman year, I developed an obsessive attraction to Anne, a graduate student who taught tennis at the college. By my second year, I was so terrified of acting on my sexual desires for her that I made an appointment to see a therapist at the college counseling center.

It was the first time I'd ever told anyone my secret, and having confessed, I felt immediately relieved. However, the counselor's nonchalant response was disappointing. "After all," she observed with the calm certainty that comes from self-appointed authority, "you haven't even tried it with men yet; so, how can you know what it is you truly want?" She implied that I was resisting nature. I was resisting something.

"What you need to do," she instructed, as I held my breath waiting for her solution, "is to date more men. Put your femininity forward."

Angry, I acted on her suggestion and slept with as many different men as I could find. This was before AIDS, and I was on The Pill; so, why not? Behaving like an over-sexed Maria Magdalena, I slept with students I'd only casually met in the college cafeteria, picked up guys in bars, and carried on in the parking lots of discotheques. While sampling this smorgasbord of men, I continued to be obsessively attracted to Anne. My behavior and my thoughts would have horrified *As Marias*—had they known.

As Marias never asked how my studies were going, but always wanted to know, "You have *um namorado*?" Of course I couldn't tell them about my one-night stands, and I could see how disappointed they were when I completed four years of college and was still *solteira*.

After graduating, I got a job as a social worker. *As Marias* approved. Helping others was acceptable work for a woman until she was able to get married. I had other motives; by becoming a career woman, I hoped to avoid both marriage and being ostracized by *As Marias*.

I rented my first apartment, furnished it with Danish modern, melmac and aluminum cookware, and proceeded to settle in. I began living two separate lives. On the surface, I pretended I was interested in finding a husband—I told *As Marias* that the right one just hadn't come along yet—while my unspoken desires continued to be toward women.

After graduation, Anne and I became friends, but she had a boyfriend, and I felt so jealous and tense whenever I was around the two of them, I thought I'd explode. I wondered how much longer I would be able to suppress my sexual attraction for her. Still, the thought of acting on my desire scared me to death. I just wanted my lustful feelings to go away, and they always did, temporarily, after I'd had a few drinks or smoked a joint.

These were the early days of the feminist movement, and as my feminist consciousness developed, I began feeling guilty about treating myself like such a commodity. So, I gave up slutting around. This abrupt, self-imposed isolation created an emptiness inside me, and I felt like a misfit caught between two unacceptable options. My loneliness, combined with pressure from my friends to be dating and from my family to be married, put me back on the lookout for a decent, available man. That's when I started dating Mario.

Mario and I had gone to high school together. We were friends, at first mostly by association as we ran with some of the same crowd. During our senior year we became intellectual buddies, hotly debating the relevance of Richard Wright's *Native Son* to Mario's life. We also began playing tennis together. Mario was slow and clumsy, and I consistently beat him, which might have discouraged another man, but only made Mario more interested in a rematch and in our relationship. I found Mario physically attractive and a nice guy although he was somewhat passive and lacked ambition.

After graduation, we had both planned to go on to college. Unfortunately, in response to the escalation of the Vietnam War, the selective service had discontinued student deferments and established a draft lottery. When the numbers were pulled, Mario's birthday came up number one. It was bad luck for Mario and foreshadowed big changes for me.

Mario wouldn't go to Nam, a decision I supported and respected. I wouldn't have gone either. Mario also wasn't willing to go to prison or to Canada into exile for the rest of his life. Mario was Italian-American, his mother's youngest, and leaving his family was out of the question. So, he joined the Peace Corps and was sent to Nicaragua.

In his absence, Mario became more attractive; after a couple of months, our letters became urgently passionate. At the same time, As Marias stepped up the pressure to marry Mario when he returned from the Peace Corps. They said things like, "How many *crianças* are you and Mario going to have?" or "So what, you don't have *anel promessa*… You can still wait for him."

During WW II, my mother had waited for my father to return from overseas, just as As Marias had waited during WWI for their husbands. As Marias had always married their men before packing them off to war, and although my situation was different—I wasn't sending Mario off to war—it was similar enough that they were able to apply their rules to my life.

As Marias' persistent interrogations and assumptions made me feel even more guilty about my secret attraction for women. Behind their words, I always sensed the Blessed Virgin, or the figure of some saint, eavesdropping from across the room, ready to pass judgment. Despite carrying on with Mario through the mail, I didn't want to get married. I was attracted to women, and, specifically, to Anne. I felt afraid and trapped. I became depressed.

After six months, Mario wrote and asked me to marry him. I wrote back and said, yes. Did I love him? Who knows. I felt cornered, and I guess I panicked and acted without thinking, taking what felt at the time like the easiest path.

Mario couldn't get permission from the Peace Corps to come home to marry me, but they agreed to let me sign up as a volunteer. Now, as I look back, I see how fortunate it was for me to get married away from home. Without the witness of my family, it would feel less real.

After all their encouragement, *As Marias* complained that I was running away to get married. They wanted a church wedding. They wanted me in white, looking like a virgin, and Mario in his tuxedo, looking manly and debonair. They wanted a gaggle of bridesmaids and ushers lined up at the altar, a reception at the Portuguese Hall with a buffet table of cold cuts and deviled eggs, and a live band for dancing until long after we'd left for our honeymoon. But when *As Marias* saw how determined I was to do it my way—I had sold my car and given notice at work—they calmed down. After all, married in Nicaragua was better than not married at all.

When I broke the news to Anne, she threw her arms around me and said, "Congratulations!" Then she laughed and blurted out, "Why don't you marry me?!" Was she serious, I thought? My stomach lurched at the possibilities. Had she been attracted to me all these months? But the moment was lost when her boyfriend put his arm around Anne's waist and said, "Hey, honey, why don't you marry me?!"

I was terrified by Anne's suggestion, and to avoid thinking about it, I told myself that taking back my promise to Mario was impossible. I knew *As Marias* would disapprove if I ran out on my marriage plans; and doubly so, if I were to abandon my fiancé to go shack-up with a female jock.

I moved forward with my plans and joined the Peace Corps. After training in Puerto Rico for three months, I was shipped to El Viejo, a village in northwestern Nicaragua, where Mario and I were reunited. We decided to be married at the Peace Corps Center in Managua; the Chief Justice of the Nicaraguan Supreme Court agreed to officiate. The fiesta that we planned for after the ceremony included a piñata made in the likeness of Uncle Sam.

As a wedding dress, I chose a traditional Nicaraguan white, cotton shift, embroidered down the front with curlicues of varying pastels. Mario's wedding shirt was a cutoff version of my dress.

The other women volunteers helped me make bowls of macaroni salad, trays of deviled eggs and tiny ham sandwiches on Bimbo bread. It didn't occur to me to have black beans, rice, guacamole and tortillas. I had avoided a church wedding witnessed by my family, but without thinking, had created a celebration that felt familiar and legitimate.

While planning the wedding, I had been aware of a little voice inside me, protesting. The voice was certain I was doing the wrong thing. On the day of my wedding it became louder, more frantic.

"I don't want to get married!" it screamed inside my head.

"Oh, of course you do." Another voice tried soothing it with denial.

"Turning back is not allowed," said yet another voice, echoing *As Marias*.

After we were married, I became very angry and took it out on Mario. It seemed like everything Mario did got on my nerves. The way he laughed, trimmed his moustache and combed his hair—even the way his breath quietly whistled through his nostrils—made me rabid. I struggled to regain control over my life by trying to control Mario; I started picking petty arguments with him. I withheld sex and intimacy; sex had become so entwined with my rage that making love was dangerously volatile.

I didn't tell Mario what was eating away at me; he thought my moodiness and cranky disposition were side effects of birth control pills, or the stress of being away from home, or the oppressive, tropical climate. Mario was incredibly patient with me and my consistent foulness.

As a Peace Corps volunteer, I got plenty of positive reinforcement for being married—and for having babies. I felt as though *As Marias* had followed me to El Viejo. The women in the village pitied me for my childless state; Doña Louisa, the *viejita* who lived next door, teased Mario, using words like *huevos* and *pelotas*. There was no such thing as a career woman in Nicaragua; women were defined by their relationship to their family—particularly, by how many children they had. The last thing I wanted was to have a child, and thankfully, Mario agreed, although for different reasons.

For two years, I used work, cigarettes, food and beer to contain my rage. I was so far removed from who I really was, I didn't even know the Spanish word for queer. I felt as if I were living someone else's life, as if I was always waiting for something to happen that would finally bring me into my own.

I wrote to Anne every week, and we developed an intimacy we hadn't enjoyed before being separated by continents. Yet, even with the safety of the distance between us, I wasn't able to tell Anne about my passion for her.

Miraculously, Mario and I survived our two years in the Peace Corps without getting me pregnant, or otherwise seriously harming each other, and when we returned home from Nicaragua, my parents threw us a big wedding reception. There was a champagne fountain that inspired a long string of toasts to the eternal happiness of the newlyweds—who by that time weren't so newly wed, and were on the brink of divorce. Anne and her boyfriend sat with Mario and me at the main table, while moist-eyed and at a table by themselves, *As Marias* thanked the Blessed Virgin and all the saints for my marriage.

"Now *minha neta*, it's time for the *crianças*," chided my grandmother, her cheeks rosy from the champagne. Before she could carry on any further, Maria Helena, my great-grandmother, interrupted us. She was wearing her customary black jersey dress and carrying a flat rectangular gift, wrapped in silver and pink paper.

"*Avó bençõa*," I greeted her, asking for her blessing.

"*Bençõa neta*," she said, handing me the package. She stood by waiting for me to open it, and so I did, revealing an 11x14 picture of the Blessed Virgin.

"Santa Maria, abençõan," she said, crossing herself.

Adjusting to life back in the States would have been hard enough for two people in a well-functioning relationship, but for Mario and me, the transition was hellish. One day, faced with another of my refusals to have sex, Mario was unable to contain his frustration and punched a hole in the closet door. We both knew that that door could have been my face. We decided to make an appointment to see a marriage counselor.

"Why don't you want to stay at home and be a wife and mother for your husband?" the counselor asked, having immediately identified the problem with our marriage as my unwillingness to adjust to my role as Mario's wife.

The counselor's ignorance only strengthened my resolve not to disclose the real reason I wanted out of the marriage. "I don't want to be Mario's appendage," I said, furious. I'd gone back to my old job as a social worker, and so I added, righteously, "Besides, I'm the one who has a job."

Within a year after returning from Nicaragua, Mario and I were divorced; we both agreed it was for the best. I never did tell Mario about my attraction for women. I told him that I just wasn't in love with him anymore, and he believed me. The court listed the reason for our divorce as "irreconcilable differences," which was closer to the truth than anything I was able to admit.

The actual separation was uncomplicated. Mario and I had a dog, but we didn't own anything except what we had been given as wedding gifts—things like electric can openers, a hot air corn popper, and a donut maker. I kept the dog and Mario got the gifts. By default, the car stayed with me; it wasn't paid for and Mario still wasn't working.

I packed the dog and my clothes into the back seat of the blue Pinto sedan; Mario didn't see me off and I didn't look back. As I sped off into my future, I felt exhilarated, intoxicated with the promises of freedom. I never saw Mario again.

I think for most of us there are a handful of decisions we make that end up having an immeasurable impact on our lives. For me, finding the courage to divorce Mario was one of those. By choosing not to adjust to being Mario's wife, but to honor my feelings toward women, I had given myself the gift of possibilities, the potential to be who I really was.

As Marias were more disappointed than disapproving of my divorce. After their initial concern for the sanctity of my soul, they decided that because we hadn't been married in the Church, it hadn't really counted. They always referred to my divorce as an annulment.

My coming out wasn't a single act of cathartic honesty; it happened a bit at a time over a period of years. First, I had to be truthful with myself, then I was able to come out to a few, select others, which did not include *As Marias* or my parents, who I still feared would shame me. So, I traded one compartmentalized lifestyle for another, although this time without the emotional and social isolation I had lived in for so many years.

Coming out was scary, but being congruent with who I was, was such a joyous liberation from so many years of containment that at first I barely noticed the discomfort. Initially, coming out meant having sex with women. I put the squeeze on Anne; her response was eager and unambiguous. It was such a great relief finally to have had sex with her, that afterward, while cuddling among the tangled sheets, I absently commented, "Now, that wasn't so bad, was it?"

"Should it have been?" she asked, a little offended.

It took ten years before I felt strong and self-confident enough to come out to my parents. My father accepted the news calmly; he said that he had known for years. My father had never objected to me remaining single after divorcing Mario. I don't think he thought any man would have been good enough for me. When I came out to my mother, she physically recoiled. Clearly sickened by the idea of sex between women, her first response was, "I'll love you no matter what, but just don't blame this on me." Over the years, she has made good her promise to love me and has tried hard to overcome, or at least to contain, her repulsion to my lesbianism.

I didn't come out to As Marias before they died. Would they have judged my sexual preference sinful and disgusting? Probably. But As Marias thought sex per se was sinful and disgusting, I think they might have gotten over their initial shock and continued to love me.

I want to believe As Marias wouldn't have been able to forget the precocious little girl who followed them around their kitchens, learning the recipes that were never written down, or trailed along through the chicken pens and into the gardens on treasure hunts for eggs and giant pipinellas, or the child who uncomplainingly knelt beside them on the cold, marble floor of the church, while they clicked through several passes of the rosary. As Marias, with their penchant for creating reality to their own liking, would have kept me in their hearts forever as an obedient and precious child; just as I choose to remember them as perfectly strong and wise, unpredictable and funny.

Coming out did not immediately simplify my life. The pressure to be straight that I had attributed entirely to my family, I soon learned came from everywhere—my coworkers, the mechanic who worked on my car, my next-door neighbors. Even the other women in my feminist support group weren't comfortable with what looked like the sudden change in my sexual preference.

Nor did coming out eliminate my bouts of depression and insecurity. The same destructive behaviors I had engaged in with men—promiscuity to avoid intimacy, the dance of ambivalence—I carried over into my relationships with women. All of which pointed to the need for me to do some deeper healing.

Through numerous, unconscious acts of self-betrayal, I had come dangerously close to spiritual death. My unexpressed sexuality had a powerful, obsessive quality, while coming out gave my sexuality its solid, rightful place among the many parts that make up who I am. Ironically, acknowledging my sexual preference liberated the rest of me.

Since leaving Mario, I've had plenty of moments of self-loathing; you can't live in this society and not suffer the effects of internalized homophobia. But the strength that has come from living with integrity has allowed me to create my life with consistent wisdom, courage, and humor. Like As Marias used to say whenever I whined about how difficult something was: "Não pica daloroso, não saber sabroso." "You can't know joy, if you haven't known pain."

The Bridge Builder

KATHLEEN BOATWRIGHT

The first time I met Jean, she was having a nice conversation with my fifteen-year-old daughter at our church. I was very impressed by the mature way in which she spoke to my daughter. Then, during the service, I sat in the front row and watched Jean sing. I was so enamored by her presence that she stuck in my mind. But then she left town and was gone until January the following year.

Come January, I was sitting in church and I looked across the room, and there was Jean, carrying her guitar, walking down the aisle with such determination. I had this incredible lump in my throat, and I said to myself, Jean's back. After the service, and despite my difficulty talking to new people, I just had to ask Jean where she had been. I had to talk to her.

I found out that she was back in Corvallis for five months to finish her degree. She didn't have a place to live. So I said to her, "Don't worry, my parents have always wanted to take in a college student. You're redheaded like Dad. They'll love it!" I went and dragged my mother away from where she was talking and I said, "You remember Jean, she's looking for a place to stay. Why don't you and Dad take her in and board her?"

From early on my parents encouraged the friendship because they saw how much Jean meant to me. Meeting her brought me to life in a way they hadn't seen before. They knew that I used to cry for hours on end when I was a child because no girls liked me at school. My mother would come in and rub my leg or pat my hand. I was extremely intelligent and bright, but I had low self-esteem because I wasn't able to find friendship. So my parents encouraged Jean to invite me to lunch or to take me for a drive or go horseback riding. They felt her friendship was really wonderful for me. They were glad I was happy. For a while.

My husband didn't pay much attention—at first. He was a state policeman and had always been nonparticipatory, both as a parent and a spouse.

After four months of being friends, of having this wonderful platonic relationship, Jean had to go away for a month for her externship. While she was away she met a fundamentalist couple. Well, Jean sent me a postcard and said, "Something's going on. I'm playing with fire. I can't handle it. I've got to talk to you." My heart wrenched. What was going on?

When we were finally able to meet and talk, Jean explained to me how she and this fundamentalist woman started sharing in an intimate way. My response was to put my arm through hers and say, "Don't worry. We'll get it fixed." Jean couldn't be homosexual because it was wrong. Besides, if she was homosexual, then she would be leaving my life. And I think on a deeper level, I didn't want Jean exploring these things with anyone but me.

After her externship, Jean wanted to be more sensual with me. Her attitude was, "Now I'm going to show *you*." She said, "I'll give you a back rub some night." So one night—after Bible study, no less—she was over at my house and said, "Why don't you lay down on the blanket on the floor and take off your blouse and bra and I'll rub your back?" And I was like "Okaaay!" My husband was working all night, and this just seemed like a great setup. So this nice little Christian lady rubbed my back, and I said to myself, *Gee, this is it!*

All the little pieces, all the little feelings came together. Even comments my mother made to me over the years began to make sense. She'd say things like, "Don't cut your hair too short." "You can't wear tailored clothes." It was then that I also realized that the neighbors I had grown up with were a lesbian couple, even though I had never thought about that before. I recalled the feeling of walking through the Waldenbooks bookstore, looking at *The Joy of Lesbian Sex* and longing for that kind of intimacy. It all came upon me at that moment, and I felt a real willingness to release myself to this person in a way I had never done before. Then the phone rang. It was my son from Bible college. I thought, *Oh, God, saved by the bell! I don't know where this would have gone.*

By the end of the month, Jean was graduating, taking her national boards, and trying to figure out what to do about her feelings toward me and what to do about the fundamentalist woman. It was Pentecostal hysteria.

Now, at this time I still had a husband and four kids. I had a nineteen-year-old son at a conservative Bible college. I had a sixteen-year-old daughter in the evangelical Christian high school, of which I was a board member. Two children were in a parochial day school. My father was the worship leader at church. And I was still very bound to my parents for emotional support. I was the favorite child. And my grandparents lived in town.

Well, shit, I was in way over my head. I was really painted into a corner because there wasn't a single place I could turn to for even questioning. So I started looking to some Christian sources. Some of the advice was so incredible, like, "If you feel homosexual tendencies, you can't have the person you have those feelings for over to your house in the evening." "You can never let a member of the same sex sit on your bed while you're chatting." "Meet only in a public place." I thought this advice was ridiculous, but I also thought it was my only option because my spiritual nature was more important than my physical nature. Intellectually and emotionally, I was so hungry and so turned on that I didn't know what to do with my feelings.

At this point, people pull the trigger, turn to the bottle, take drugs, leave town. But I didn't do any of those things because I was madly in love. If I had pulled the trigger, I wouldn't have been able to express the part of me I had discovered. I had found someone, someone who shared the same sort of values I had.

Everything reached a crisis point. I acknowledged to myself and to Jean that I was a lesbian and that I loved her. By this time we had already been sexually active. My husband began to get suspicious that something was going on, and he and I went into counseling. Jean was leaving for a job in Colorado and told me that I couldn't go with her because she was a responsible woman and didn't want to destroy my family. And I still hadn't found the spiritual guidance that I needed.

I had to get away and do some soul-searching. I needed to figure out if there was any Christian support somewhere that said I could reconcile my love for Jean and love for my faith. I didn't feel I could build a life of love if I rejected my faith. So I packed my bags and told my parents that I was leaving to go to stay with my great-aunt in Los Angeles for ten days. I told my husband, "I am going to get away and I'm going to think about a bunch of issues, and then I'm coming back."

For the first time in my entire life, at the age of thirty-six, I was by myself with my own agenda. I had left my husband, my children, my parents, my support structures, got into a car, and started driving to West Hollywood, where I knew there was a lesbian mayor and a gay community. So surely, I thought, there had to be a spiritual gay community.

In West Hollywood I found Evangelicals Together. It's not a church, just a storefront ministry to the gay community for people coming out of an evangelical Christian background. It's led by a former American Baptist minister who talked my language. He said to me, "In order to deal with your dilemma, you have to take a step back from your relationsip with Jean. Lay her aside and ask yourself, *Who did God create me to be?*"

Through our sharing, and by looking from a different perspective at the gospel and what Jesus had to say, I could embrace the theology that said, "God knew me before I was born. He accepted me as I was made to be, uniquely and wholly." Ultimately, in an obedience to God, you answer that call to be all that He has created you to be. I felt firmly and wholly that what I had experienced with Jean was no demonic possession, was not Satan tempting me with sins of lust, but an intimacy and a love that was beautiful and was God-given. So now I had to figure out how to deal with it.

When you're my age, you're either going to go back to the way it's always been—go for the security you've always known—or take a chance. I felt that for the love I felt for Jean I was willing to risk all. Of course, having Jean there, I was hedging my bet a bit. I was jumping off a cliff, but I was holding somebody's hand.

Jean flew down a few days later to join me in Los Angeles. She agreed to commit to me and I to her. The first Sunday after we affirmed our relationship, we worshiped at All Saints' Episcopal Church in Pasadena because I was told that the Episcopals had the framework of faith I loved, as well as an ability to use reason in light of tradition and scripture.

It was God answering the cry of my heart to send me to that worshiping place. Jean and I had never been to an Episcopal church before. We went into this beautiful place with the largest Episcopal congregation west of the Mississippi River. We sat in the fourth row. It was just this incredible Gothic wonderful place. It was All Saints' Day at All Saints' Church. They played the Mozart Requiem with a full choir and a chamber ensemble, and a female celebrant sang the liturgy. We held hands and wept and wept. We could go forward because in the Anglican tradition, the Eucharist is open for everyone. God extends himself. There are no outcasts in the Episcopal church.

When I got back to town, I met with my husband at a counselor's office. I said, "Yes, you're right. I am gay and I'm going to ask for a divorce. I'm going to take this stand. I want to meet with my older children and my parents to talk about the decisions I've made." I felt at least I had a right to make my own decisions. I went to pick up my two youngest girls at my father's house. I went to open the door and I heard a flurry of activity, and the children saw me. "Oh, Mommy's home! Mommy's home!" And my dad stepped out on the front porch and pushed the children away and slammed the door. He took me forcibly by the arm and led me down the stairs and said, "You're never seeing your children again without a court order! Just go shack up with your girlfriend!" And he forced me down to the street.

It took going to court to see my two youngest children. They hadn't seen me for two weeks. They asked, "Mommy, Mommy, what's wrong?" I leaned over and whispered in their ears, "Mommy loves you." My husband wanted to know, "What are you telling the children?" I had only a minute with them, then went downstairs, and my husband told me that he wanted me to come back, that he would be my brother, not my husband.

I tell you, my whole world came down upon my ears. I wasn't allowed to see my children. I was denied access to my residence. The church had an open prayer meeting disclosing my relationship with Jean. They tried to get Jean fired from her job. And when that didn't work, they called Jean's parents, who then tried to have her committed or have me arrested. My older daughter, upon the advice of her counselor-pastor, shook my hand and said, "Thank you for being my biological mother. I never want to have anything to do with you again." After that, whenever she saw me in town, she hid from me. I saw her lie flat on the asphalt in the grocery store parking lot so I wouldn't see her. People I'd known all my life avoided me like I had the plague. I was surprised that Jean didn't just say, "Hey, lady, I'm out of here!"

Fortunately, I wasn't entirely without support. I went to Parents and Friends of Lesbians and Gays (PFLAG) and I met some wonderful loving, Christian, supportive parents and gay children who said, "You're not sick. You're not weird. Everybody's hysterical." They offered any kind of assistance possible. Through their emotional support, I felt like it was possible to survive the crush.

Living in a small rural county in Oregon, I didn't know anything about women's rights, let alone gay rights. So it's not surprising that I bought into the lie that children of lesbians or gays are better off living with the custodial heterosexual parent. I believed my husband could provide a sense of normality that I could not. So I signed away my custodial rights and became a secondary parent. After being the primary-care parent for twenty devoted years, the judge only let me see the children two days a week.

By then I'd had enough. So I packed one suitcase and a few things in grocery sacks and left my family and children behind. Jean and I just rode quietly out of town in the sunset to her job in Denver, Colorado.

As you drive into Denver, you go over this big hill about fifteen miles from town. We stopped at a phone booth and called the local PFLAG president to ask if there was a supportive Episcopal parish in town. She said, "Yes, go to this place, look up this person." It was getting to be evening. It was clear, and we were going over the mountain. It was a whole new adventure. It was real closure to my past and a real opening toward my future. Still, the guiding force in my life was, "The church has the answers."

Jean and I called the church and found out when services were and asked if they had an Integrity chapter. Integrity is the Episcopal ministry to the gay and lesbian community. There was one, so two nights later we walked into our first Integrity meeting. There were twelve attractive men in their thirties and the rector. They were shocked to see two women because it's unusual for women to be in Integrity. The only thing dirtier than being a lesbian in a Christian community is being a Christian in the lesbian community because it brings in so many other issues besides sexual orientation, like patriarchy and all that stuff.

Denver Integrity was an affirming congregation. We were out as a couple. We were healed of so many things through the unconditional love and acceptance of this parish of eighty people. The rector there encouraged me to become involved. Out of his own pocket he sent me to the first regional convention I went to, in 1987 in San Francisco. Now, I'm vice president of the Western Region for Integrity, and I'm on the national board of directors. I'm one of only maybe 125 women in Integrity's membership of about 1,500.

Integrity gives me a forum for the things I want to say, both as a lesbian woman and as a committed Christian. And because of my background and experience, I can speak to the church I love on a variety of issues that others cannot. I can say, "I call you into accountability. You are bastardizing children raised in nontraditional households. You're not affirming the people that love and guide them. You say you welcome us, but on the other hand you don't affirm us. You don't give us rites of passage and ritual and celebration like you do for heterosexual families."

The church needs to change. What we're asking for are equal rites. We're asking the church to bless same-sex unions. I'm asking for canonical changes that affirm my wholeness as a child of Christ who is at the same time in a loving committed relationship with a woman. We're also challenging the church to make statements asking the government to legitimize our relationships and give us the same sorts of tax breaks, pension benefits, et cetera. But most importantly, we need the church to get off the dime and start affirming gay and lesbian children's lives. I never want a girl to go through what I went through. I want to spare everybody right up front.

My husband remarried; he married the baby-sitter. At Easter of 1987, I got a call informing me that he had removed my ten-year-old daughter from his house, accusing her of using "inappropriate touch" with his new stepsons. He wanted to unload the difficult child. Then he used that child as a weapon to try and deny me visitation for the younger one. The end result was that I had one child and he had one child. I filed suit against him without any hope or prayer of winning back custody of my other child.

I went to a lesbian minister to ask her about finding a lawyer to handle my case, and she said to me, "The best attorney in this town is Hal Harding, but he's your husband's attorney. Maybe that will prove to be a blessing." So I had to find another attorney.

As part of the custody proceedings, Jean and I eventually met with my husband's attorney. He took depositions and asked Jean and me really heartfelt questions. Then he advised his client—my ex-husband—to go ahead and have a psychological evaluation. The court had not ordered it and, in fact, would not order it because there was no precedent in that county. But my former husband agreed to go to the psychologist of his choice. That psychologist, a woman, took the time and energy to interview every person involved and recommended to the court that Jean and I become custodial parents. We now have custody of both children, sole custody. It was indeed a blessing.

We just added Jean's ninety-one-year-old grandmother to our family. So we are all-American lesbians living here in Greenacres, Washington. We are Miss and Mrs. America living together. The thing that we need in our life now that our faith doesn't give us is a community of supportive women. We have yet to find that place.

Gale (Sky) Edeawo, 1995.

"If It Feels Right, Do It"

GALE (SKY) EDEAWO

As a child, I played with dolls, helped mom clean house, and hid blushingly from little boys. My girlfriends and I were crazy about boys. We loved them to chase us and hunt for us. We wanted to get caught. When they did catch us, they would pull our hair and push us around. We would break away and run home giggling, predicting which boy we would marry when we grew up.

The boys chased us only when they were bored. We longed for their company, knowing that one day they would grow up and begin pursuing us like the older guys who sat on the porches and held hands with our big sisters. In our early teens the change came about. The boys started to walk, not chase, us home. They also began to carry our books rather than throw them at us.

I was very boy crazy in my teens, and always managed to have a boyfriend or admirer. This said a lot for me, because in those days black men and boys liked girls and women with big legs and nice round behinds, of which I had neither. I was a size 3 with skinny legs and no ass at all...However, I was always a bit top heavy (runs on my mother's side of the family) with a strong ego (my father's side of the family). I had big eyes, a slight over-bite, deep brown skin, and thought I was sorta-cute. My inner pride must have attracted the young men because I always had someone's class ring around my neck or letterman's jacket over my shoulders. Usually, I had my pick of the litter.

Then along came Earl, good-looking, well built, bow-legged Earl. This time I knew, at age 17, I was hopelessly in love. Earl drove a red Buick, and we went everyplace together. We were an item. After Earl and I had been together for over three months, his friend, Bill, emerged. I had never met him, only heard talk he was in Virginia visiting his grandmother, staying out of trouble. The girls who knew him were forever talking about how gorgeous he was and how he always worked and had money. When Bill returned to L.A., everyone was excited. Except me. Yes, he was very handsome and yes, he always worked, had money and a car. But for some reason he wanted to come between Earl and me. He would bring beautiful girls to Earl's home and they would all go out on dates, leaving me to keep company with Earl's drinking mother.

I would beg Earl not to leave, only to be laughed at by Bill and his entourage of pretty women. I could not get Earl to see that this friend of his was up to no good.

Wanting to insult Bill, I told Earl that he was either funny (the word we used for gay) or just trying to destroy our relationship. Earl wouldn't listen to me. He would not treat me correctly, but he could not let me go.

I hated Bill and vowed to get even with him. I tried to run him down once with my automobile as he was leaving Earl's house, but he was too quick. I realized killing Bill was not a good form of vengeance, so instead I married him!

Here's how it happened: It turned out that good buddy Bill had always wanted Earl's girlfriend (i.e., me), and the best way to get her was to make her angry enough to leave. Leave Earl, I did. It hurt me, but it had to be done. There were more fish in the sea and I was tired of looking and feeling like the fool of fools.

Not a week after I left Earl, Bill started pursuing me. He would come to my house, charm my parents, bring me gifts, and take me anywhere I wanted to go. Bill was a very attractive man, part East Indian, part African American, tall with keen features, and dark, silky, naturally curly hair. I was the envy of many women who thought I had made the number one catch. I asked him once what the deal was with him. "You can have any good-looking girl you want, why do you want Earl's girl? And besides, I will never love you."

It turned out that Bill was a challenge freak, and I was the ultimate challenge. He had never known a girl to dislike him with the intensity that I did. He also envied the way I worshipped Earl and wanted me to worship him in the same manner. Bill convinced me to start dating him so that I could get even with Earl. I agreed. He convinced me to have sex with him, to really make Earl crazy. I agreed. He asked me to marry him, the ultimate revenge. At first, I declined.

When Earl found out about our affair, he was enraged. He denounced Bill as a friend, finally. He labeled me a slut, then went on a week-long drinking spree. He cried to my parents and Bill's mother, and enlisted in the Army where he begged to be sent to Vietnam so he could die for his country… They sent him to Germany instead, where he served his entire tour of duty.

Soon after graduation, and after becoming pregnant with Bill's baby, I married him. I had two girlfriends who were also pregnant and married. We formed a group of six and had some great times together. Dee was the first to deliver her baby. We were all at the hospital asking her what it felt like, did it hurt, was it worth the nine months? Vera was second to give birth. I was last. In February, 1965, I gave birth to a baby girl, my only child.

Bill and I tried to make our marriage work, although I never learned to love him. In my heart, I would always be Earl's girl. I must admit, Bill and I did have some good times. Since I remained his great challenge, he went out of his way to please me. We actually became friends and enjoyed great sex. Bill worked hard at Firestone Rubber and brought home his entire paycheck. We had two cars, a nice apartment in a nice middle-class area. Most of our furniture was new. I managed money well and turned out to be a very good housewife.

However there was another side to Bill, that same deceitful side that tore Earl and me apart. Bill was a big liar, and he had a temper. While he never beat me up, we had many arguments. I believe he was afraid of me after I pulled a knife on him in the middle of one of his tantrums and invited him to push me to use it. When you're not in love with the person you are living with, your tolerance level is quite low. I had no tolerance at all. If it had not been for my circle of friends, and the fact that my belly was big, I probably would have gone home to my parents in the middle of our first argument.

Firestone had offered my husband a management position several times. He always turned them down because a written test was involved. Although my husband had completed the 12th grade, he could not read or write. He was good at faking it, but not good enough to comprehend the test. I suggested he take a reading class at night school. He said he did not have time. I bought elementary school reading material from the bookstore so I could help him learn to read. He soon grew bored with this, and we would begin to argue. He was fired from his job for continuing to break the safety rules. I am certain he got himself fired purposely so that they would never learn of his reading disability.

After I gave birth to my 7 pound 6 ounce baby girl, life with my husband became unbearable. He was not working or looking for work. We argued constantly. Dee's husband was now in jail because he had decided to become a hustler and got involved in some get-rich scheme that backfired. Vera's husband had left her as soon as their baby was born, taking all but $10 from their joint bank account. When I heard about Vera's husband, I pulled some money out of the bank and hid it among my photo equipment. I don't know how, but my husband managed to find it and spend every penny on only God knows what. When the rent was due, I went to my private stash, and there was nothing there—no money for rent or groceries either. Bill had just started a new job and made some sort of deal with the landlord to pay in full on payday. He also told me he would be handling the money from then on, and would give me a food and household expense allowance. This new job paid 50% less than what he was making at Firestone, and my husband knew nothing about handling money. That was the day I said to myself, "I'm out of here."

I left my husband one afternoon while he was at work. I had a van come and take all our furniture to a storage locker. Bill arrived home to find only his clothes hanging in the closet. Everything else was gone, including his baby and Earl's girlfriend.

After leaving Bill, I stayed with a friend he didn't know in Echo Park. He went all over looking for me, full of angry threats. It was only his ego at stake. He soon got over it and had to admit that he never won the challenge.

I soon came out of hiding and moved back to my parents' home with baby in tow. Bill and I went separate ways and he never in 29 years has paid $1 in child support...

Pickings were slim in the late '60s; I could see that my days of being pampered were over. I became less and less interested in the men I met. They all seemed to be a mass of confusion, especially the ones returning from the war. I made a mental note to stay away from drug addicts, ex-cons and war veterans. Needless to say, I seldom dated. I was prepared to be single for quite some time.

I remember the first time I caught myself looking at a woman's legs and ass, in the "wrong way." Donna was a dark complexioned, Italian secretary at my job. I was not looking at her with envy or admiration. I was looking at Donna daily, constantly, with pure lust. I did not know what the hell was wrong with me. I was beginning to feel like one of *those funny people*. Oh! God forbid, I told myself, don't let that happen! I started going out with any man who asked me, just to prove to myself that I was all right. The men I dated were boring, brain-dead, had no money, or drank heavily. I soon got over my secret crush, decided it was just a passing fancy, and stopped dating. After that I only went out alone or with girlfriends.

One night I was out alone at the La Rouge, a club known for its sexy, topless go-go dancers. These dancers had the most beautiful bodies I had ever seen. They could make parts of their bodies—tits, navel, arms, thighs, legs and ass—move like they were run by batteries. I would become spellbound, sightless to anything in the room except these voluptuous, half naked women. I ignored the man across the room who tried to catch my eye, and refused a drink from the handsome guy at the bar. I just wanted to be alone and enjoy this feeling.

I did not know what was coming over me but this time I was going to let it run its cycle. These were straight women, I supposed, and I was also straight. All I could do was cross my legs and go home later and masturbate. I cursed myself for not knowing any gay men or women or any gay clubs until one night I was out with two of my girlfriends at a club on Main Street. There was a small stage there with a single go-go dancer. She was not as sexy as the girls at the La Rouge. She was around 5' 2", and wore about a 5\6 dress, about the same size I was at that time. She had small, pear-shaped breasts with large erect nipples, a small ass, small legs. I remember thinking to myself, "Too little—throw her back." My straight friend Gertie, who knew nothing about my hidden desires, leaned across the table to say to me above the music "Don't go into the restroom alone if that dancer is in there. She likes to get real close to women. She's one of those funny women, and she don't like men."

I thanked Gertie for the warning and decided to turn around and give this dancer another once-over. She had a thin, tight dancer's body, lovely chocolate brown skin, and a cute narrow face with high cheekbones. Her hair was cut short and was naturally waved. She wasn't such a throw-back after all. She had been drinking a bottle of champagne and was obviously feeling quite good as she moved her body seductively, teasing the men in the audience. I figured she had been on stage long enough to be taking a break soon.

Gertie was out on the floor dancing, and Irma was in a deep conversation; so I eased my way unnoticed to the restroom. I prayed that none of the five women patronizing the club that night would enter the restroom, especially not

Irma or Gertie. The restroom was very small, situated at the end of a narrow hallway. It only had one door, one stall with a door that locked, and a small washing area. I stood by the sink with the water running, pretending to wash my hands. The music had stopped for several minutes and I was hoping the dancer would enter. As soon as I gave up and turned off the water, I heard a soft knock at the door. It sounded like Gertie, coming to rescue me. I reluctantly said, rather harshly, "Come in girl, it ain't locked."

As I reached for the door to make my exit, in walked the go-go dancer. She entered the small space and closed the door behind her. She stood with her back against the door. She looked me up and down in a way that I had never been examined before by man or woman. In a throaty, seductive voice that did not match her small frame, she said "Is anyone in here besides us?" I said "No, I just came out of the stall myself." She was now wearing a thin tee-shirt over her bare breasts and I could feel every inch of her body, nipples and all as she brushed past me to enter. I ran the water again, pretending to wash my hands. She began a conversation with me from the stall, asking me which perfume I was wearing. I began to apply make-up to play for more time. I just wanted to be near her. I reached over and locked the door leading to the hallway, not caring what I would say if anyone tried to enter. I only knew I was living for this moment. I needed to know where it would take me. She came out of the stall and stood purposely close as she washed her hands, smiling at me in the mirror. She winked. I guess that was my sign, to take my leave or stay. I chose the latter. She then turned to face me, her right nipple pressing hard against my arm. I felt a wicked sensation—something I had never experienced before. She said, "Do you like women?" I replied, "Sure, some of my best friends happen to be women." She was now standing so close I could feel the moist heat from her body and smell the soft musk fragrance she was wearing. When she spoke, I could smell the champagne she had been drinking, softened by mints.

"Don't play dumb. You know what I mean, let me show you." By then she was kissing me softly on my lips, closed mouth at first. Then her tongue slowly slid past my lips to search for mine. A woman's tongue—I felt like fainting.

Then I heard a distant knock at the door, which brought me back to reality. She slowly moved away, looking at me, smiling while licking her lips. She seemed pleased with what she had accomplished. I left the dancer standing alone in the small restroom and entered the hallway to meet Gertie, who was looking wide-eyed and concerned. "Was that woman in there with you? Did she hit on you? Did she try to hem you up?"

I said "Calm down, Gertie, she knew better than to mess with me, and besides, they only go as far as you let them."

I soon learned that the dancer's name was Vicki. When she returned to the stage, someone had sent her another bottle of champagne. She beckoned me from my table. Not giving any concern to the stares coming from my friends, I practically ran to the stage and stood there waiting to serve her or do whatever she may have wanted me to do. She slipped me a piece of paper with her home and work numbers on it. Then she told the waitress to bring an extra champagne glass, because she wanted me to drink with her. She poured the bubbles, held her glass up, and toasted, "To us." I went back to my table oblivious to what my naïve friends were thinking. A new episode was about to begin in my life and it felt so right...

Vicki turned out to be a very good friend. She was my introduction into *the life*. She showed me the lesbian scene, the gay men's bars. She and I never completely made love because she lived with an auntie and I was back at home with my parents. But we did a lot of hugging, kissing and heavy petting in the back seat of my Ford.

Vicki got off work early on Friday nights: 10:00 p.m. I would be parked in front of her club, and off we would go to our favorite lesbian night spot, the club Hi Dollie, which was set a bit off the street on the corner of El Segundo and Western. This club was full of beautiful black lesbians—little ones, large ones, black skin, brown skin, yellow lesbian women. Women as masculine as my Uncle Willie, women as sexy as my Aunty Kay. Many of the harder butches were bouncers and made sure there was no trouble. A few gay men patronized the club, and a handful of straight men who fancied lesbians were regulars. Other than those few, the club was strictly women.

There were many very feminine women who patronized the Hi Dollie, all very attractive. I soon found out that women like Vicki and myself were considered queers among queers, because we were femmes who liked other femmes. I never really got into serious role-playing. About the best I could do was be attracted to a soft butch, boyish but femme. The bartender was a soft butch. In the straight life she would be considered a pretty man. Now known as lipstick dykes, I guess Vicki and I were ahead of our time.

There were always female players in the club. They had a rap that could set super pimps to shame. These women wore silk suits, gold watches, satin ties. They would dress down to their toenails.

The Hi Dollie had a lesbian singer named Ray. Ray was everything a good-looking man would want to be, but could not be unless he were a woman. The woman was super fine and kept the women screaming in the aisles. She stood about 5' 9", with a stocky, solid build. Coffee brown, with soft features, she was a sensitive butch, a soft stud broad. On top of being charming, she could sing, her control of the mike was professional, and her stage presence awesome. I couldn't get enough of the Hi Dollie or of Ray.

Vicki and her aunt soon moved back to Arizona, running from her aunt's crazy husband who had wrecked the car, tore up the house, and was temporarily in jail on drunk charges. They fled town before his release, but not before Vicki and I could do one last night on the town. She told me to play safe and be careful. To this day I still have a thing for dancers, and I always think of Vicki, my go-go dancing friend.

I came out to my mother in the late '60s after introducing her to Vicki. Mom had no trouble with my choice of lifestyle. She had been very protected by gays and lesbians when she arrived on her own in New York City from Smalltown, Georgia. She remained friends with the homosexual community until she married her first husband and moved to Detroit.

I didn't enjoy the set as much after Vicki left. I needed a running buddy, and it was difficult to meet friends. On the lesbian set it was easy to feel alone in a crowd. I began to spend more time at home with my daughter. I had my own apartment by now, and had just left one low-paying insurance company to work for another no-paying insurance company. But the new place had a better work environment, free lunches, and a new friend named Barbara.

Barbara sat at the desk across from me, and we became instant friends. We were the same age, we were both single parents. Barbara had a four-year-old daughter, my daughter would soon be four. Barbara was straight, and she enjoyed the nightlife. We became running buddies. We went to all the straight happening clubs. Barbara enjoyed the company of older men—much older. She always had one helping with the rent, or a late car payment. Her 70-year-old Grandma once ran one of the most notorious bordellos in Louisiana. From the age of eight, Barbara would help her grandma clean the place and count money. So Barbara was used to the high life, having men and money around.

One night we had been dancing at a local club until closing time. Neither one of us wanted to go home. Barb asked if I knew of any happening after-hours clubs. I hesitated because I only knew of gay ones. Then I figured, what the hell, girlfriend's been around, nothing should shock her...it didn't. Off we went. The club was on Hoover and Colden. When we arrived, it had a nice, mellow crowd. We were able to get a table and enjoy the view. We weren't there five minutes before an aggressive butch came over to ask Barbara to dance. Barb threw her purse on my lap, and in no time was out on the dance floor. First they were fast dancing off of an old Supremes tune called "Let Me Go The Right Way." Next a slow jam came on, and Barbara was holding that woman closer and tighter than I ever saw her hold one of her ancient men. We had a great time that night. On the way home she asked me why didn't I tell her of those clubs long ago. It turned out that Barbara had always been excited by butch broads. They would often bring their women into her grandma's bordello. They would rent a room, stay for hours, sometimes all night, then leave. Barbara said she was only allowed to sneak glances at them, until now.

Soon we were not going to the straight clubs at all. The Hi Dollie, The Clowns, and other gay clubs were our turf. One Friday night we were at the Hi Dollie when I spotted a table occupied by six of the finest butches I had ever seen. I recognized one of them. She had been Vicki's barber, and her name was Ann. This barber had a style about her like I had never seen before. She performed while she cut hair. She handled her barber's drape like a matador takes control of his red cape. She would dance around her patron's head until she was certain she had it right. She intrigued all of the women, which angered most of her male co-workers. I would accompany Vicki every time she went to get her hair done. I enjoyed sitting there watching Ann perform, hoping she might notice me. She never had.

But now here, at this club, she and another sleepy-eyed butch were smiling, looking in our direction. I quickly turned to Barbara and said, "Don't look now, girl, but we are being observed." I was sitting as stiff as a board trying to appear composed, looking directly in front of me at absolutely nothing. Barb immediately looked over at the table, even though I told her not to. She turned around quickly and joined me in looking straight ahead at absolutely nothing.

"Oh, God, one of them is walking over here." "Which one?" I asked. Soon a voice was saying, "How are you ladies doing this evening? May I buy you a drink?"

Ann became my first lesbian lover. She later told us that she approached our table because the group of butches said they would give $5 to whichever one of them would go over and talk to the two square ladies sitting up front. The club was not full yet so they felt like having a little fun. Ann was a naughty daredevil. She took the $5 and the dare. We lived together as lovers for seven months, and have remained friends for more than 24 years. I often tease her and say, "That $5 dare you took over two decades ago has you stuck with me for life."

Ann and I broke up because I was not sure of what direction I wanted to take in life. I was not sure if I wanted my daughter to grow up in a lesbian household. I was not sure if I wanted to deal with the stigma that society placed on gays and lesbians. I was very confused. I became argumentative, angry, and began to over-drink. When Ann and I broke up, I thought the world would collapse. I did not know if I wanted to return to the straight life for appearance's sake or if I should tip-toe around the gay life and have a clandestine relationship with another woman. It did not take long for me to realize I would not easily find a woman like Ann, especially one who would accept a clandestine affair.

Barbara met an older man and married him, giving him four sons, naming them all after her husband: Junior, The Second, The Third, and The Fourth. Barb should have remained a lesbian so she would not have had to put those boys through that naming sacrifice.

I began exploring the lesbian world in Los Angeles, yet could never find the niche I was looking for in the gay set of the '60s. I was searching for more of a political arena, which seemed not to exist. Where were the activists and writers to uphold lesbian and gay life?

There were parties and more parties. Confusion, fights, drinking. This was not me. I had no handle in the gay world. It left me no choice but to return to the straight life. I remained straight for 22 years. I always remained close to my gay guy friends, continued to go to their parties and other functions. I kept in contact with Ann as well. She became the barber to most of my men friends, and I met most of her lovers throughout the years.

I never did find Mr. Right. I would tell my men that I had had only one man in my life, and She was a Woman. I began to date men from Africa and the Caribbean, thinking maybe they would be different—stronger, wiser; but after the novelty wore off, they were all the same.

I went back to college and majored in international black history. I also became active in the black community working on prison reform, hotlines, at drug prevention centers, and women's literacy programs. Upon graduation I started travelling the world. I lived in Paris for three years, in Amsterdam for two. I travelled to West Africa seven times and maintained an apartment in Dakar, Senegal for one year. From there I returned to France. My 16-year-old daughter was living with me. She was pregnant with my grandchild. Her young boyfriend lived in the States. I was living a bohemian life, but with a pregnant daughter I had to put down roots. So, for security's sake, I married my second husband, my penpal from an African magazine. His dream was to live in America; my dream was to live abroad. We had what the French called a "Blanc" marriage—a business marriage, a marriage on paper only. We had absolutely nothing in common. The happiest day of my marriage was when I placed him on the plane at Charles DeGaulle airport and bid him farewell. He left for America. The year was 1982. Other than him sending me money for one year as we had agreed, we never laid eyes on one another again.

Two months after my husband left Paris, I packed up my daughter and three-month-old grandchild and sent them back to my parents in the States. Now Paris was all mine. I could enjoy the freedom of no longer being a wife, a mother, a grandmother and housekeeper. I was free to sleep late, read in bed, and hang out at night. Unfortunately I never moved on the gay and lesbian set while living in Paris. My sole purpose in being there was to write and continue becoming one with the African communities of Europe.

I now had several gentlemen friends: a restaurant owner who fed me, a night-club owner who kept me well dressed and happy, and a musician who kept me entertained. Even in Paris, the city of love, I couldn't find Mr. Right. I was quite happy with my freedom. I received a small amount of money from my husband every month—enough to pay rent, buy food, and play around a bit. I became a small celebrity in France, reading my poetry at coffee shops, bookstores, the Sorbonne, and private businesses. When the year was up, and my husband's checks stopped coming, I moved to Amsterdam to work in a friend's cafe bar. Amsterdam—another wild city known for its open gay activities—which I learned nothing about. By 1985 I realized I was homesick for the States. I missed my parents, my daughter and granddaughter. I missed the California weather, and melt-in-your-mouth soul food. Little did I know how much I also missed the women.

It didn't take long for me to get back into the swing of things. I spent time with all of my friends, began working through the temp agency, and after 12 years, began dating African American men once again. I thought I had missed them. I started travelling for the first time in the southern states, Louisiana and Georgia being my favorites. I also became involved with several women's groups and realized how much in awe I was of women—not just their bodies anymore. This time their wisdom, resilience, and perseverance made a lasting impression. I had watched the women of the world carry entire countries on their backs and not break under the pressure. I began to love and admire these wonderful women. I started writing stirring poems about them and began to realize I was also writing about myself.

By the late '80s, I stopped being in the company of men altogether. Although I was still basically straight, I realized I had no interest in the male gender. I worked as a volunteer with several different womanist organizations. Eventually I got my hands on some lesbian magazines. I realized the lesbian community had come a long way since the '60s. There were active political groups, peer counseling sessions, coming out workshops, self-help programs and literary gatherings. The lesbian community seemed to be as busy, if not more so, than the straight community of women.

This time around I had something to give to the life, as well as receive. My time to give was January, 1991. I had just returned from island-hopping in the Eastern Caribbean, and knew I had to decide where I was taking my life. I had a straight friend named Robyn who was active in women's rights and also loved to club hop. She liked good jazz and African/Caribbean music. I had begun visiting the Catch One Club, a black-owned, lesbian and gay club over on Pico Blvd. with black entertainers. I kept these outings a secret from my straight friends.

In the beginning I even kept them a secret from Robyn. One evening I invited Robyn to follow me to the club in her car so that we could enjoy some great jazz. I was partially truthful with her. I let her know it was a gay club, but downplayed it, saying the entertainment was great. Robyn was a well-rounded young lady and told me she had no problems with gays at all. She went on to tell me about some high school friends who were lesbians whom she had always remained close to. I did not tell my friend, immediately, about my past history. When I finally did, some weeks later, she took it quite well. In fact, Robyn remains straight to this day but can be seen with me at lesbian parties, poetry readings, and other functions.

The day that I knew lesbian life was where I permanently planned to be was on a Sunday evening when Robyn and I went to the Catch to hear some jazz. Our plan was to leave there about 8:30 and get to the African/Caribbean club before they enforced the 9 p.m. cover charge. At 8:40, Robyn stood up from her bar seat, quickly finished her drink and looked at her watch. She said, "Gale, we only have 20 minutes, are you ready?" We always traveled in two cars just in case one of us wanted to leave a place before the other. My beer had barely been touched and I was quite relaxed. She went on to say, "You can meet me there later. I just don't want to pay that cover charge."

I was becoming very bored with straight clubs; it did not matter if they were African, African/Caribbean, or African/American, they just were no longer the space I preferred to be in. I tuned Robyn out for a moment, trying to decide what to do. The jazz quartet was taking their 20-minute intermission. The attractive female jazz singer who stood about 5'2" and had the body of life, was circulating around the oval-shaped bar greeting smiling patrons with hand-shakes and genuine hugs. The jukebox started up with Stephanie Mills singing her song "Home," from the long-running broadway play "The Wiz." I thought "What great timing." I felt as if Stephanie were singing that song for me.

I looked toward the entrance in time to see two handsome butches enter who looked to be in their mid-40's. Both were wearing white suits, and one was wear-ing a cashmere Stetson hat. They looked as if they had taken careful time in grooming, just so that they could make this dynamic double entrance. I was impressed. Their entrance gave me a feeling of knowing, of belonging. Across from me on the other side of the bar sat a lesbian couple, one speaking softly into the other's ear. Two olive complexioned gay guys at the jukebox were laughing, while glancing flirtatiously over their shoulders seeking attention. The bartender, a round-bellied, friendly man, who seemed to know everybody's business, was giving a "3 snaps up" sign to an interested patron leaning on the counter.

At the far end of the bar a woman sat alone. I had seen her there before. She was a good-looking lipstick dyke, and everything about her said trouble. She had been eyeing me for a long time, giving me a half warm smile. She never said a word, only looked. A part of me warned, "Leave that alone." Another part of me said, "What harm can she do you? If nothing else, she looks as if she could give you something great to write about." I decided to go for it. I felt like Dorothy, going in the right direction down the yellow brick road, brave enough to start this life once again...

"Gale, you want me to save a seat for you at the other club?" It was then I realized my friend was still there. One foot was gearing for the door, but at that moment she had not yet gone. The jukebox had Stephanie belting out the last words of her song as I turned to Robyn and said, "No girl, I won't be leaving at this moment. You go on without me. Don't save a seat for me either." I knew I would remain here for the rest of the evening, or longer, adjusting to my brand new world of Oz...

Juana Maria Gonzalez Paz with her daughter, 1982 and
years later on lesbian land.

From Battered Wife to Lesbian Land

JUANA MARIA GONZALEZ PAZ

In 1976 my husband, Brion, began beating me with a frequency and intensity that caused me to fear for my life and that of my nine-month-old baby, Mary Ann. We lived in a small cottage on the Florida coast, and I supported all three of us with my veteran's benefit that enabled me to go to college for the first time.

I dropped out of school when Brion sabotaged the car. The campus was several miles away and public transportation inadequate, so that was the end of my steady income. (I'm a Vietnam-era Navy veteran; I was going to school under my G.I. Bill.) Brion had quit his job so he could watch me every minute. I didn't trust him to stay home with the baby while I went out to work. I tried to get welfare but I wasn't eligible while Brion lived with me, and he refused to leave.

In June of that year, Brion admitted some startling things—that he'd made sure he slept with me every day until I got pregnant and that he'd manipulated me during the entire relationship through an elaborate system of lies and deceptions. He laughed and said it was easy, that I had a moral code I lived by, and he could always anticipate how I'd react to any situation. He also said he wasn't letting me go alive. I threatened to leave and he threatened to kill all of us, including the baby and the dog.

The night he dragged me around the house closing windows with one hand (to muffle the noise) and covering my mouth with the other, I knew he was serious. I held the baby with one arm and with the other I tried to loosen his grip on my mouth so I could breathe. I broke free long enough to scream bloody murder. The police arrived within minutes, checked me for external injuries and tried to get me to make a statement. But the inside of my mouth was cut, and I couldn't talk. They assured me that my neighbors were looking out for me and urged me to yell if I needed help. They said someone in the neighborhood would hear me and call them.

The police left, and Brion apologized. Actually, he wanted to have sex. I refused, and he waited until the next day to rape me. Things went from bad to worse. I made plans to leave town. I was all packed and waiting for a ride to the bus station when he came home drunk and carrying a loaded gun. He held me hostage for four hours and slapped me and knocked me down so many times I can't remember them all.

He wanted to kill me but I think he was afraid to live without me. He raped me until he couldn't get an erection anymore. Mary Ann cried at first, but I closed the door so she couldn't watch, and she sat down in her crib to play her red piano.

Brion decided I should cook one more dinner before he killed me, and I ran away from him on our way to the grocery store, despite his promise to shoot me in the back if I made any false moves. He disappeared when I started screaming. I got to a phone and called the police. Since I looked like a victim from a horror movie by then and I'd called many times before, they had no trouble believing my story, but they did think I might change my mind later and refuse to press charges. I explained that the only way for me to get out of town alive was for them to keep him in jail overnight. The bus to Los Angeles left once a day and I had already missed it.

I had to get out of town to save my life, and I had to get to a major city with emergency social services. I chose Los Angeles because it was far away and on the west coast. I knew how to survive on my own in a big city but I didn't want to go back to New York.

I arrived in L.A. after three days on the bus. I didn't know a soul there. I got on welfare quickly and again, no one had trouble believing my story. My bruises were starting to get large, purple and yellow. My face was sore and swollen, too. There I was, a young woman walking around a strange city with a baby, a suitcase, and signs of a recent beating. I guess I was pretty obvious. "I know, I've been there," women on buses and street corners seemed to say to me with their eyes. Wherever I went, people seemed to know I was on the run.

I spent nine months staying home, taking care of the baby, healing, forgetting, remembering and letting go. Some days I was too upset to leave the house. When I did, I often returned to my roach-infested apartment near MacArthur Park to face a dreaded vision of my husband standing in the shadows, red-faced with beer and the threat of violence, holding a gun and sneering, "Hello, honey...get undressed." "That it could come to this," I thought as I calmed down and assured myself it was just my old fear welling up inside me and making his image seem so real. Surely he could never find us. After all, the police had arrested him.

I basically liked living alone and didn't miss having a mate. I never wanted to marry again, although in the beginning I did despair of ever resuming "normal relations" with men. Then I decided I didn't know what "normal" was and didn't care. I was not afraid to face the world alone and never thought I needed another person to co-parent my child, although a lot of my plans were postponed for years while she was little.

After the better part of a year, I was ready to face the world again. I went to a welfare conference and plunged headlong into welfare rights work. I gave and gave and gave, trying to change a system that basically never budged, though minor concessions were made, and I, personally, could have become a token Puerto Rican minority at a low-paying social service agency job.

When welfare rights became a never-ending cycle of infighting and meetings that went nowhere, I went on to other things—school again, feminism, writing, lesbianism, and women's land. I saw an article about lesbian land in Arizona. I was ready to change my life, so I called and arranged a visit. From there I heard about other lesbian lands and I've been in the lesbian community ever since. Mary Ann and I lived on lesbian lands for a few years, then settled in Arkansas, where I was on welfare for most of the 1980's.

Being on welfare has given me the freedom to stay celibate as long as I want. I've had to acknowledge that white lovers, male and female, usually represent an opportunity to increase my access to money or privilege. It's too easy to look toward the relationship for security rather than love, whether financial gains are realized or not. So, I've opted out of the whole lover game by concentrating on myself and my own process and progress.

Mary Ann will be 20 this year and is attending college studying theater. I am developing grassroots study groups called *Women, Values and Community*. It is time we start applauding each others' freedom, choices, and movement—in many different directions.

Christine Berrier

Reflections on a Life

CHRISTINE BERRIER

We headed south on I-35 in a borrowed car, leaving behind several feet of dirty snow and the dark clouds that hung over Minneapolis, threatening more. We wore goose down coats and heavy boots with thick wool socks. Worn leather gloves gleaned from the Rag and Stock Company bins kept our hands alive. We pulled our caps down over our ears and tucked the knitted scarves more securely into place to fend off the cold as we loaded the trunk with our suitcases. It had been hard to pack the short-sleeved shirts and sandals we would need; hard to believe that it was warm anywhere. It was early morning. If we traveled all day and all night we could get there tomorrow. It was March, 1978, and I was going home to Texas to be married.

I had come to Minnesota more than two years earlier, in a desperate escape from the oppression of Texas' August heat, running away from a life that had too many unanswered questions and unmet needs. The move had created an instant and positive change for me. There was something refreshing about leaving the familiar conservative politics and values of the Southwest and experiencing a whole new place. The men were different, they expected different things from women, and I fit. For the first time, I wasn't too tall, or too talkative, too articulate, too intimidating.

I met David at a fundraising concert to benefit victims of the Guatemalan earthquake in February of 1976. Behind his unassuming wire-rimmed glasses he hid fluid green eyes with long lashes. His whole body was as pliant and inviting as the curls of his beard. He was a teddy bear of a man with a disarming smile. His mind was constantly active, his mental energy barely containable. He was an outrageous flirt, and a persistent one, and in just a few weeks we found enough in each other to love. In just a few months, he convinced me that we should live together.

Our apartment had big sunny rooms and uneven wood floors. The three flights of creaking wooden stairs we climbed to reach our door were carpeted in burgundy flowers, left over from a decade that required such finery. Our apartment's enormous windows overlooked a small courtyard ringed by ornate iron gates. In the winter, the radiators hissed and clanged and gave off unmanageable amounts of heat. We took turns feeding peanuts to an albino squirrel who was brazen enough to climb up the brick wall and perch on the icy windowsill.

We shared endless trips on dependable red buses that shuttled us to and from the university, in all kinds of weather, free of charge. David knew my schedule better than I did, and on days when he arrived home first, he would amble back down the hill to meet me at the bus stop, carrying some surprise, some offering aimed at pleasing me, clenched in his awkward hands. Over the next two years, his consistent tenderness touched me, and the certainty of his love for me was clear. My love for him seemed unshakable. He seemed like "the one." I asked him to marry me.

Until then, marriage was something he hadn't considered. Among our friends, legal marriage was considered out of date, an unnecessary acquiescence to social norms. Neither of us had been with anyone else since we began to date, but he was reluctant to commit to monogamy as a way of life.

In the beginning of our relationship, sexual intimacy had been compelling for both of us. I accepted whatever David offered me sexually, flattered by the constancy of his attentions. After a few months, I began to realize that David knew how to get what he needed sexually, but had little interest in satisfying me. Sex was an extension of his consistent physical affection, only the touches were deeper, the caresses carried more urgency. He would touch my breasts and stroke my thighs enough to insure my willing participation, but his fingers would not brave that dangerous, dark, territory that terrified him so. Oral sex was never even discussed. It took us a long time to talk about the fact that I was not orgasmic with him (though orgasm was always easy for me without a partner), or to discuss why he had so much trouble controlling his ejaculation.

We sought help through the university counseling center, where we were referred for couples counseling in a "sexual dysfunction" clinic. Our counselors were a male and female co-counseling team who used an approach developed by Masters and Johnson. We were urged to examine many aspects of sexuality within the context of our relationship and instructed on ways to change our communication patterns. There were exercises designed to help David learn to prolong his erections and help us focus on mutual satisfaction. Some of the ideas were helpful, but the discussion about sexual responsibility led us seriously offtrack. The principal idea was that each person in a couple is responsible for their own pleasure, responsible for communicating what they need and being graceful enough to allow their partner to learn how to please them. When there are two willing partners, that works. When either partner is shut down, it can be dangerous. For us, it translated into David continuing to get the sexual satisfaction he wanted from penetration, while I was left wondering what I had a right to ask for. My version of taking "responsibility" for my orgasm was to touch myself while David penetrated me. At least I was orgasmic, and we didn't have to face our fears.

When the counseling was over, in our mutual discomfort, we created and enforced an impenetrable silence around sexual issues and returned to our previous status quo. Things went from bad to worse sexually, while our emotional intimacy, our sweetness, and the convergence of our values and political commitments got stronger by the day. The conflict between what was exchanged between us emotionally and what went on in the bedroom was difficult to reconcile and painful to admit, so we ignored it. It was nothing new to me. I expected it.

From childhood, I had been imprinted with shame about my body, a feeling that there was something intrinsically unattractive about me. My first venture into romance had been with a young man who celebrated me as an emotional intimate while essentially ignoring my sexual needs. It was 1970, and the social discussion was Vietnam. We were eighteen. Frank and I didn't really date, we communicated. We wore beaded headbands and sandals, and wandered through the city parks in those summer evenings after work, wild with excitement that was only slightly subdued by the Texas heat, mustering the courage to buy marijuana from strangers, to be grown up. He could talk endlessly about his feelings, about political ideas, about socialism and change. We kissed and held each other and talked about the revolution and then went off to different colleges and filled each other's mailboxes with dreamy monologues. But the dreams weren't enough after a while. I wanted a real person in my life, someone tangible who could love me and touch me. There was teenage sexual play but nothing else. I began to feel cheated. When I asked Frank why he set such narrow limits with sex, he always had an idealistic, moral answer for me. Those answers satisfied me for a time; I wanted to believe him, but reasoning couldn't override what was happening inside of me. One Sunday evening, as he was putting me on the bus to return to Austin, I pleaded with him to explain himself to me. He managed to admit to me that he was gay.

That admission propelled me into what was the beginning of a whole new part of my life. By the time I was 23, I had fallen in love with two other gay men, fallen in love and been celebrated as an intimate friend while my sexuality was essentially ignored. One of them made a repeated plea for me to marry him, trying desperately to deny his own sexual orientation in order to keep me.

Aside from these experiences, there had only been one brief and mysterious lesbian encounter that left me breathless and confused. I met Catherine when I was 21, and had just returned from a year abroad. In Europe I had walked arm in arm through the city streets with women friends who kissed me at every greeting, every parting, without hesitation. I knew the scent of them, was comforted by their closeness, shared their dreams, but had never translated that intimacy to sex. Meeting Catherine reminded me of that lovely innocence and lustiness. Her auburn hair fell down around her shoulders, cascading in loose waves, touching translucent skin, softening the angular frame of her face. We were in a women's group together, we talked about "issues" and dredged up private thoughts to give each other like presents. At the time, I didn't understand that I had a crush on her. I didn't have the language.

One weekend we borrowed her grandmother's car and went camping on the Pedernales River, which crawled through a canyon in the limestone's white heat. Toward evening we were surprised by a thunderstorm that found us far from the tent. By the time we made it back to camp, the wet clothes had become second skins, draping our curves, clinging to clefts. The wind brought a chill that rushed us into the tent, where we took off our clothes so spontaneously that our nakedness came almost as an embarrassment. We kneeled in the too short, too narrow space, our faces inches apart. She kissed me. More kisses followed, then touching, and there was no way to get enough of her. In the morning, we struck camp in silence, both unsure of what to say. We rode back to town without speaking. I never saw her again and I edited her from memory. It was easier to pretend nothing had happened than to try to make sense of it.

The confusing consequences of the brief intimacy with Catherine, along with the dissatisfaction of frustrating attempts at relating to gay men, reinforced my fears that I was sexually unacceptable. I needed to be loved and known as a woman, but I hadn't been able to draw that into my life. I left Texas, hoping that everything would change. I had no way to explain my consistent attraction to gay men, even though I had spent many hours in therapy trying to understand, and I had no tools for breaking out of that pattern.

In so many ways, the love that David and I shared seemed like the realization of all my romantic dreams. I chose a man with whom I felt safe, safe from the threat of real intimacy yet satisfied with what we shared. Especially in the bedroom, there was no invasion into the private heart of me.

We were married in Austin, Texas on a beautiful spring day, standing within the circle of a gazebo in a public park. I wore a borrowed dress. We carried daisies. A banner hung overhead, bearing the words "If I keep a green bough in my heart, the singing bird will come." There were only a few friends, a simple flute serenade, romantic vows we wrote ourselves, without the benefit of clergy. No diamond ring, just a silver band bearing a stylized bough.

Marriage helped me feel validated as a woman, and soothed a dissonant relationship with my parents. I had finally accomplished the one thing that would make me a success in my mother's eyes. The public joining of our lives helped establish separateness from my parents on a deeper level than had been possible before. They began to treat me like an adult, and I began to act like one.

Now, for the first time in my life, loneliness was not an issue. There was ample psychic space for autonomy without the nagging isolation I had known before. There was immense comfort in finding David home each evening, in sharing the events of the day, and believing that he would be there for the rest of my life. I deepened my investment in the relationship, allowed myself to become more vulnerable now that I knew he would stay. I let my shoulders come down from my ears, learned to breathe easier, relax. We graduated from college and moved into professional careers. We became active in anti-nuclear work, lost our naïvete about political activism, and kept on going.

In 1980 we packed our meager belongings and moved to New York City so that David could be involved in international human rights law. We made a pact. If I moved to New York with him for two years, he agreed to let me decide where we would spend the next two years. I worked in a school for multihand-icapped children. We saw plays and ate inexpensive, exotic foods, wandered through the city feeling like explorers soaking up adventures on every block, and worked hard for very little money.

After one year in New York, David and I had other issues to face. He want-ed to continue with his work in New York City; I was ready to consider a move. We fought about having a child, about who paid more of the bills, about what our future would look like. We went into counseling again to try and resolve our differences. Within weeks we both became infatuated with our female counselor. No level of professional expertise could have diverted our attentions away from her and back to the real issues at hand, so our involvement with her was quick and unproductive. In 1982 we moved to Texas together so that I could be available to my mother, whose health was failing due to cancer. The rock-bottom real estate market allowed us to become first-time home buyers. The big sky was a relief from the urban intensity we had just left. I planted crepe myrtles and oleanders around our predictable suburban tract house with its brick facade. I stripped floors, laid down tiles, refinished cabinets and made a home.

We began yet another round of a seemingly endless arguments about having a child. When we finally agreed to try, we took a hole-punch to my diaphragm to ceremoniously destroy that circular latex shield with which we were both so familiar. Then we drank wine and cried, both recognizing that inviting a child into our lives would put an end to our relationship as we knew it.

The level of ambiguity I felt regarding the pregnancy surprised me. It was physically difficult, there were months of nausea and headaches, and my dis-comfort with my body increased with every added pound. Fatigue took on a new meaning, and my moods changed almost as quickly as my appetite. Yet, deep down inside in that inarticulate place that knows, I was excited to bring our child into the world. I felt enormous pride to have accomplished this phys-ical, sexual deed, and felt a new connection with mothers everywhere. With David as coach throughout the ridiculously long labor, I gave birth to our daughter, Laurel, in November of 1984.

My life changed dramatically in January of that next year. My father was arrested on a felony sexual assault of a minor. He had molested a young boy from his church. My mother retrieved her husband from the downtown jail, paid his bail, and maintained his silence. They each had their own anger and shame. He was convicted of a felony and, because of my mother's cancer, was given a deferred adjudication with probation, which meant that he paid hardly any penalty for what we discovered was a history of deception and illicit sexual behavior. When we learned the scope of his pathology, the cloud of confusion about my sexual attractions and experiences began to dissipate. For years, in dealing with questions about my attraction to gay men, counselors had asked me if my father was gay. I never understood why. In intimacies, I had exhibited many responses common to women who survive childhood sexual abuse: difficulty being in my body, shame when I was sexually aroused, an inarticulate fear that intimacy would suffocate me. Though I had not articulated any specific memories of childhood sexual abuse, now it seemed possible that much of my confusion and tension around sexual identity could have had its origins in family dynamics. For some reason, that made me feel less crazy.

By the early spring, my mother began to require more physical care than my father could provide. My sisters and I each took two days a week, made the three-hour drive, and went to help. I took Laurel with me; she was still nursing. I was faced with caring for my mother and my child while working at a full-time job. I wanted desperately to do both, but barely had enough energy to do either well.

My mother was living in her home with someone who had become a stranger to her. My parents sat in silence, their old patterns shattered. I came into their home every week wanting to be with my mother, confronted with the awkward distance between my father and me. Each visit brought tenderness, sadness, confusion, anger, and a host of other emotions.

During her last weeks, Mother and I talked about the many things she had kept secret over the years. When the talking was over, and I sat beside her in the days of quiet before her death, I knew her story: that she had entered her marriage with very low self-esteem and had found a partner who participated in devaluing her sexuality. He mirrored her own distrust of and negativity about her sexual self. They had tried to negotiate a relationship while neither of them had understood even the most basic facts about themselves. My father had repressed his homosexual orientation to the point that it erupted into behaviors he could not admit or control. My parents assisted each other in denying the uncomfortable dynamics of their relationship and of their individual lives.

My mother died in August, 1985. I was 35 years old, my daughter was still in diapers. In October, I began writing in my journal about the sexual attraction I felt for one of my lesbian friends. Deanna had been with me at the birth of my daughter; she had listened, helped and encouraged me for years. In November, my husband began to tease me about my attraction to her. In December, she and I stopped avoiding that attraction. The lessons of both my parents' denial had come home to me so dramatically that I could not ignore what was happening in my own life. I could not close my eyes to the essential negativity in my sexual relationship with my husband, could no longer ignore my attractions to women.

There was no deceit; David knew from the beginning that Deanna and I had begun a sexual relationship. I tried for many months to maintain a sexual connection with my husband, to articulate to him what I needed. We continued to live together, and I tried to juggle work responsibilities and time with my child, and divide the rest between both of my lovers. The logistics were practically impossible. Sex with my lesbian lover was total erotic fulfillment, a release of desire and a satisfaction that I had never known. With her, sex was breathing in, taking, getting. Her delight in arousing me, the celebration of wetness, of smells and sounds, released a primal passion in me. Intimacy took on new meaning. I knew emotional immediacy for the first time. Heterosexual sex had been a joining of myself to "the other." Lesbian sex was coming home. Each time I went to be with her, I had to walk away from a man I loved, leave my daughter and my home, and learn to be comfortable in her physical space. We met in borrowed snatches of time, compressing our involvement into moments that always passed too quickly. Sex with my husband was the same negative message it had always been, yet with the comfort of familiar territory, and our closeness was accompanied by the special tenderness of spending time with and sharing love for Laurel. After a few months, I gave myself permission to say no to him. Having been touched by Deanna, who was motivated from sensuality and sexual hunger, and having touched that same way and been received with such openness, something inside of me shifted. There was little David could do to draw me back to him.

We were divorced a year later. We legalized the joint custody arrangement that we had begun when we were separated, an arrangement that continues today. When I discuss my divorce with other people, they are always pleasantly surprised to hear how amicable it all was. What they don't hear about is the tremendous disruption of shuffling my child back and forth between households every week, packing her little suitcase and saying so many reluctant goodbyes, each time experiencing a small but acutely painful death. They don't know about needing not to cry when I hand her off, so that she can go happily to her Daddy, or missing exactly half of her everyday life.

Divorce meant leaving a house that I had made into a home, and moving into an apartment. In order to meet my monthly expenses I had to change jobs, and for at least the first year, it was a constant struggle. I had virtually no furniture, very little credit, a meager income; all the predictable hardships faced by women who divorce, only slightly lessened for me because I had a profession.

Single parenting demanded much more from me than I had prepared myself to give. I had my own grief about losing the nuclear family I had tried to believe in, and found myself also having to deal with my daughter's. There were long periods of time, months, when she cried easily and showed her frustration about having to deal with each of us, apart. In that early period, my lesbian lover was just that, a lover, who maintained her own apartment and her own lifestyle, and spent time with me when she wanted to. She offered a certain amount of emotional support, but was never there to drive the carpool to day care or pick up my sick child from school. I missed having someone share those daily duties, missed feeling confident that I was not in this alone.

Not all of the changes brought by divorce were negative ones. I began to understand and appreciate that I had extricated myself from a relationship that had misogyny at its very core. David's love for me had been complicated. He loved the intelligent, articulate me, but was repelled by my physical sexuality. Even when he wanted to, he couldn't be successfully sexual with me because of his own deep mistrust and fear of women. Away from his consistent sexual rejection, I began to be less critical of myself. Having moved beyond the roles and expectations that were so woven into our marriage relationship, David and I had an opportunity to become real friends.

There was a new sense of my own power. For the first time in my life I faced my needs and demanded what I wanted. I was proud of that. The nuclear family myth was exposed, with all its limitations. I began to understand that I was more than a wife or a mother, that my life could have a broader context. I admitted that the "stability" of marriage had often felt like confinement to me. I had lost my sense of being in charge of my own life because I had shifted my focus to maintaining a family unit. I began to be comfortable in my attempt to redefine family for myself. Whenever I was with my daughter, it was just the two of us, and we developed a whole new way of relating that was simple and direct, and very satisfying to me.

My new status as a woman in a lesbian relationship gave me a different social position with lesbians who had been my friends for many years. I was introduced into a fairly well organized lesbian community, shown the ropes in a way that many newly out women never have an opportunity to experience.

Soon after the divorce the dynamics in my lesbian relationship also began to shift. Sensing the possibility of legitimizing our relationship, of becoming a couple, Deanna became more available to me. With her I was understood, and seen, really known. She knew why it was important to me that the dishes get done tonight instead of tomorrow. She knew intuitively when I spoke with my mother's voice instead of my own, and she knew how to answer either of us. She saw vulnerabilities no man had ever seen. She learned the way my face changes when I'm scared in sex; knew why my body froze sometimes as my mind drifted off to some safer place. She knew how to call me home.

Since as lesbians we were outside mainstream assumptions about relationship, we had a greater freedom to articulate to each other and ourselves just what the current nature of our relationship was. Without the heterosexual script of love, marriage and baby carriage, there was no sense that we had to achieve any specific goals in our relationship. I felt a greater sense of privacy and originality than when I was married, as if a certain mystique about lesbian sexuality prohibited people from assuming that they knew what my life was like. I could give or withhold information about my life as I pleased, since my relationship was essentially invisible.

Over time, the invisibility became a burden. When we had arguments or problems, there were very few people on whom I could call for help. It was difficult to get leave from work to drive Deanna to an important appointment with a physician or miss a few days to attend a funeral in her family when the relationship was not recognized or legitimized by my co-workers. There was tension around defining me as "family" for the annual Christmas photo, or dividing inheritance money fairly among her married siblings and her "single" self, long after we had moved into a house together. I had the unfailing support of one of my sisters, but had not come out to my father or my other sister. We were invisible to them, no matter how many dinners we shared or family occasions we attended. That invisibility saved me their consternation, at the expense of their support.

Other issues interrupted our harmony. Deanna was physically lovely and younger than me. While I enjoyed her physical beauty, there were times when I longed to be the one who was pretty and sensual and feminine. In bed we were careful not to take on rigid roles, and it was in sex that I felt most honored and enjoyed as woman, but in many social contexts I felt like a second-class citizen. I missed being the only female in the couple, being female to someone's male, even while I intensely enjoyed having a woman as my lover. My old issues of not being attractive, or not being good enough, were constantly stimulated by remarks from people who were surprised to see someone as striking as my lover with someone as plain as me.

Early in the relationship, Deanna began what was to be a long pattern of leaving me and beginning new sexual relationships when things would settle down between us. She had a gnawing sense of restlessness, some need to act out her sexual prowess and get distance from me whenever our intimacy became too intense. I was constantly anxious that she would leave me, which she did over and over again. There were many comings and goings, households put together and then dismantled, and the safety in our relationship eroded with each event.

The dance we did in an attempt to get our basic intimacy needs met was immensely confusing and disrupting. Periods of unity and sweetness were interwoven with almost total breakdowns of communication. Neither of us had been prepared to deal with the grief process that unfolded in me in the wake of the divorce. The kinds of feelings that emerged were unexpected, and our emotional resources were not well enough developed to allow us to handle them effectively. The levels of ambiguity, the disappointment that went right down to the marrow of me, were startling. Deanna would press me for commitment, then threaten to leave. I would shut down when she pressed me, fearing a repetition of the kind of pain with which I was already too familiar.

Our most intense and final struggle was about children. Though Deanna and I did live together after my divorce was final, she never became fully engaged as a parent to my child. Laurel already had two parents, who were actively co-parenting. Deanna participated in nightly bedtime rituals, and shared the daily meals, was a consistently willing and cheerful playmate, and her relationship with my daughter was deep and affectionate. Yet she resisted taking responsibilities as a parent; she was unwilling to change her work schedule to be available for the frequent interruptions of caring for a child, never buying her the inevitable next pair of sneakers or getting the right food for the lunch box. Hindsight tells me she felt like the outsider, though she never said so. She began to verbalize her desire for a child of her own and gathered information about insemination. She had in mind a lesbian version of "Ozzie and Harriet." She would be the mommy, and I would be the daddy. We would live in a lesbian copy of a heterosexual marriage. My stomach began to tighten.

I had fantasized for years about us having a child together, about finally achieving the kind of closeness I had missed by raising my own child in the context of divorce. There had been dreamy ideas of the attachment, of the joy of sharing the day-to-day amazement of watching our child grow. But we had never seriously discussed the possibility of having a child together. Now when it came up, the prospect was tainted by the lack of commitment I felt from her, the damaged trust that had become intrinsic to our connection, and my issues around defining my femininity. I wasn't sure I could take on the "other mother" role. On a daily basis I had to face the painful realities of my relationship with my daughter, face the frustration of not being able to be as fully involved in her life as I would like to be. The idea of having a child in a lesbian couple, without any legal rights to that child in the event of a break-up, posed too great a threat. The risk felt huge. I knew I couldn't bear to go through separating from a child again, and with Deanna's history of leaving, I had no reason to feel secure that we would raise her child to adulthood together. I was in the process of applying for admission to graduate school, ready to divest myself of fourteen years of taking care of other people's needs in a health care profession and move into a field that would allow me more personal growth. The financial, physical and emotional drain of taking care of a newborn would make that impossible.

Even more important than all of those issues was my discomfort with conceiving and raising a child without a father. It was hard for me to admit that I had trouble with that, to disclose such a traditional value. I had friends with children who had been conceived through insemination, and felt no judgment about their choice, but I experienced an intractable negative response to the idea of conceiving that way myself. It is a constant comfort to me that my daughter has a healthy relationship with a man who loves her dearly, that she experiences a daddy. He offers her things I cannot, and their relationship will enable her to have a better relationship with men than I will ever have. Even though I recognize my sexual orientation as lesbian, it saddens me to be so disconnected from men, and I didn't want to participate in a life that took that disconnection for granted. The fact that my conviction is tantamount to treason in the lesbian community made it difficult for me to articulate, but I did, and Deanna left, putting an end to five years of the most powerfully intimate and confusing relationship of my life.

When Deanna left, she took with her all the validation and real closeness I have known. What followed was not the simple loneliness of loss, but the complex experience of living in an absence, with so many of the things I wanted now seeming out of reach. The dependency had to be dealt with.

Alone, at 40, a lesbian single mom with a seven-year-old daughter, I am left with a lot of questions and frustrations. The isolation within the lesbian community has come as a surprise. The comfort I derived from relationships with other lesbian couples has disappeared. The break-up of my relationship with Deanna somehow has disappointed and alienated them and made them inaccessible to me at a time when I desperately need support. Because so many women my age already have lives filled with work, family and community responsibilities, it has been next to impossible to meet women who are ready and available for relationship. The physical, sexual isolation seems almost unbearable at times. Facing the fact that I cannot create relationship, cannot replace my loss, has forced me to focus my energies on myself and try to develop a new support system. Building that back into my life is a slow and difficult process, but well worth the effort.

The work for now is to come to some point of peace about myself, reaffirm my own value, and stay open to what the future may hold. I face the future with a broader sense of what I have to offer, with a more forgiving attitude about my own shortcomings. My sincere hope is that the best of lesbian life is still ahead.

Ellen Bass at a high school prom and, left, with her family.

Change

ELLEN BASS

This is where I yank the old roots
from my chest, like the tomatoes
we let grow until December, stalks
thick as saplings.

This is the moment when the ancient fears
race like thoroughbreds, asking for more
and more rein. And I, the driver,
for some reason they know nothing of
strain to hold them back.

Terror grips me like a virus
and I sweat, fevered,
trying to burn it out.

This feat is so invisible. All you can see
is a woman going about her ordinary day,
drinking tea, taking herself to the movies,
reading in bed. If victorious
I will look exactly the same.

Yet I am hoisting a car from mud ruts
half a century deep. I am hacking
a clearing through the fallen slash
of my heart. Without laser precision,
with only the primitive knife of need, I cut
and splice the circuitry of my brain.
I change.

Author's note: "Change" was not originally written about coming out, but
the poem captures the process of change many of us have experienced.

Shutting Down/Breaking Out: Snapshots from a Life

ZANNIE KYD

As a fourth grader, I loved Esther; although I knew I couldn't tell anyone, I definitely planned to marry her. Later, I loved Judy and Barbara and Barbara...I sure was taken with those Barbaras...and I loved Jane and, in different ways, the Helens. And there were other fleeting crushes, passionate desires to share a word or a touch with interesting women in classrooms and churches, on beaches and busses, at libraries and luncheonettes. And, there were the radio voices, invisible strong women whom I longed to know and whom I did encounter, ever so coolly and casually, in my daydreams. Oh, the pleasure and the joy!

And then, in a few short hours ripped from some other life and forced into my own, *they* found out. Classmates called me "lesbian," a strange new word not to be found in my collegiate dictionary...they avoided, sought out, sneered and pointed at me. They talked about, at, and to me: "I'm so sorry for you," said one; "We can never trust you again," said another. They burned cigarette holes in my favorite jacket; with nail polish they wrote on it "Burn the Lesbians" and they hung it in a public place. As for my elders, they treated my "affliction" with all their sciences and creeds. While the college psychologist educated me on the "evil women" portrayed by Krafft-Ebing, my preacher dad expounded the religious view and accompanied me to our drug-dispensing family doctor and thence to the specialist at the local state hospital. My mom thought Arthur Murray dance lessons might be some help...and all of them opined from time-to-time that, really, there is no such thing as a lesbian. Their efforts were persistent and they fucked with my mind...ultimately, they won.

Shutting Down

I gave up women, and transferred my passion to scotch and silence. But scotch was a demanding lover and a fickle friend; never satisfied, she always demanded one more round...and when the bar was closing or the bottle empty she left me alone to deal with the fixes we'd gotten into together. I needed help in controlling her and someone to run my life better than I could by myself. Perhaps those magazine messages of my '50s adolescence held the answer: A Man. And, indeed, I knew a man who wanted to marry me. He treated me better than I treated myself; older and wiser, he would fix me, straighten me out. I married him... my sister claims I told her it was for "two years, max."

But two years stretched into twenty-odd, and in this marriage forged in loneliness and despair, I grew more lonely and desperate. Oh, we had lots of nice things: fine china, travel, and credit cards. I had my privileges: school and then work, fancy clothes and cooking gadgets that he perceived I needed. There were no fights with the in-laws, no financial setbacks, no battering, rape, or extra-marital affairs. We were parents, professionals, nice people...a picture-perfect couple, some thought. But, let me show you a few pictures, some snap-shots from my marriage.

History

It's not that P. and I don't talk at all. Parts of our past lives flourish in our con-versations, relived and revisited, extended into the present. The patterns of streets in the towns where we grew up, the names of our teachers, and the col-ors of our tricycles become shared knowledge. The mahogany tables and floor lamps of our childhood homes people our reminiscences. Certificated events — confirmation, scout merit badges, and high school graduation—verify that we did not spring full-grown from the earth. A few Christmas cards and an occa-sional engraved announcement reawaken each of us to the suspicion that the other once had a different life.

But, the joys and agonies of those previous lives remain unspoken secrets. Occasionally something from P.'s past appears...an object I hadn't noticed or a letter in the mail. If I inquire, I am told not to pry...and soon the letter or the object disappears, presumably put in the large drawer where P. keeps his past, safe from my knowledge or intrusion. For me the drawer is a symbol, an ever-present reminder that not revealing the past is one of the unspoken bargains, perhaps the cornerstone of this marriage.

...and another history snapshot

I have saved no objects to conjure up memories of lost loves and adolescent crushes, and my history must survive in my mind. To write it would be to make it too real and open it to the potential scrutiny of P. Secretly, I read some of my history in the stories of others, rereading and rehearsing to keep it alive. Parts of my history I forget, and some persons I kill off with stories whose sources I can never know. I remember with bitterness and sweetness that I am a lesbian. I remember that I tried to be a lesbian and failed. I remember that it may be in my genes, that my daughter, too, may be a lesbian. I remember that it may be my mother's mothering that caused me to be a lesbian, that my daughter, too, may be a lesbian if I mother her that way...but I cannot remember what that way was. I remember that lesbians love other women, that I have loved women, that women have loved me...and I remember that I cannot let this happen again. I remember that I must not talk about these things: doctors, counselors, preachers, teachers, friends, family…all will turn on me if I speak of it. I remember that it is important to remember that I am a lesbian.

…how does your garden grow?

It's just a small garden plot, 6 feet by 25 between the house and the garage, but it gives me a lot of pleasure. I dug it myself, and planted it densely. It doesn't have rows, but vegetables and flowers are interspersed for compatible growth and to be pleasing to the eye. I'm trying to do it organically, and I've read about companion gardening…tomatoes and basil belong together; each repels the other's pests, and when harvested they taste good together, too! But every year, the biggest pest is P. and his demanding questions. Can't he dig the garden for me? Don't I want him to fertilize it? Don't I know that planting in rows would be better? Don't I want him to use something stronger on the squash beetles? Daily I refuse and resist; I protect the garden from his incursions. The garden is my "room of my own." I talk kindly to the plants as I weed and water them; and they reward me with their beauty and their fruits.

Alcohol

Fortunately, I think (or at least I did then), P. likes to drink. What I don't think much about is that he also likes to control…or if I do think about it I think that it is good. He controls the flow of alcohol in our house; although he does it fairly liberally, he does it very authoritatively: two drinks before dinner, a bottle of wine with, and later some sort of "nightcap." With some cunning I can stretch the two drinks into three…by accidentally setting the oven on low instead of high, and thus creating an empty time, or by drinking from his glass when he is not looking, or by other ruses.

For many years I never enter a liquor store, I never pour whiskey nor uncork the fine wines that P. prefers…this is part of the unspoken bargain of our marriage vows. Somewhere along the line, however, I discover boxed wine and suggest that we use it for cooking; P. agrees…and now I have my own supply! No transparent bottles he can mark…and I buy it myself with the groceries! Before dinner I sip wine not only from my glass, but also from my pyrex measuring cup; if he's watching too closely, I can always pour the cupful into the chicken and boil it off.

I could tell you many such tricks I play on him, but really on myself. Every day I practice letting him control me the way a child is controlled. Instead of challenging his authority I become the naughty child…and as time goes on this role becomes a way of life. The way we deal with alcohol becomes the way we deal with almost everything.

There are no pictures here of my daughter or of the mother I was, the mother I hope was a "good mother" whatever that might mean considering the context. There are no snapshots of women friends; to tell you the truth, I couldn't allow myself to develop close relationships with my female acquaintances…it was simply too threatening to what I saw as the stability in my life. And, there are no photos of that other person that I was…the competent professional academic, the "feminist" teacher who could leave her other wifely life at home.

Breaking Out!

At least a dozen things had to happen before I could set myself free of my marriage. Looking back, it seems that my parents and maternal grandparents had to die, and with them not only the threats to my body and freedom, but also the guilt that would have been mine if, as my parents predicted earlier "it would kill your grandparents." Even more compelling was my parents' earlier insistence that in declaring myself a lesbian I was deliberately, conspicuously, arbitrarily and unnecessarily doing something *to them*. That is, they (or at least my father) viewed my assertion of my own lesbianism as ungrounded in any truth, a fiction I had deliberately concocted in order to punish them. Because my parsonage upbringing had taught me the importance of not offending or hurting others (and I had practiced self-repressive inoffensiveness for many years), there was great conflict between the lesbian and the preacher's kid inside me. By staying married, I could avoid the recurrence of these conflicts, which I knew would be inevitable were I to hit the streets as a "free womyn."

In this and other regards, there was also my daughter to think about. At one level, P. had convinced me early on that he was by far the better parent, at another level I retained the belief that I contributed importantly to the quality of her life. I could not bear the thought of leaving her. Nor could I conceive of the possibility that alone I could be a reliable mother (whatever a court might decide). I was, and knew I was, too depressed, too prone to drunkenness and isolation. Were I to seek companionship it would be among bar dykes…and that knowledge raised issues of its own. And so, in order for me to leave, my daughter had to grow up and go off to school.

More than a year before I left, I screwed up my courage and told her of my intention to leave. Her response was both shocking and strangely affirming: "I've been worrying about what would happen to you when I went away to college." Together we worked out my departure schedule; as I had already waited this long, I would wait until she was safely out of the state and could not be pressured to live with her dad and go to the local university.

In some sense, these issues of parents and child were structural matters; they framed the situation. While they were important, by themselves these changes would not have allowed me to "run away." In order to escape, I needed to have the will and the energy to do so, and the belief and determination that I could. These came from many sources. Again, some snapshots tell the story.

Treasure to Trash

There's a feminist bookstore in town, and by the early '80s I have started to frequent the lesbian section. Furtively, I enter and pretend I'm looking at women's history or some other genre. Quickly surveying the lesbian shelves, I grab one, pay for it, and leave. On later trips, I get braver and idly pick up the free papers and flyers before I leave. From the bookstore I go to an out-of-the-way restaurant where I devour the reading material and play with my food. I leave the restaurant and drive around until I find just the right dumpster where I ditch the reading material before going back to my office or home. I am amassing a wealth of knowledge and information, and with it some courage. I am beginning to feel that I might be real.

Kathy

Suddenly I realize that Kathy is in my life...and that I am madly, totally, wonderfully in love with her. She is a secretary in my office, but our time together starts to expand well beyond the 8 to 5. At one of our first get-togethers she queries me; before she asks, I know her question will be "have you ever been in a lesbian relationship?" When I respond affirmatively she asserts that ours will be a wonderful loving platonic friendship. Disappointed and exploding with passion, I accept her ground rules...she is the first friend I have had in nearly two decades.

What a wonderful gift she is! We go out after work and she talks a mile a minute filling the spaces between the one- or two-word remarks I am able to venture. Soon she teaches me to say more and to look at her when I'm talking. One Saturday afternoon we go shopping; she cannot believe I have never before gone to a mall with a woman friend. There are many similar trips; in teaching me how to shop for myself, she teaches me that there are many simple ways in which my life can be different. She openly tells me how odd and unfree I am, how her other friends' husbands don't follow them around or call up to check on their whereabouts, how her other working friends have their own cars. She teaches me to laugh at myself (sometimes), and she goes to the bank with me when I start my own savings account; we've decided, Kathy and I, that I'm going to save any cash I can spare and a small sum I inherited to buy my own car! And she gives me presents...small items that are beautiful because they are from her. At first I am fearful that she will not like them, but I start to give her presents too. She comes to my house when P. is not there—the first friend I have ever "had over." We talk and talk, out in the sunshine and at Wendy's before work. With her, I start to laugh at some of P.'s habits...but P. is starting to be mean to Kathy; he glowers at her when he sees her; she is upset by him and perhaps a little afraid. A year and a half goes by...and Kathy is looking for another job. I encourage her, but when she gets it I congratulate her and then I cry almost steadily for a week. I see her much less often, and soon I rarely see her at all. I miss her terribly...but I know I will always love her and be grateful for the great gift she has been to me, indeed the miracle she has worked in my life. I can talk a little and I can laugh; I can buy personal things without P.'s approval; most importantly, I have gone places without him and now I have my own car.

The Bar

It's the early '80s, and I know where the gay bars are in town...at least I know their addresses. I begin to seek them out whenever I have the car. No neon beer signs, no party noise, often no street numbers announce their presence and they are hard to find. But find them I do, and I begin to circle them regularly, hoping to see women entering or leaving. One has a sign "every night is ladies' night" and I decide it will be my bar. After months of circling, I recognize some of the regulars. They wear jeans, I discover, and I buy a pair and break them in. Soon I have the courage to pocket my wedding rings and, knowing there will be no return, I walk in.

Once having been inside, I cannot stay away. My life takes on new rituals. As I leave the office I take the phone off the hook knowing I will tell P. I need to return to work after dinner (and knowing just as well that he will call me to check that I am there). After I have my own car, sometimes the grocery is my "destination"; planning ahead as I leave work, I stop and fill the trunk with sacks of cans and paper goods to be carried into the house at midnight. The same trick works with the library, I discover. With one excuse or another, I get to the bar several nights a week, sometimes for an hour or two, sometimes for longer. But it is never long enough. By now, I am meeting many womyn...and I know that my life is going to change...indeed, my life has changed for a few hours almost every day.

"God is Love"

Like many a grownup "preacher's kid," I am ambivalent about the church and have cycled in and out of it; most often I resist church influence on my life, but at times I have sought comfort in the rituals of my childhood. On this spring day, I am sitting in church as a woman pastor preaches about loving others different from ourselves. When the service ends the congregation sits down for a meeting called to decide whether a denominational group of lesbians and gays can use a room in the building for bimonthly meetings and worship. Many infrequent attenders have come to participate in this decision and to deliver their homophobic diatribes against the pastors and against all "deviants" and "queers," "dykes and fags" everywhere. A few people, men and women, speak eloquently in favor of opening the church to the gay and lesbian group. But, as they speak, they are shouted down with abusive remarks. Hatred swells and fills this "sanctuary of God." The hatred is so palpable, so real and so large that it spills out of the building and back through time and makes visible to me the hatred that I had neither recognized nor named those twenty-odd years ago. My hands tremble as I mark "yes" on my quivering paper ballot; my body is shaking and my head is light. The gays and lesbians are voted down by a narrow margin, and as I leave the church for the last time ever, the pastor says, "I guess this wasn't the right issue. The congregation just isn't ready." But for me it is the right issue and now I am ready...ready to name the hatred and to name myself among those hated.

AA

For the first time in all these years, I am noticing how much I drink and what it is doing to me. I notice that I regularly get the shakes and that I am often the only one with wine at lunch. My head feels funny, almost vacuous, and my vision is increasingly obstructed. I am feeling caught. I make resolutions not to drink and keep them by day; but come dinnertime I cannot be at home and not drink. I feel a circle tightening around me: I need to get out before I can stop drinking, and I need to stop drinking before I can get out. Wine and whiskey give me the courage to say no to P. in my newfound voice; but they sap my energy. I drink rather than look for an apartment; I drink rather than sort through my things; I drink whenever I am in that house. I drink a lot and I cry a lot and I know that I have to do something to stop this cycle, but I cannot find the answer.

In the yellow pages I read those idyllic ads for alcohol treatment centers (the kind with the parklike setting and vacation allure) and I call some on the phone. The whole family will need to be involved, they say, and I know that they are not for me. I talk with a woman I know who goes to AA...but I don't ask her to take me to a meeting...I am too scared of all those people who are fixing their lives...I am afraid they will try again to fix the lesbian in me. I go to the bar...surprisingly I don't drink much while there; I am too busy watching, dancing, talking, listening. I overhear a conversation about a lesbian AA group; I listen more carefully and I inquire around. Several weeks later, I have had my last drink and I go to the lesbian AA meeting.

One often hears at AA meetings that for many people coming into those rooms feels like coming home. For me this is not the case; I had already come home when I stepped into the lesbian bar. Nor is the AA program itself my salvation; I go to over 400 AA meetings in my first year of sobriety, and many more in the next few years, but I never "work a step." What I get from AA is the opportunity to be in the company of people, many of them lesbians, who affirm that I do not have to drink today. More importantly for me, they accept me as a lesbian, and they do not punish me or try to fix me. With this acceptance, they give me all that I wanted in the early '60s...and exactly what I need in the mid-'80s.

Out and About

In October, 1985, I stopped drinking. By January, I had been convinced that I should consult a lesbian therapist who helped me greatly as I worked through a number of issues and plans. On Labor Day, 1986, I took my daughter to school in New England and within a week I moved out of my husband's home and into an apartment with the woman who would soon become my partner. Together, we participate in the lesbian cultures of our community. Proudly, we are dykes.

As I have come to new life, I have been shocked to learn the extent to which my every thought and deed was affected by the marriage in which I lived. Since leaving, my political consciousness and activism have been reborn, and the focus of my academic work has changed. It is still very hard for me to consider being "out" in situations which involve family members or male authority figures. But I grow continuously and each day brings new bravery and new realities.

It is almost nine years since I made my escape and, although I sometimes regret painfully all the "lost years" of my life, to date I have "lived happily ever after." Do you have time for a few more snapshots?

Herstory Today

One of the greatest joys in my new life is the long languid hours my partner and I spend weaving together the threads of experience from our past lives, our current thoughts, and our hopes and fears for the future. We share, and thus mitigate, the anguish, pain, and despair we each have carried so long. We create futures without fear and presents filled with joy. In some magical moments we speak spontaneously our identical thoughts, and at these times our history together seems ageless and infinite in all of its many dimensions.

Gardening Today

Today I tend to many aspects of my life with the loving care I lavished on my kitchen garden. In fact, that garden is an apt metaphor for my lesbian world. My friendships and activities cannot be put into rows and columns; instead they form themselves in beautiful, fruitful, and mutually supportive clusters. To be sure, just as my garden had squash beetles, my world has its own nagging problems...but we get along, my problems and I, in a kind of organic and productive way. In my new life I have a little kitchen garden much like the one I had before, and I love the herbs and vegetables that grow there; but today I do not need them to love me in return.

Alcohol Today

Actually, alcohol has no place in my life today. We don't use it or keep it around our house; if friends want to drink here they may, but they usually have to bring their own. Generally speaking, when I know someone who often gets drunk, my heart goes out to her; I'll spend time with her, but I'd rather not spend time with her drinks. It's very much like divorce. For years, alcohol was my lover and life-partner; now that it's over, I'd rather not see it or have anything to do with it.

But if alcohol was my life partner, then who was P.? I'm not sure I know enough about him to say; besides, his story is not mine to tell. We spent a lot of years together in a legal union, a joint venture of sorts. We shared many things, but not confidence and trust. I wonder if either of us had enough confidence or trust to share. For years I thought I would never leave him, that I somehow owed him my life. Today I know I owe my life to myself.

Star-Crossed Lovers:
An Interview

WITH TRISTAN WONG AND PATSY CHU

On a rainy spring day in Seattle, two women from Chinese American families agreed to tell Ellen the story of the love affair they've been engaged in for more than eight years. They don't know how it's going to come out yet. Nothing is resolved. Both are still legally married to their husbands of 25 and 30 years and both still live with them. Their husbands know of the affair and want it to end. Patsy has assured her husband she's "working on it," but admits during our interview that she's not. Tristan acknowledges to her husband that they are growing apart and doesn't know what to tell him when he asks about their life together after he retires. She's active as a community volunteer but has never worked outside the home and would have no income if she left him. Patsy has a low-paying, part-time retail sales job and had always planned to depend on her husband's pension in her old age. Now in their mid-50's, neither Tristan or Patsy expected life to go this way. Their concern and love for each other is apparent as they sit side by side on a friend's couch. Tears fall easily as they take turns relaying their story.

Tristan: We got to know each other because our families were good friends. We met as mothers when our children were in the third grade. We began taking family vacations together and became very good friends. Our friendship was very important to us, and it developed over seven or eight years. I think we were both very busy but we made our friendship a priority.

Patsy: Now our children are in college and moving away from home, gradually. All of this has developed in the last few years. One time we went on a trip together with a group of women friends—"the girls." And when I came back, I just had a really different feeling. I was very depressed when I got home, and I know my husband noticed it. He didn't say anything. But soon I realized it had to do with feelings I had for Tristan, and it really bothered me. I couldn't understand it. I guess for the next five years I knew I had these feelings, but I put them in the back of my head. I said, "This can't be. It doesn't fit my life."

Then finally one time Tristan and I took a trip together, and again, it was just the two of us and some other friends. I guess we had a long time to talk and we became better acquainted. Not that anything happened—because we didn't room together. But when Tristan came back, she felt differently too. That's when she told me how she felt and things started.

Tristan: I knew that Patsy was growing closer to me. It didn't scare me, but I realized she wanted to get closer. These were the only times I had ever gone on a vacation without my family. I really had a good time and enjoyed all the company. When we came back, I was surprised when she told me about her feelings the five years before. In that five years I remember feeling that she was my good friend, and she always made me feel special. There were times when I could tell she wanted to get closer in our relationship—closer meaning just being closer friends and doing more things together. I can remember I thought, "I just don't have time for this. I can't fit it in." It was always like, we'll keep it at our friendship level.

I tease Patsy because the reason she told me about her feelings for me was that she'd tried really hard to get us the best seats on the train, but we had to ride backwards, and that always makes me carsick. So she was trying to distract me by telling me how important I was to her! And it *really did* take my mind off getting sick. I remember her saying it verbally and I was thinking "I know these feelings," but I'd never heard it verbally before, so it made a lot of difference to me.

When we got to our destination, she and I shared a room. I remember waking up at 3 o'clock in the morning and then she'd say something, so we'd start our conversation at 3 a.m. It was like "I have to tell her how I feel." But it didn't happen then, it happened when we came back. Still, it was amazing to be able to talk with her.

Patsy: During all this, my husband has been very interested in staying married to me and making our marriage work. And he does know now about Tristan and me. When you try to hide something like that, it gets pretty obvious after a while. He knew, but because I denied it, he wanted to believe me, so he allowed it to continue. After a year it was just too difficult to hide, so he said that he knew. I finally said that he was right. He wasn't really angry at that point, he was just very upset. But I guess because I kept saying, "I can handle this, I can take care of it, I'll straighten it out," it became a problem in the sense that I didn't. That's what really made him angry. And that's what's made the next three years extremely difficult.

He sent me to therapy because he thought that was going to solve it. We went to therapy together for a year. But see, I didn't feel comfortable with the therapist (which was stupid—I probably shouldn't have continued). Except my husband felt that it was helping. Finally it got to the point where he didn't think it was helping either because we were just going over the same ground. All it would do was rekindle all the anger he had after each therapy session because there was really nothing he could do.

What's sad is that he wants to stay in the marriage according to how things were before—he cannot accept any changes in me. He wants things to go back to "normal." I have not been honest with him at all because I keep telling him that's what I want for us and that's what I'm trying to do, but I'm not. Up until the time I had these feelings, my husband and I were really very much in love with each other. To a certain extent we still are, but it's just that there's been a new dimension added to my life, and he can't cope with it. We had a big wedding with tons of community support. We've always done youth work and Christian work in a Presbyterian church with a Chinese American congregation. We are very well-established in the community and our marriage is very public. More than once we've been set up as an example of the perfect married couple.

I guess the first person that I told was my minister. It's interesting because he wasn't judgmental, which I think was very helpful, but he said that if you make the decision to be with Tristan, you know you can't stay in this church. He was being very honest, very concerned.

Tristan: I also want to tell the story of when my husband found out. We don't hide it real well. His first reaction was for me to work it out so that we (Patsy and I) could continue to be friends and the family could stay intact. If not, then there was a possibility of a divorce. His next reaction was that I should get therapy. I eventually did find a supportive therapist, but I felt like I was just spilling my guts and nothing was happening. The best thing she did was to suggest that Patsy and I go find support groups and meet other people. I remember telling her that Patsy's my good friend, and we've gone in very deep, but I think I could be her friend again. The therapist laughed at me. I thought—"I'm serious…I think I can do that. I think I can go back to being her friend." I guess when she laughed at me, it really made me think.

So, we went to a lot of support groups and told our story. We saw one advertised for women of color and both of us thought, "that's for black women," but we went anyway and everyone was black, but they were very nice to us. Then we found an Asian lesbian support group but all the women were really young; however Patsy was moved when one young girl heard our story and said "I wish you were my mommy." It felt good to tell the story verbally. I really surprised Patsy by how much I talked.

Patsy: Yeah, I would just sit next to her and cry.

Tristan: That's one of the things I've learned through this—to be verbal. I think I was a typical Asian woman—sit back, watch life go by. I mean, I have feelings, but I was supposed to grow up, get married, have children. I wasn't supposed to talk it over with anyone or question my future.

When I was young, I was very interested in sports, and people thought that I could be lesbian. I played softball and was always in a group of girls. I remember I wanted to go into P.E., but my parents said "that's not a good profession for a woman," so I did what they asked. I wasn't completely happy about it, but I wasn't unhappy either. I didn't want to go against them. I had a sister who kind of did her own thing, and I knew I didn't want to buck the system.

I think my husband felt that if I would go to therapy, the therapist would change my mind and "cure" me. Recently we've gone through this again because he wants to go to therapy together. But my therapist taught me to investigate the parts of life I was interested in, and I can't share them with my husband. I've always said that if he asks me directly, I'll tell him, but I'm not volunteering anything. And he's not asking me anything.

Patsy: So we've both given in to our husbands a lot. It goes back to the old Chinese ways where the man is right about everything and has all the power and the woman has none. The man can divorce his wife for any reason or no reason—if he doesn't like the way she does her hair or she doesn't bear him a son. These traditional feelings run deep and affect us, I'm sure, but we also live in modern times and we are affected by the modern world around us. Mostly I think it's that these two men just don't want things to change.

Patsy: So when we want to make dates and spend time together, I'm very clever. I guess it will all come out in the wash. My husband wants so very hard to believe me, that it's not that difficult for me to pretty much do what I want, although he's drawn up some very clear rules. For instance, she's not to call me, she's not to come to the house, no more trips together for the last three years.

Tristan: But we just came back from Mexico City two months ago.

Patsy: I take groups on missions for the church. We had eight women on this trip. Of course my husband thinks I roomed with this other person. Tristan came on at the last minute. I mean, I engineered the fact that she was on the trip, but in his mind, I had nothing to do with it.

Tristan: On top of all this, our husbands call each other best friends!

Patsy: My husband always says that her husband is a very good friend of his, yet he never phones or goes anyplace with him. When Tristan's husband asks him to go out and do something together, he usually says no. But that's what my husband thinks a friend is: you don't have any connection with him, but then you're best friends, you know.

Tristan: Our husbands do have their differences. My husband is Buddhist. He maintains a very calm and dignified attitude toward life. I married into his religion and have a great deal of respect for him and the religion. Patsy's husband is very righteous. He says "What you have done is bad, you've misbehaved. So if you open your mouth about this, we're not going to talk about it. We've already solved that problem. We've had 20 years of perfect marriage and she comes into your life...*is this the way you want to live?*" Then Patsy tells me, "I don't want to get him upset, I don't want to go through that," and I say "If you're lying to him and he finds out, do you think it's going to be easier than right now?"

I guess I've put her on the spot a lot. I say: "Tell me why it's gonna be easier down the line. Is our health gonna be any better? We could wait if you can tell me why it's easier."

Patsy: I guess I'm expecting to wait a long time. It's like I have to finish this life before I can start another. I can't convince my husband that this is my future and not just a stage. He threatens me that I'll end up in poverty.

Tristan: If I could have my ideal life, I would share my life with Patsy.

Patsy: I guess I always have to say to myself, if I love her that much, I should be willing to leave. I don't seem to be able to. There is something stopping me.

Tristan: I won't force her if she's not ready.

Patsy: A lot of it goes back to one's childhood. I was the kind of kid who was so ashamed of getting in trouble. I never wanted to be scolded or told that I was in the wrong. I haven't changed.

Tristan: Well, when I was growing up, if my mother said jump, I would never question why she was asking me to jump. I would say, "How high do you want me to jump?" That's how I've been in my marriage too. I'd do anything my husband wanted me to do, whether I liked it or not, and usually it was okay. I guess just okay isn't good enough anymore.

What I told Patsy is that if I loved my husband as much as I love her, in the way I love her, she would never have gotten into my life. When I first realized I could leave my family for her, I was very upset. It was a shock to me. But it was true. And in the end, I will never give up my relationship with her.

Margarethe Cammermeyer on her wedding day.

...and today with her partner.

Excerpts from *Serving in Silence*

MARGARETHE CAMMERMEYER WITH CHRIS FISHER

Germany and Marriage
Nuremburg Germany, August 1964

I met Harvey in August, 1964. I'd been in Germany for five months, enough time to feel comfortable with my work and establish a good circle of friends. Frequently, Judy and other friends would set me up on blind dates. The only recollection I have of these unmemorable evenings was that I was as tall as, or taller than, my poor dates. I wasn't a particularly good conversationalist when I wasn't interested in someone. That quiet aspect of my personality, coupled with my date's uneasiness at being with a taller woman, made these evenings exercises in polite boredom. Since my goal in the service was to excel, not to marry, when my friend said he knew a surgeon who knew a lieutenant who wanted to meet a tall girl, I agreed with reluctance.

So I went out on a blind date with Harvey Hawken. For the first time, when I opened the door, I had to look up to someone. Harvey was six feet, six inches tall, weighed more than 230 pounds, and was definitely not a pushover. I think he was as shocked as I to meet someone so tall. Standing at the door in my high heels, I nearly looked him straight in the eye.

He was from a rural area just south of Seattle. He'd gone to the University of Washington on a track scholarship, joined the ROTC program, and was now a second lieutenant in an armor battalion. He was a professional soldier. It was a role he proudly cultivated, as did I. We found each other familiar, and amazingly comfortable, even from the beginning. Our families were similar—-both conservative, Lutheran, and middle-class. We were both first-born children, each of us with three siblings. There were three boys and one girl in each of our families. We both skipped fourth grade. We were both college graduates, had serious, intense natures, and wanted to excel in everything we did. Also, without modesty, I can say we made a good-looking couple.

From August through December, seeing Harvey in the evenings and weekends was as natural a part of my schedule as work at the hospital. We were a couple. People expected to see us together. By then, both of my best friends, Judy and Deanna, had married and moved in with their new husbands. I lived alone, and spent time with Harvey. He was a very personable, easy friend to everyone he met. When we showed up almost nightly at the officers' club, people exclaimed at how great the two of us looked together. The encouragement from all around us was not very subtle.

But Harvey never mentioned the possibility of marriage, though he wrote several notes to my mother telling her how fond he was of me. And I didn't want to consider marriage because I viewed it as a loss of freedom. I had no role model to demonstrate that a woman could be a wife and pursue a career. My mother hadn't. In marrying, she lost her autonomy, became subservient. Marriage meant losing all the things I enjoyed and had worked to achieve. Even though Harvey and I didn't discuss it, always being together, having our married friends tell us we made a handsome couple—all that pointed to an expectation of marriage, and I was beginning to feel trapped.

Harvey had a very strong personality. Like his physique, it's very imposing. It seemed to me that as long as his expectations were met, things went smoothly. But if something he didn't like happened, I feared major confrontation.

I sensed that even those first months together. Though I felt he was taking me for granted, that no matter what the event, he would expect me to dutifully be his date, I didn't feel I could talk to him about it. So I bottled up my feelings of being irritated or discounted, and was obediently available all the time. In those days, that's what a woman was supposed to do. Any magazine or film told me that. And I was used to taking care of others' wants and needs.

Yet there were times when I felt I couldn't breathe around him. Reconciling his constant presence in my life with my own needs seemed impossible. The only solution I saw was to stop seeing him; then maybe I'd get some breathing space. But that meant a confrontation, which I did not want. Finally, in January, he developed a muscle spasm in his back and had to stay in the hospital for several weeks. This gave me an opportunity to escape.

I'm not proud that I told him I wanted to stop seeing him when he was on his back in the hospital. But it seemed my best opportunity to get some distance in order to think things through. I didn't have the courage or didn't feel I had the right to do it until he was in the hospital. Disappointing him because of my needs was very difficult. On his second day there, I came into his room, listened to how he was feeling and how he'd be off his feet for a couple of weeks. Then, rather suddenly, I told him I needed time alone.

I said, "I don't want to see you anymore. I am not in love with you, so why don't we just back off."

He seemed crushed. It pained me a great deal. He insisted I not do this. I needed time alone, but I compromised when he persisted. I said that I did not want to see him for thirty days. And then I left. I got time off from the hospital and went to the Bavarian Alps for a few days by myself.

It was a great relief to be alone in the mountains, walking, thinking, reading. I had time to reflect on the last months. I never expected to be married, only to continue my military career unattached. I wanted to become Chief Nurse of the Army Nurse Corps and a general, and that mattered more to me than becoming a wife.

When I got gack to work, it started. Though Harvey honored my thirty-day moratorium on seeing him, I felt he conducted a rigorous campaign to get me to change my mind. I was astounded by his persistence. It seemed to me that he courted me from a distance, in ways he never had while we dated. I got calls from his friends, who said, "What are you doing to Harvey? He can't work, he can't eat." My friends and colleagues said he called them. I'd come home from work and there would be flowers at my door with notes saying he was counting the days until my self-imposed separation was over. I'd go to my car in the morning, and written in the frost on my windshield would be the words "I love you."

I couldn't tell you how much of this was because he wanted me, and how much was because he wanted to get his way. I hadn't intended to provoke him to be more attentive; I simply needed time alone to understand my own feelings. Whenever some memento appeared, I blushed, and felt relieved no one was there to witness my response. His displays of attention were embarrassingly public; I'd been brought up to be a very private person, and I was frustrated by the continuous intrusion and bombardment.

But then, the heat increased. He called and politely, even sweetly, asked to see me when the thirty days were over. I couldn't turn down such persistence and intensity, and agreed to have a quiet dinner with him in my apartment. So the very first evening after the moratorium ended, he came courting. He arrived in splendid military attire, dressed in his most pressed and polished fashion, looking more as if he were coming to an inspection than to a dinner. In his arms were flowers for me. The whole business.

Then, at dinner, he asked me to marry him. I was stunned. I looked at him absolutely dumbfounded. I wondered to myself what on earth I was going to say to this. After a minute, I said to him, "I need to think about it." We finished dinner and went to my weekly bowling league tournament as we'd planned. Now I was in turmoil. During the game, I struggled to figure out what I was supposed to do or say.

I didn't believe I had any options. If someone had said to me back then that my decision about marriage should be based on what I needed, I would have replied, "Well, I need to do what I'm supposed to do." My role as a daughter, woman, and nurse was to be there for other people. That was reinforced by my family, school, the military, and the media.

In addition, there was Harvey's commitment to win me over. Before this, no one had ever gone to such trouble to convince me to do something. My decision seemed to matter to him. I felt that not seeing me for just thirty days had sent him into a state of desperation and pain. If I agreed to marry him, I believed I would make him very happy; if I turned him down, I feared he would be devastated.

I tried to put the jumble of feelings and "shoulds" in some kind of order. Harvey and I had spent a lot of time together, and I felt comfortable with him. We had a foundation for our relationship. We looked good together as a couple—that was important, or everyone said it was. I wasn't sure what love was, but I did care for him. So as I thought about Harvey's proposal, his bombardment of attention, and his pain when it wasn't returned, I decided maybe marrying him was what I was supposed to do.

We got back to my apartment after bowling. I said to him, "Remember that question you asked me earlier? The answer is yes."

He said he was delighted!

And I certainly got caught in the moment and acted pleased. But I wondered what I had just committed myself to. I had felt trapped before. Now I believed my autonomy was gone. But, I thought, perhaps that's the way it's supposed to be.

Looking back, I find it hard to explain my passivity in those years. I approached marriage with a blind optimism and a superficiality. Harvey and I both came from traditional families, both of us confirmed in the Lutheran church. No relative of ours had ever gotten divorced. All we knew was that when you married, you married for life. I assumed that once we decided to marry, we'd live happily ever after. It was real storybook stuff—-but it was a view of life, relationship, and marriage shared by our friends and families.

I did believe, however, that my own career dreams were ended. Moments after I agreed to marry him, I sighed and said, "I guess I'll never make it to be Chief Nurse and the first female general." Remember, in those days, women with children under the age of sixteen could not serve in the armed forces. Naturally, marriage meant children, and that would end my military career. I would have to return to civilian nursing (if I worked at all and I wanted to work). I was losing control over my own life and, at the same time, agreeing to the most "normal" thing in the world. I felt both those contrasting forces; it was a price a woman paid. Though I was ambivalent about getting married, it meant doing what I was supposed to do and was a cause for happiness. That view would be confirmed by everyone around me in the following days.

Becoming Whole
Lincoln City, Fourth of July, 1988

The boys and I arrived at Aagot's in a flurry of hugs and hellos. Her place had become as familiar as our own home, having served as the boy's and my vacation place during the time I lived in San Francisco. The other women were staying at a motel on the beach, just blocks away.

After we settled in, Phyllis called to ask if I would drive her to the bus station to pick up her friend Diane. Phyllis didn't like to drive in the rain. I said I'd be happy to play chauffeur.

I picked up Phyllis at the motel, then drove to the bus station. On the way, Phyllis gave me a quick history. She'd known Diane for more than thirty years. They shared their passion as artists. Diane had also taught art at a university for almost as long as their friendship had lasted, so they saw each other only about once a year, but had a great time when they got together.

We pulled up to the station and Phyllis jumped out to find her friend while I waited in the car. When they returned, Diane and I met through the rearview mirror. We exchanged glances. But it was dark and raining, and as the chauffeur, I was quiet for the rest of the trip back to the motel. After dropping them off, I went to feed my tribe at Aagot's.

That evening, the boys, Aagot, and I joined the five women at their rooms overlooking the ocean. The kids, kept in by the rain, wanted to play a game of Pictionary. Everyone else, except Diane, agreed to participate. As the women and young men began a raucous game, Diane stretched out on a couch with a book. Andy, Mr. Persistence, continued to badger her to join the game. She politely repeated, "No, thank you," several times and went back to her reading. Undeterred, Andy vehemently challenged her again. Finally, she said, "I don't play games. I'm just a dud." Without missing a beat, Andy calmly replied, "Well, come on, Dud, play." She laughed with great delight, put down her book, and joined us. From that moment on, the boys called her Dud.

The next evening was the Fourth of July celebration on the beach. Aagot decided to stay at home. The rest of us staked out a good spot early. The boys built a large fire pit and, since the weather had been unseasonably cold and windy, put up a rain tarp. We left Jean's wheelchair at the sidewalk and carried her down to our beach camp.

The sun disappeared into the waves and the entire town congregated at the beach to watch the fireworks. There were campfires and laughing children as far as you could see. As we had done every year since they were very little, the boys and I made Somemores over the fire—-marshmallows, apple slices, and chocolate piled and melted on graham crackers. I had also brought my guitar. We sang folk songs together until the fireworks display began.

Near midnight, the fireworks over and conversation dying down, Jean said she needed to call it a night. I drove the adults back to their motel. However, I'd promised the boys I'd come back to the beach. There was going to be a very low tide at 3:00 a.m. and they wanted to stay and go crabbing. As I helped Jean to the room, I gave an open invitation to everyone to return with me. I expected Phyllis to jump at the chance, since Jean would have others available should she need anything. Instead, Phyllis encouraged Diane to join me. Diane and I had not spoken more than a few casual sentences to each other, and I suspected the poor woman only wanted to get some sleep. But Phyllis pushed Diane until she agreed to keep me company while I watched the boys. We drove back to the beach together.

By now the boys were crabbing with single-minded devotion. Diane and I got the fire going again. Here I was, sitting on a log across from a near stranger in the middle of the night. I felt rather awkward.

Then I did something contrary to my style. I began to talk, and while I spoke, I found Diane listening in the most extraordinary way. I talked more, and she asked a few questions, and listened with an intensity that illuminated everything. So I continued on about everything and anything. But most amazing, I talked about me. Perhaps it was the fact that here was someone who lived thirteen hundred miles away, someone I thought I would never see again. In the dark, with a kind stranger, it was safe to share what I felt. It was, in fact, wonderful.

Not only was Diane a superb audience with inspiring questions and inexhaustible interest; she had great stamina. In what felt like no time at all, I looked up from the fire and noticed the sun was rising. I'd talked until dawn. We were alone together. The boys were asleep against the logs. The beach was deserted. We smiled at each other and chatted about how quickly the night had passed.

No one listens like Diane. No one I have ever known. Hers is a receptivity that's intelligent, compassionate, and amused. Her heart is light, her laughter warm and ready. It's laughter that is never mean or petty, but embraces, loves, values. The laughter of an artist and teacher who inquires into the mysteries of religion with the same intensity she gives to a succession of Scottie dogs.

I'd never known what it means to be understood by one person. It is that simple. It is no different from what every other person in the world wants: to be special to one other person.

Meeting Diane and experiencing the rightness of being with her made me realize I am a lesbian. Finally being able to acknowledge that gave me the last, connecting piece to the puzzle of my identity.

It was a puzzle I'd tried and failed to solve since my adolescence. Not understanding—-or not accepting—-my sexual orientation was like looking at myself through a faulty lens. If something didn't feel right, I couldn't find the reason because I couldn't see myself clearly. I attributed my social discomfort in school to various sources. I was shy because I was Norwegian, I didn't want to date because my clothes weren't fashionable—-but none of those explanations was entirely right. My on-and-off reclusiveness in college seemed to have no cause at all.

I so wanted to fit in. I wanted to be accepted, to be like all the women in the movies I saw, like the heroines in the books I read, like the classmates I knew, like my mother, whom I loved. I tried to play the role of a woman they played: a woman who desires a man. But I really didn't.

But when I acknowledged I am a lesbian, I could look back and see clearly for the first time. All my life I had recoiled at being intimate with a man, but I believed that I could change those feelings with time. I enjoyed working with my male colleagues, I had affection for male friends like Doug and cared for Harvey. But when I dated and when I married, not only was I not attracted to my male partners, I felt physically violated whenever I was kissed or touched by them. Despite trying, wanting to be an accommodating wife, I withdrew physically whenever possible. Being sexual with a man felt like a violation. It wasn't Harvey's fault. It wasn't any man's fault. Some unchangeable part of myself felt that sex with a man was an invasion and I resented it. Over fifteen years of marriage, those feelings only got stronger. At the age of forty-six, I finally had to face the fact that being straight wasn't a choice I had.

Yet, when I left my marriage, all I knew about my identity was contained in a negative statement: Being in a relationship with a man is not who I am. When a friend wanted to fix me up with an eligible man, I said no. My friend assumed that as an older, divorced woman, I was going to stay single and unattached for the duration and was not looking for another relationship. I wasn't asked to explain my lack of interest in dating, so I didn't. But silently I tried to understand my disinterest in men. I read books and studied scientific reports. I learned that the medical profession does not consider homosexuality to be a mental illness, and many scientists believe it is genetically determined.

I didn't want to have a relationship with a man. I accepted that in the years after my divorce. But I didn't want to be with a woman, either. I feared being a member of a despised and stigmatized minority. And there was something more. Like the world around me, I was homophobic—fearful of those who are labeled gays and lesbians. In my ignorance, I had only negative images of them: they were taunted, beaten up, fired from jobs, rejected by friends and families. I didn't want to be part of that group.

My homophobia was also unconscious. Just recently, a former colleague told me that when we served together in Vietnam I mentioned that I thought some of the women on my high-school softball team had been lesbians and that I didn't approve. I was very surprised by his memory. First, because it's hard to acknowledge my own intolerance and prejudice, and second, because I have no memory at all of saying or feeling such a thing.

Only once from the time of my divorce until I met Diane did I let down my armor. In San Francisco, I began to care for a person. I avoided thinking this special feeling linked me to an ostracized minority by telling myself that this person "just happens to be a woman." That relationship never evolved but the memory of new kinds of feelings remained.

After that, as much as I might have liked to, I couldn't be as naïve as I was in my youth. And I couldn't deny my suspicions that I might be homosexual. But my own homophobia continued to hold that self-knowledge in a kind of intellectual prison. I wondered if I was a homosexual, but I banished any feelings that might go with the concept. Also, I never said or thought the word "lesbian." "Lesbian" was too personal. It had ownership—and I wasn't ready for ownership. I could only use the term "homosexual"—it locked the feelings in a theoretical trap, keeping them impersonal, like the word itself.

Over the next couple of years, I focused on my military and professional work and my sons. But when I met Diane, I realized how lonely I'd been. I cared for her, and I realized that this caring was more than friendship. It was love. For the first time in my life I felt: I can talk to this person. We discuss things. We have feelings for each other. We express those feelings easily, and I don't try to keep my distance as I always had done with men. One of the things that most surprised me was that my feelings came not from attraction but from an emotional connectedness. For the first time, I experienced completely fulfilling love.

I remember how resentful I felt when the true deal about marriage hit me and I realized that all the people who had been urging me along that path knew the truth about it but no one had told me. I'd asked all the women I could talk to what marriage was really like. And everyone—including those who professed to care about me—were under societal pressure to uphold the myth so they wouldn't disillusion young women. Didn't want people to accuse them of being bitter. Then when I made the discovery that I'd been rooked, and wanted to know was this all, what I heard was, "Oh, girl, of course that's what marriage is, you should know that, what did you expect? Don't be so naïve."

—Angela Bowen,
from "Another View of Lesbians Choosing Children,"
in *Lesbians at Midlife: The Creative Transition*

Blake C. Aarens with her former husband, 1986.

...1991.

"Take Care of My Best Friend for Me"

BLAKE C. AARENS

It's what we say to each other just before we hang up the phone. In the process of coming apart as a couple, we have come together as the closest of friends. I am a lesbian of African descent; Doug is a blond, blue-eyed, Jewish, heterosexual man. We talk regularly on the phone, sharing in each other's triumphs and consoling each other through the hardships. We joke about growing old together—not sharing a bed, but sharing the meat of our lives, breaking bread together when we can—but more often than not, the telephone is what holds the tangible connection. He is my biggest fan. I am his closest confidante.

We scare people: his parents—who I believe want him to hate me, or at least not support me financially, and my ex-lover—who questioned my lesbian identity and wanted to offer me only limited access to Club Dyke. When we told our married and very pregnant neighbor we were splitting up, she panicked and grabbed Doug's hand like a supplicant. Instinctively she jumped to protect the male ego, to shame me for having the audacity to leave and live as a lesbian. "You're such a great guy; somebody'll snatch you up in a minute," she said.

Doug responded in kind. "The great guy you talk about is a direct result of seven years of this woman's influence—c'mon Blake, let me take you to dinner."

We left our neighbor with the knowledge that we'd created monsters of each other, Godzillas smashing the intricate and shaky structure of patriarchal marriage and setting fire to the mandatory meanness that is supposed to accompany its dissolution.

We were married on 27 December, 1986. Doug wore a deep brown tuxedo; I wore a dress of white lace and Chinese silk that my mother made. We wrote our own vows and even sang to each other as part of the ceremony. The love we expressed on that day remains; it's just taken a different form. The license we signed had little to do with how we actually felt about each other. Proof positive comes from the fact that the license has ceased to exist and yet the relationship remains, alive and viable on terms that the institution never intended and could never support.

In many ways, my time with Douglas turned me into a lesbian. I know most men would probably blanch at that (or resort to violence) but what I mean is that Doug gave me space to find out who the hell I am. And who I am is a lesbian. I have known this since I was in third grade. But I got brainwashed by the compulsory hetdom that is the world we live in. Our marriage was unconventional enough to allow me to get real. I was blessed to have found a man who didn't require me to reflect him at twice his natural size, so I could take the time to check out my own reflection.

There is a belief among straight people that lesbianism is a phase. It is interesting for me to note that I look at the time I spent married in that light. It was a period of transition between the little girl I had been under my mother's roof and the woman I needed to become under a roof of my own. My marriage to Doug was a safe place for me to grow up. I earned the freedoms I have now by being willing to do time in the system. However, I wouldn't advise getting married as a way of finding yourself. My experience is the exception, not the rule. I wore the mask and costume that were required of me for entrance into the world of heterosexual privilege, but once I entered that world, my true nature began to surface. I didn't go into my marriage with the idea of coming out—I sincerely believed I had found my fairy tale—but once the spell began to break, I had to make the best of the situation.

Unlike most women, I'm in better financial shape than I was when I got married. I was raised on welfare in Brooklyn, New York. Bergen Street and Kingston Avenue—the heart of Bed-Stuy—an area known as the war zone. When I met Professor Douglas West, I was living in a studio apartment off campus and working three jobs to put myself through college. He helped send me to Japan for my junior year. We bought a house together—an 80-year-old bungalow with hardwood floors and a fireplace. We took trips to the Caribbean, and today I can afford to live in the gourmet ghetto of North Oakland.

The journey to this place has been a rough one, full of wrong turns, dead ends, and misremembered directions. You see, I knew I was a lesbian at the age of eight. I was in love with a girl in my class, and in my precociousness, I had sought out and found the word that described my feelings. That kind of clear-headed self-knowledge is a thing of beauty in a black girl-child. What was less than beautiful was the response I got when I shared that knowledge with the adults around me. The girl's mother patted my head and said, "Of course you love her, and she loves you too." Her father looked at me sideways but said nothing. And my mother did her damnedest to beat that knowledge out of me with a switch from one of the bushes out front.

That beating taught me to make myself over to conform to others' images of me, to do whatever it took to get attention and approval. It gave me an adversarial relationship to my body, and to the emotions that coursed through it. Added to that was my internalized racism which controlled everything from how I wore my hair, to my choice of friends. I cop to the part I played in my own repression. At the same time, I acknowledge how much of my behavior was supported by the institution of marriage.

The best metaphor for the difference between my married life and my life now is the image of the sleepwalker waking up. I was so unconscious when I got married. And in order to keep myself in my marriage and in the straight white way of doing things, I had to keep myself sedated. Heavily. Smoking pot and drinking until the center as well as the edges of my life became fuzzy.

Many of the changes in me came through therapy. As a faculty wife, I had health care like I had never had before, physical as well as mental health care. I had the resources to seek out therapy and heal the wounds that had placed me so deeply in the closet. The regimen my therapists put me on has led to a sobriety that's self-referenced and based on truth-telling. If I can look myself in the mirror and call my true name out loud—lesbian—I don't need to hide behind a bottle or a joint.

I didn't come out because I fell in love with another woman. I came out because in therapy the layers of pain that began forming when I was eight fell away. It's been a process, not an event. But the event that accelerated the process was leaving my marriage. It was the biggest risk I had ever taken in my life, the biggest permission I'd ever given myself to do what I knew in my gut to be right for me. Because of that, I am more alert to paradox in my life and less able to sit with psychic uneasiness. I've learned to listen to the beating of my own heart, whereas before I left my marriage, I was more worried that my heart would beat too loudly and disturb other people. I am no longer afraid of disturbing other people.

There are profound physical changes also. I have a couple of pictures that tell the story beautifully. In the first one, my hair is straightened and down around my shoulders and I'm wearing makeup. I have on a white lace blouse which is cut low enough to expose the curve of my right breast. You can see the outline of my hip through the fabric of the hot pink, skin tight skirt I'm wearing. It's a size eight and bunches up across my belly. My balled fist mostly covers my mouth. The picture was taken in Princeton, New Jersey in 1987. I used to show this photo to prospective lovers—almost like a spread in a girlie magazine—to turn them on and prove to them that I was beautiful. I stopped doing it when one woman noticed the fear in my eyes. She said I looked sad in the picture—frightened and uncomfortable. She told me she was glad I'd found my smile.

The other picture was taken in 1992. I am straddling a driftwood log out at the Marin Headlands. My hair is short and natural—a crop of unruly curls and wild kink—and I have a tail that reaches to my elbow. I am wearing a flannel shirt, jeans, and hiking boots. My face holds a sleepy and relaxed smile. It is currently my favorite picture of myself—typical dyke image that it is—for it shows me with a level of self-possession and ease in my body that I never thought possible. The nice part is that the breasts and hips of the other picture are still there; I just don't feel the need to put them on display. I don't have anything to prove.

No, I didn't have to come out as a lesbian to change my clothes or the way I wore my hair. But before I came out, I judged clothes by how they would make my body look, not by how they felt. Now, if it ain't comfortable, it doesn't go home with me.

I was trained in the necessity of putting my body on favorable display in order to even hope for access to the goodies. And favorable display in the het sense is all about helplessness and control. Beat your naturally kinky hair into artificial straightness. Confine the contours of your body, except for the all-important pillow-like breasts. Imprison your feet in shoes that make it impossible to kick, let alone run. Shave the hair off your body in a sick parody of prepubescence.

I'm much easier on myself physically. Gone are the days of burn marks on my neck from the hot comb or sores on my scalp from the lye. I don't force myself into the nearly impossible straight, manmade, white notion of femininity. My body can find its own contours. Plain and simply, I weigh more than I used to and wear larger-sized clothes. My breasts are fuller, and my belly and hips and ass have serious curves. I walk more firmly on the earth—in flat shoes and clothes that I can take deep breaths in. I feel good about this physical abundance and like my reflection in the mirror at 32 much more than I ever did at 24. I don't deprive myself of food or affection or decent treatment in relationships. They all go hand in hand. Allowing myself to take up more physical space greatly affects my experience of psychic and even economic space. I allow myself to have. I take better care of myself, and it shows.

Another big change between then and now are the people I have in my life and the quality of my relationships with them. I no longer spend time with people who are trying to hide from their own truths with drugs or alcohol. It was as if lying to myself about who I was and where I was going made it necessary for me to interact with people who were telling themselves similar lies. I have experienced the flip side of this in that now people who aren't ready to wake up and look at their truths don't want to be around me. It's as if they preferred me drugged and stupid, walking through life like a zombie. It makes me sad to know this about the people I sincerely believed were my best friends, but it's another one of the truths I don't flinch from anymore.

When Douglas and I got married, the invitation list was mostly his colleagues in the math department. There were a handful of people I knew before I met him, and only one friend I had made on my own during college. I had little contact with people my own age. Doug is nine years older than I am, and he's considered one of the young ones in the department. It was like spending all my time with my parents' friends and having no friends of my own. I was desperately lonely and I lost the skills for making and sustaining friendships. It is still a struggle for me to reach out and make contact with other people. I fell for the myth that my husband would provide my world for me and I ended up very isolated. I, who as a little girl would walk up to any new face and introduce herself, am having to learn all over again how to make myself open and available to friendship.

In leaving my marriage and keeping my friendship with Doug I learned the lesson that love of the deepest kind, the kind that nurtures, is about being able to show up and tell the truth and still be loved. I began to exercise my possession of the word "no" and that has made all the difference in the strength and clarity of my "yes." My leaving wasn't about him being wrong or being a horrible man; it was about me being somewhere I really didn't want to be. About me living my mother's dreams for me and not living my own dreams for myself. When I told Doug I was leaving, we had our tears together and our disappointment that we wouldn't have "happily ever after." We also managed to still have our love for each other. I learned that relationships can change and grow and that they don't have to end. That experience has changed me. It has made me demand in all of my relationships the space to tell the truth, to say when something isn't working for me, to clear up misunderstandings, and to voice my hurt and anger. I expect the other person to be willing to show up in the same kind of risk-taking honesty.

The personal changes are easy to delineate. It's the changes in other people that are harder to set down on paper. I cannot judge the changes in my familial relationships from "Blake the married woman" to "Blake the lesbian," because for the most part, my family doesn't know. Or more precisely, they know but would rather they didn't. I believe my family was more open and accepting of my marrying a white man than they will ever be of my lesbianism. They could understand it from a "marrying up" standpoint, an economic or genetic maneuver to get ahead in the world, to "lighten up." I think on the advantages I got through my marriage, and I can't help but wonder whether or not the marriage would have ever happened if I were darker, or if I'd worn my hair natural back then.

My entry into the middle-class, white world was solely because of Douglas. I did nothing to earn the car, the house, the trips, nothing except marry Douglas B. West, Ph.D. Losing the courtesy and privilege I had as the wife of a white man has been one of the hardest losses to adjust to in my day-to-day life. True, the courtesy only came when Douglas was actually with me. But once we'd shown ourselves to be a married couple, I became legitimate in the eyes of store owners and academics, people who would otherwise have written me off as just another nigger gal, interacting with me through all the racist and sexist stories in their ears.

In truth, my presence on Doug's arm didn't always protect me. I can remember a dinner party at the home of one of Doug's colleagues where I was the only person of color present. One white man saw fit to wink at me from across the room and lick his lips. I was outraged and insulted, but I didn't do anything except express how hurt I was to my husband when we got home. I tried to explain to him why it was both racism and sexism that allowed the man to behave that way. I was sure he wouldn't have acted that way toward the white women there. Unconsciously he may have registered my fear around fitting in and read me as a target who wouldn't want to draw undue attention to herself by calling him on his behavior. He was right.

Approval-seeking got me into the marriage and the straight white way in the first place. I wanted to be loved and cared for, to be thought well of, to have everyone's acceptance. Not only did I want it, I thought I needed it to keep breathing. To be allowed to keep breathing. I ignored the fact that I needed other young women in my life and other black people. That's the other big issue for me. I married into Doug's world and there were almost no other black people in it. I think I remember meeting one black mathematician the entire time we were together. And I missed my people. But I never pushed the issue of bringing a group of black people into my white husband's home.

Now there are more black women in my life than there have ever been. Regardless of who I'm with, I demand time and space in my life for gatherings with only women of color and with only black women. I remember the times as a young girl when my mother's sisters and cousins and neighbors and friends would come together—the laughing and shouting they would do. I am making my own memories of those kinds of times.

Douglas never stood over me saying, "Straighten your hair! Go on a diet! Defer to me, my colleagues, my male friends, and my parents! Dress a certain way! Hide your intelligence! Break all your cultural ties! Change your name to mine!" No, he never told me to do those things. He also didn't actively support me in not doing them. He was tied into his modified straight white male role just as I tied myself into mine as a female impersonator of the patriarchal kind. He didn't know how to be my ally in times of conflict. I think part of him realized that the path I was forging was going to change his life as well, and he wasn't all that sure he wanted his life changed.

One of the blessings of leaving the mainstream is that people watch their step with me. Straight, white people in particular. There's a certain kind of respect I get as an outcast that I never got as a black woman playing by the rules. The man who winked at me at the party felt safe interacting with me through the stories in his ears about black women. Walking in the world as a lesbian gives people pause. If I'm willing to be loud and clear about who I am, I probably won't have any qualms about publicly embarrassing people for their rude and racist behavior.

People no longer feel free to ask intimate questions. When we were married, siblings, cousins, even strangers on the street felt free to question us about when (not if) we were having children. No one invades my privacy that way now. Even though I've only formally come out to one brother, they know enough about San Francisco's reputation and about who I've always been to know not to ask me about my personal life if they don't want to hear the "L" word. The tradeoff is that it often feels more like disinterest than respect. Come to think of it, no one really asked me how I was truly doing when I was married; I was just willing to reinterpret prying questions as inquiries about my well-being.

There are tradeoffs in my living as a lesbian. I don't have a built-in Friday night date. None of my plans for holidays are set up for me in advance. I have to take an active part in my life as I never did in my marriage. I had certain things I could count on that I don't have anymore. I had a buffer against loneliness and protection against solitude. I don't necessarily see those as good things. They served as additional ways for me not to be present in my life, for me to take things for granted, for me to never have time alone to listen to my own thoughts. Now I get to check in with what I really want to do instead of just dropping myself into the preestablished customs. I have to really think about whether I want to celebrate a holiday and what that celebration might look like from my own desires and beliefs. I don't always welcome this kind of freedom. There are cold December nights when I wish I had the Kodak Christmas—the house with the fireplace, the tree with the trimmings, the husband, the family pulling for our survival as a couple and sharing their warm wishes for us. But then I remember the price tag.

When I was married, the vast majority of people I came into contact with knew me solely through my husband; they often didn't even know my name! Though the words of our ceremony were unique, Doug and I had still become "a man and his wife." Even with the best laid plans and the budding consciousness we both brought to our marriage, we were fighting an uphill battle. In many ways, we lost. Or more to the point, I lost. I lost my friends, my people, my individuality, and my autonomy.

In coming out as a lesbian, I have regained all of that and gotten some new things to boot. I have financial support to write. I live where I've always wanted to live. I make decisions about my life without having to consult anyone else. And I know I deserve all these things. I am my own person in ways that even the most progressive of marriages cannot support. I am a lesbian of African descent. And that has made all the difference.

Ellen Farmer with former husband on their wedding day, 1980.

...left, with her partner and children, 1991.

The Children of Lesbians

ELLEN FARMER

Your children live in your home,
and instead of picking up their socks,
pick up your vibes.
They tell you, in not-so-subtle ways:
"Get it together, Mom.
Don't go having an identity crisis on me.
I need your attention.
I'm the one growing up here!"
They say: "Why did you and dad get divorced?
What's a lesbian?
Why did you bring me to a parade with guys in dresses?"

They can't seem to leave you alone.
They never let up
until they hear that familiar, resigned tone in your voice:
your own true story.

And you do owe them an explanation—
at least a PG version of what it means to love—
and the tools to build
a strong identity for themselves
in a world still swirling with hate.

You are the tour guide to the beginning of their lives,
a trip they won on a game show
somewhere out in the universe.
They are: *The Children of Lesbians!*
charter members of a "Head Start" program
without government funding,
a country club without a country,
a loose affiliation of dauntless spirits
launched from the cutting edge.

Home Improvement

Reva Talleygrone

I didn't have an orgasm until I read how to in *Ms.* at the age of 33. By 39 I had become a raging maniac of sex. So far, only in my own mind, but part of me knew it was just a matter of time until this animal broke out. At night I dreamed of making crude love to women in my car, my bed, on the balcony off the bedroom. Dreamed exactly how full-breasted women would feel under my body, my hands, my tongue. One night in a dream Freud would have loved, my clitoris grew several inches long. By day, I felt my brain was in that organ. I rose from my desk, prepared to teach "The Love Song of J. Alfred Prufrock" to my Intro to Lit students, dizzy from lust, hardly able to stand and walk, the sensation so strong it gagged me.

The more outrageous the lust, the less I wanted my husband John. That poking nose of a penis which rose and prodded my rear in bed, I edged away from. I kissed him goodnight, shutting my mouth against his tongue. My hands on his man's chest, I mourned its flatness, then turned away and lay for hours before going to sleep, my palm cupped over a breast that wasn't there, only the flat sheet mocking me. Why couldn't I enjoy him? I reasoned with myself. He was deprived by me, always. Aren't we all the same cells, women and men? The fetus in the womb starts out with undifferentiated tissue. Each becomes beautiful. I thought of Michelangelo's David, that magnificent boy called forth from stone like a prayer. I'd never been a hater of men. But I longed for a woman till I felt like baying at the moon, my mouth in an open howl of sorrow like the silent, open mouth on the face of the old woman in the moon.

But we had sons, John and I, sons nine and eleven, who thought our house held them safe as arms. To confirm their faith, to nail down a future for us, I got us started remodeling. First we beamed up a bearing wall and added a new kitchen, something we'd thought for years would be impossible. As triumphal as the new room was, I feared it as soon as it was done. A large crack appeared in the plaster on the landing where the new beam tied into the old, and I eyed it every time I went upstairs. Was it spreading? What if the house rejected the addition, as a body rejects an unsuitable transplant, and the whole thing crumpled?

Such fears made me weary, as if I were knitting a garment which was being unraveled at the other end. To keep ahead of the weariness, I stepped up the pace of remodeling—which is why we were redoing the bedroom at the very time my lust for women and my inability to tolerate John's advances were on a collision course. Which is why I was in a fever to spackle over all the cracks and nail holes, sand the woodwork to silk and spread satin latex like heavy cream over all the imperfections.

While we redid the bedroom, John and I slept in the spare room on a mattress on the floor, surrounded by the clutter which would normally go on bedside tables—phone, reading lamps, books, scraps of paper with phone numbers written on them, ballpoint pens.

One night I was sitting up in bed, cushioned by pillows against the wall, writing in my new journal. I hadn't kept a journal in twenty years, and suddenly I was compelled to write in this one. I said this to John who was wearing only a T-shirt, pacing around the room looking under things.

"Huh?" he said. "Compelled?"

"Like people with dietary deficiencies are compelled to eat strange things. That's what it feels like. My grandmother had a deficiency like that. She ate whole cabbages and lettuces. Couldn't stop herself. What are you looking for?"

"My book. Whole cabbages?"

"She cut them up first, into quarters or something, I think, but she ate them raw." I sat thinking about this, how her body knew what it needed.

"Have you seen my book?" John persisted. "Is it over on your side?"

I rummaged through my pile of books—I was reading the diaries of Anaïs Nin and a book on dream interpretation by Fritz Perls. "No," I said, "keep looking. It's got to be here. John?" I asked. "Behind that crack on the landing, is that where the beam is tied into the joist?" I decided to bring this up casually, interject it into the conversation. "What if it isn't hooked in right or something and it gives way."

John bent over, digging through his piles of stuff. "Are you sure you haven't picked it up?" he asked. When my question about the crack in the wall got through to him, he stood up and considered, his penis dangling from under his T-shirt like a chicken neck. "Give way?" he said. "It's not going to."

"But what if it did?"

"Then we'd fix it."

"It would be fixable?"

"Everything's fixable."

I was annoyed with myself for being annoyed with him for not wearing shorts. Not everything, I thought.

"We'd jack up the side of the house again," he said. "Like we did in the first place, and go in there and fix it. Aha!"

He found his book under a shirt under the cat and crawled into bed to read it.

I was still thinking about my grandmother, about compulsions and how my life had been changing. A few years ago, I went through a stage of not wanting to do anything but watch junky TV shows like "Trapper John." At bedtime I would go fix something wonderfully rank—a sliced liver sandwich and a glass of port—to fortify myself against the long loneliness of the night ahead.

But now TV sickened me. I'd shed the twenty-five pounds gained from late night snacks and was developing an unexpected urge to start jogging—I could already feel, from imagining it, the muscles stirring in my legs. And most recently, because things were going on that needed recording, I'd found myself shopping for this yellow spiral notebook.

Things like the house dreams.

In the first dream, I looked out the window and saw menacing people headed for our house. I begged John to protect us, but he piddled around trying to build a paper sword while a man entered and pressed a gun to my temple. I cried for my life, then thought, no, I'll die composed, so I mustered calm, and then awoke.

In the next dream, a woman entered through a skylight. When I accosted her, she invited me outside to talk. We sat at a picnic table where I asked her what right she had to break into people's homes. She only smiled, and I didn't want her to go away.

Every night it was like this. People kept breaking into our house. First bad people, then crazy people, then ordinary people. Last night, men and women, perfectly pleasant people, carried babies and bags of groceries up and down our stairs, nodding to me as they passed.

As I sat beside John on our makeshift bed recording this dream, I realized something: I wasn't afraid of the intruders anymore. I put the notebook down and stared at the walls around me, old plaster walls we hadn't redone, with stains like undiscovered continents and cracks like long rivers.

Beside me, John lay on his back holding his book over his face. Every few minutes his face slackened and his book dropped to his chin, rousing him just enough to lift the book so it could begin its descent again. I took the book and closed it. He fell sound asleep then, his face empty. *Don't Push the River* was the title of the book he was reading, the one he kept telling me I should read. Little did either of us know how fast that river was already pushing me.

Our two cats, a young brother and sister, groomed one another at my feet with loud smackings and chompings. Piramis kissed his sister Thisbe all over her face, nibbling ecstatically around her mouth while getting into position to mount her. Those two are going to have to be neutered quick, I reminded myself.

I knew even as I turned out the light I would not be able to sleep. Before long I eased up off the mattress, slipped out the door and went down the stairs in the dark.

I opened the refrigerator and, by its light, poured milk which I heated in the microwave. The clock on the coffeemaker glowed as the microwave timer counted off seconds digitally. One is never alone in the dark anymore, I thought. Always little lights glowing, little clocks counting out one's life. The other day I'd come in from the backyard, and the digital display on the microwave said "YES." I stopped in my tracks. What was the question? I stood staring at it, thinking it must be an optical illusion. But it said, "YES." One of the kids must have entered a command I didn't know about.

The milk was hot, steaming, with a skin forming. I sat at the counter and sipped it in the dark, thinking of the kittens upstairs, of the warm milk smell of new kittens, feeling comforted by the milk's flat blandness and even by the electronic eyes, better company than none.

Before the milk was gone, an idea came. I turned on one dim light and opened the phone directory. This is ridiculous, I said to myself. It won't be here. I'm glad no one can see me. E. F. G. It *was* there: *Gay Hotline.* Suddenly shaking, I dialed the number. When a woman's voice answered, I depressed the button and disconnected the call. But I called again, this time with a piece of paper and pencil beside me. Was this my voice? I wondered.

"Are there organizations?" I was asking her. "Places people can meet? Are there therapists people can go to who don't—" My voice was constricted, odd. But the woman on the other end didn't seem to notice. She answered my questions in a matter-of-fact voice as if I were asking about home repair.

Back upstairs in the dark room where John breathed evenly, I put a small piece of paper in one of the pocket dividers of my journal, kicked the cats off the bed, and descended toward sleep. Even after I closed my eyes, I was pulling the brush along the edge of the bedroom molding, pushing the fullness of paint right up to but not past the edge.

Two weeks later, we were ready to spend the first night in our newly remodeled bedroom. John came in while I was folding the new comforter over the new quilt stand.

"What do you think? Nice, huh?" he said, carrying in two drinks. On Sunday nights, he got very solicitous about my having enough to drink. Still holding both drinks, he sat down on the edge of the bed to look over the results of our work: a peaceful, monochromatic room—walls, satiny woodwork, and plush carpeting all in the same creamy white.

I stood in the middle of the room and studied the effect. It looked like a magazine picture, like someone else's house.

John put my drink down on my bedside table for me, put his arms around me, and bent down for a kiss. I controlled my response before I recoiled more than a fraction of an inch and kissed him back.

"Let's celebrate our new room tonight," he said. "After 'Masterpiece.'"

I pushed away from him, gently. "It looks like I wanted it to look," I said. "We're getting pretty good at this." At fixing rooms, I thought. I only wish we could live in them.

I got in bed modestly, keeping my gown around my legs. John turned on the TV and got in bed beside me.

On the screen, the camera panned over the books and memorabilia of past "Masterpiece Theater" series to the strains of "Trumpet Voluntaire." Over the years, we'd seen all the shows together, so this was like looking through a museum we'd been in many times, or through a family photo album. The memories it stirred in me were mixed. Sunday nights I usually fixed a fun dinner, often homemade pizza, and back when the kids were little, we'd pile in bed together and watch "Wonderful World of Disney." Then we'd put the boys down for the night and watch yet another episode of a great drama we'd looked forward to all week—"The Duchess of Duke Street" or "I, Claudius," for example. Then, after I had drunk enough to fold a large part of myself away, enough so that sometimes I couldn't remember when or how the segment of "Masterpiece Theater" ended, I felt obligated to pay the price exacted of me by marriage. The sex never lasted long, and I was left sticky and ashamed, but virtuous, too, because what I'd done one more time was the only right and decent thing for me to do. As much a part of taking care of my family as painting walls.

This had been the Sunday night schedule since the kids were little. Now that they were older, they no longer watched Disney but played with their friends until bath time and read in their own beds before going to sleep.

Tonight was the beginning of a new series. Alistair Cooke came out and talked about it.

"Drink your drink," John said. He snuggled against me. I began drinking purposefully and tried to get involved in the drama, but my eyes kept leaving the screen to study the walls. I'd liked it when I was still fixing up the room. I chugged my drink, yet felt little from it. I got up to get another.

"Hurry up," John said. "You're going to miss it." In the dark kitchen I took a few swigs of whiskey straight from the bottle, being watched by the little electronic eyes, glowing red and green. I must look like a drunk, I thought, drinking from the bottle this way. I replenished my drink and headed back upstairs, relieved to be a little unsteady now.

"Come on," John said as I climbed back into bed. "You're missing the show."

"I can't concentrate," I said. On the screen, a maid dressed in old-fashioned maid's clothing with a ruffled bonnet and apron was telling a woman in bed something urgent. A gentleman came in, and the maid curtsied and left. He sat on the bed, holding the woman's hand. Then the scene dissolved to a man riding fast in a horse-drawn carriage through the English countryside.

"Do you want me to refresh that for you?" John asked.

"Maybe a little." I handed John the glass without looking at him. Men on horses were riding to intercept the man in the carriage. Is one of them the woman's husband, I wondered? I couldn't tell. The men all looked alike. John was back with the drink now, though it seemed only a second since he had left. And then Alistair Cooke was back and the music was on again.

"Drink some more of your drink," John said, and suddenly he was on me, kissing me with his tongue in my mouth. I looked up through the dark at the corner of the room which was sliding away from where it was supposed to be. I closed my eyes to stop it from moving.

John pulled up my nightgown and squeezed one nipple in his fingers, while he did something to himself down below. His tongue was still in my mouth, and I had a clear urge to do something that had never entered my mind before: bite his tongue, bite it off. Horrified, I fought the monster urge which, for the moment, passed. I am all right, I said to myself. I can do this.

Then something else happened that had never happened before. The field of vision in the dark of my closed eyelids turned scarlet. It didn't turn all at once, but filled in, one shimmering block at a time: red. I opened my eyes to get rid of it, but it was there, too. In the night around me, all the dark was red. I thought, bizarrely interested in the phenomenon at a moment like this, so that's why we have the saying, *I was so angry I saw red*. I twisted my head away because I knew what would happen if he put his tongue in my mouth again.

"What's wrong?" he asked.

"Nothing," I said. The rage faded. I can do this, I thought.

He entered me. Okay, what would happen now would be farther from my face, less personal. I could do it. But suddenly, my arms were acting independently of me. I was beating him with my fists, beating his back, his shoulders, his head.

He was so stunned, it took him a few seconds to spring out of my reach. During that time, I watched amazed as my arms flailed him.

"What in God's name?" he panted.

I couldn't say anything for a long time. I tried to make myself very small and not move. "I don't know," I said finally. I thought of the shoulder I had just been hitting. How often we had put our shoulders together to do the heavy work we did. I began to sob uncontrollably, thinking of the feel of his shoulder under my hand when I gave him back rubs. I cried silently, but the sobs shook my whole body.

"Shhh," he said. He patted me. "You're upset or something."

I lay flat on my back with my hands over my face. It was a long time before I could get the words out: "I'm sorry."

"Just go to sleep."

I lay still, stiff, cried without shaking or making noise. Remarkably, he did go to sleep, his deep breathing beside me steady as always. I was very sober now. After a long time, I couldn't cry anymore. I continued to lie still, staring into the dark, for how long I have no idea. I made no attempt to keep track of time. I had no coherent thoughts, as if I were holding my breath with my whole brain. I did not need thoughts. I knew it was time to let the river work, slip into its waters with a child under each arm and trust it to carry us to another shore.

Joan Larkin 1953, 1994.

Robert

JOAN LARKIN

Right now in Fayetteville
where it's two, not three o'clock,
you're doing what you did then:
driving a rattletrap, maybe
on a road lush with spring green,
or sharpening a Venus drawing pencil
by a river that's slowly drying out.
I see the thin green pencil,
not the hand holding it—
I can't remember your hands.
There's a dog with you, not
the one we had together—
she must be dead ten years.
I see you in worn flannel
and round gold glasses.   Those
must be gone, too,
with the hat I hated,
the square brown one with earflaps.
I want to call you on the phone.
Want us in Tucson together, 1962,
before my father died.   Before
any of it.   I want to be kind this time,
and not just to you.
I want my mother back,
the way she was then:
not thin or grey yet,
not sweet the way she was later,
starting to die. Robert, she forgave me:
for divorcing you, even for writing
that I was queer.   She didn't say
she forgave me, she just said,
Oh well, you turned out all right.

I want to call you
in Fayetteville, right now,
so you can say it too: *I love you,*
in your surprising baritone.
I want to say, *Mother,*
please sit with me in the orange kitchen.
I have something to tell you.

Want

JOAN LARKIN

She wants an old house full of cups and the ghosts
of last century's lesbians; I want a spotless
apartment, a fast computer. She wants a woodstove,
three cords of ash, an axe; I want
a clean gas flame. She wants a row of jars:
oats, coriander, thick green oil;
I want nothing to store. She wants pomanders,
linens, baby quilts, scrapbooks. She wants Wellesley
reunions. I want gleaming floorboards, the river's
reflection. She wants shrimp and sweat and salt;
she wants chocolate. I want a raku bowl,
steam rising from rice. She wants goats,
chickens, children. Feeding and weeping. I want
wind from the river freshening cleared rooms.
She wants birthdays, theaters, flags, peonies.
I want words like lasers. She wants a mother's
tenderness. Touch ancient as the river.
I want a woman's wit swift as a fox.
Meanwhile, she's in her city, meeting
her deadline; I'm in my mill village out late
with the dog, listening to the pinging wind bells, thinking
of the twelve years of wanting, apart and together.
Meanwhile, we've kissed all weekend, we want
to drive the hundred miles and try it again.

Tell Them the Wedding is Off

KAY WARDWELL

When it came my turn to say "I do" at the wedding rehearsal, my throat closed up and I couldn't speak, not even to apologize to my alarmed fiancé. The minister told him not to worry—the real ceremony was what counted, and I'd be fine by then.

But I wasn't. When the church bells began to ring, signalling the start of the wedding, I was overcome by the clear, certain knowledge that I did not want to get married. It took a moment, but I managed to convey this new information to my mother, who, to my utter amazement, put her arms around me and said I didn't *have* to get married. Few mothers, I thought, with a great deal of gratitude and relief, would be so understanding and compassionate, especially after having spent months planning their daughter's wedding.

My relief was short-lived.

"All you have to do," she said, "is tell everyone in this church that the wedding is off. *I'm* not going to do it."

I walked down the aisle and married the high school quarterback.

During our honeymoon we watched TV in the hotel room, being careful not to accidentally touch one another's bruises, which we got when our rented mopeds collided with a van. Then we packed up and drove from Maine to Georgia, where my new husband began his job as a 2nd lieutenant in the U.S. Army.

It is indeed an understatement to say that as an officer's wife, I was a miserable failure. The morning my husband began his training, I went to the gym to lift some weights, only to find that the sole activity open to me was dance aerobics, the weight room being closed during ladies' hours.

Then, because I'd wasted at least twenty minutes fighting a losing battle to keep my maiden name on my dependent I.D. card, and because there were no legal parking spaces left at the Officers' Wives' Club building, I was seven minutes late for the mandatory orientation for the wives of the men in the Officer Basic Training course. I snuck in and leaned against the back wall, but the Colonel's wife hailed me from the podium, pointed to the one empty folding chair in the front row, and waited for me to seat myself. I said I preferred to stand; she stared at me for a moment before picking up her 3x5 cards to resume what turned out to be an hour-long lecture that could have been entitled "How to Serve Your Husband Most Effectively."

The first bit of advice was to be on time for all military functions—this was important. We were to strive to be assets rather than liabilities to our husbands' careers. We were to cook good, nourishing meals—no take-out pizza, no macaroni and cheese dishes from a box, and definitely no TV dinners—because our husbands needed to be kept in optimum health. She warned us to avoid arguments with our husbands—they wouldn't be able to concentrate on their work if their home lives were turbulent. We also needed to watch our own behavior—to turn in library books on time; to avoid losing our I.D. cards, because applying for a new one would be a frustrating and time-consuming hassle for our husbands; and to avoid getting parking tickets, because after three of them, our husbands would be hauled in by the Commanding Officer and reprimanded. She said a lot more that I missed when I began to notice that of all the women in the room, I was one of only a few not wearing nylons, and the only one wearing dirty white running shoes. After the lecture, we toured the base in a big green Army bus, the Colonel's wife pointing out for us the commissary, the thrift shop (where we were encouraged to volunteer our time), the day care center, the hospital, the craft shop, the post exchange, and the housing compound. After a quick trip to the restroom when we finally returned, I hurried to my car to get to the commissary for fresh fruits and vegetables. I was trying to read the fine print on the ticket under my windshield wiper when a woman ran from the building waving my wallet (containing my 90-minutes old I.D. card), which I had left on top of the toilet paper dispenser.

I didn't fit the officer's wife mold any better at the next base to which my husband was stationed. It was there, in fact, that I first fell in love with a woman. Of course I didn't recognize it as love. I blamed my husband for all the fights that ended with me stomping out and driving straight to Nancy's apartment.

Nancy was the most beautiful, most intelligent, most interesting woman on this planet. She was so wonderful I even enjoyed running errands with her. I loved sitting with her in the waiting room at the car dealership while they serviced her car. Stopping at the supermarket for toilet paper was a big treat. I was so attracted to her that I had to look, alternately, at the ceiling or the carpet when, in the mornings, her hair still dripping from the shower, she'd stand at the ironing board in her bra and underwear to iron her clothes.

To this day, one of my biggest regrets in life is not daring to kiss that woman. I had one chance (I think). I had just settled in for the night on the carpet in her spare room when she leaned against the doorframe and said that I could sleep in her bed if I wanted to. Instead of answering right away, I panicked. If I did sleep in her bed, would she try to touch me? What would I *do* if she tried to kiss me? Even worse—what if I slept in her bed right next to her and she *didn't* try to kiss me? Either way, I'd lie awake all night long, trying not to breathe erratically. I declined her offer, only to spend the next several hours searching for the courage to walk the nine or ten steps to her bedroom and tell her I had changed my mind.

Nancy and I continued our friendship, and after a while, decided that since we were both unhappy in our marriages, (she and her husband were separated), we'd get divorces and finish college together. We wrote for, received, and filled out applications for admission to the University of Florida. We also joined the Parachute Club, but on the first day of training, I discovered I was pregnant. My husband and I moved to another Army base; Nancy moved to Florida. I was crushed.

A year after my son was born, I met Lisa, the wife of my husband's new boss, at a monthly tea and Tupperware party. She, Sharon and I bowled together on the Officers' Wives' Club bowling league; played third base, pitcher, and short-stop on the softball team; and were player-coaches of the women's volleyball team. After games we usually drank a couple pitchers of beer, and when our husbands were gone, we'd eat dinner together while our kids played. When we were especially lonely or sad, and sometimes when we'd just stayed up late talking, we slept at each others' houses.

One night Lisa and Sharon (whose husband was in Korea for 18 months) asked me to go to Maria's, a little bar off the strip where we sometimes went for a beer. Because they'd been drinking already, I tried to convince them to go home instead. When it became apparent they were going to ignore my advice, I left my son with his dad and went with them, so I could drive. After three or four shots of tequila at the bar, Lisa leaned over and asked Sharon if they should tell me or not.

"Sure, let's tell her," Sharon answered.

"Tell me what?" I asked.

Sharon grinned. "That we're sleeping together."

"So?" I replied.

They laughed.

"She doesn't understand," Lisa said to Sharon. She put her hand on Sharon's thigh. "We sleep together."

I frowned, confused. So they slept together in the same bed. I thought it was wonderful they were that close—that they could comfort each other.

They laughed and then kissed—on the lips. For a long time. I was aghast, astounded that they would go to such lengths to play a joke on me. The G.I.s in the bar stopped playing pool, stopped dancing, stopped drinking, and stopped talking. When the bartender suggested that we leave, I dragged the two women out to the station wagon and threw them in the back. They stopped kissing only long enough to salute the military guards posted at the gate to the base where we all lived.

At Sharon's, we had a few more drinks before Sharon went to her bedroom to call her husband in Korea. When she was gone a very long time, I went to check on her, only to find her sitting on the edge of the bed, crying.

"What's wrong?" I asked, sitting down beside her.

Her husband was in love with a 1st lieutenant stationed in Yongsan, she said, and he wanted a divorce. I put my arm around her, trying to comfort her. She cried for a long time, then wiped her eyes and asked how I really felt about her and Lisa. I answered, honestly, that I couldn't even see how she could kiss another woman.

She smiled. "That's the best part," she said, and then, taking my chin in her hand, she turned my face toward hers, and kissed me—on the lips. For a long time.

"Now that wasn't so bad, was it?" she asked.

I shook my head, in a mild state of shock. It had been soft, loving, tender—and I wanted her to kiss me again. Then, for the first time in my life, it occurred to me that lesbianism was a real option, even though nobody had ever asked me whether I wanted to be straight or lesbian when I grew up, nor whether I wanted to love men or women—or both.

She kissed me again, and then Lisa appeared beside the bed, asking what we were doing.

"I'm kissing Kay," Sharon explained, "because she said she couldn't see how women could kiss each other."

"Oh," Lisa said, and untied the laces of one of my dirty white running shoes. Sharon pulled the other off and tossed it into a corner of the room. If I live to be one hundred and twenty-five I will never forget the next two or three hours in that room with those two women.

Two months later, though, I was in the psychiatric ward at the base hospital. Many factors led up to that experience, but most related to the fact that our husbands were helicopter pilots in a secret anti-terrorist commando unit. This meant they were gone seven months in every twelve—they'd leave for six weeks, come home for three, leave for four days and then come back for eight before heading out again. We weren't allowed to know where our husbands were, what they were doing, or when they'd return. We did know that our phones were being tapped, and we knew that our husbands were often in bars with women, because several came home with venereal diseases. The unit's divorce rate hovered at about 75%—only one in four marriages survived a three-year assignment.

But that wasn't the worst of it: their helicopters crashed with alarming regularity—in an eighteen-month period, six crashes claimed the lives of eighteen pilots: two drowned in the ocean off Panama, four were killed instantly when they slammed into a North Virginia mountainside in the dark, four burned in a fiery collision of two helicopters. The rest of the deaths were attributed to mechanical problems. Most of the aviators, and many of the wives, including myself, coped by abusing alcohol. With enough of it, we thought, our anger, sadness and fear would wash away.

One day after driving past the guard at the gate, I started to laugh. It all seemed so ludicrous. Then suddenly, it all seemed unbearably sad, and I started to cry. Then I laughed again, then I cried. Looking back, nearly a decade later, I can see that those conflicting emotions were ones I had suppressed with alcohol in an attempt to cope with an inhumane and intolerable situation. Back then, though, when I was still crying, laughing, and then crying again three hours later, I thought I was insane. It was either me, or everyone else. When a friend offered to drive me to the hospital, I went.

I sat in the dayroom all that first night, finally drained of all emotion, watching light from the street lamps seep in around the edges and through the cracks of the window blinds. A nurse with a security clearance sat by my side all night, knitting some socks for her next grandchild: each of the few words she spoke seemed faded and weak, as if they had to travel a great distance to reach me. As the night wore on, the distance between me and the rest of the world increased; I felt like a person drifting farther and farther from her spacecraft, just waiting for the oxygen tank to empty.

I had moved to the chair beside my bed and was watching the sun rise, when another nurse tossed clean, white sheets on the foot of the bed and told me to make it. I said I hadn't slept in the bed; she repeated her order. After she left, I crumpled up the unused sheets and threw them in the laundry cart in the hall. That night, another nurse told me the doctor would release me as soon as I showed any sign of an emotion, so when my husband called later, I waited for him to hang up. After he did, I pretended to get angry, told the dial tone to go to hell, slammed down the receiver and stomped off to my room.

Apparently, they had interviewed my husband while I was locked up. Before releasing me the next morning, the doctor told me that although I was not crazy, my husband, like most of the pilots willing to volunteer for the anti-terrorist unit, was a functional psychotic, and he recommended that I leave him in the middle of the night, so to speak. I must have looked dubious, because he assured me that he knew the type. He'd written a book, he said; he'd conducted a psychological study of men who volunteered for dangerous duty—men just like my husband.

Then he smiled and leaned back in his chair. "Did you know your husband thinks you're a lesbian?"

I laughed, but I was frightened. Rather than admit the truth and risk being readmitted to the hospital, I let the doctor think whatever he wanted. All I knew for certain at that point was that I was no longer willing or able to play the role of military wife. The next time my husband went off on a mission, I packed my son's and my own clothing in the car and drove home to Maine.

For the next two years, I tried to get a divorce, dated a few men, and pretended I was not a lesbian because I didn't want to give my husband any reason to go through with his threats to sue for custody of our son. When I finally did enter a relationship with a woman, I pretended to the world that she was just a friend, and that's probably the main reason the relationship ended. The next woman I was with was strong and comfortable with herself, happy with her life.

With her encouragement, I became more out, open and honest, and I believe this is why my son today accepts my choice to love women, so much so that he really can't understand heterosexism, which he places in the same category as racism and sexism.

My own parents were a different matter altogether. My sister told them about me before I was ready to deal with their reaction, which I had suspected would be negative. It was. When I arrived at my parents' house to discuss the matter, my mother offered me coffee as if I were a total stranger, one whose presence she was barely able to tolerate. She had a checklist written on the back of an envelope that she went down, item by item. The first was to establish the truth of what my sister had said. I admitted I was a lesbian. Next, she wanted me to know they had found a man—a minister—who could cure my homosexuality, and that she and my father were willing to pay his fees. I refused her offer. Then, my mother wanted me to change my name; she wanted me to know that despite their age, they were willing to adopt my son; and she wanted to know about AIDS. She also wanted to make it clear that my lesbian friends and lovers were not welcome at her house or summer cottage. My father, who'd hugged me and said he loved me when I entered the house, was curiously silent.

I took a deep breath, told them I was sorry they felt the way they did, and that I couldn't be around them unless they accepted my lesbianism. When my sister married, but my partner was not invited, I didn't attend the wedding. When Christmas came and they asked me home, but not my partner, I stayed away. Because we had very little contact for the next year and a half, I was certain that I'd lost my parents forever. Now, I think the course of action I chose was unnecessarily rigid: I was, after all, asking my parents to instantly accept something about myself that had taken me *years* to face.

The next four or five years were difficult. My folks included my partner in their invitations, but because everything even remotely relating to lesbianism was off limits as a topic of conversation, I still felt like a stranger in their home. It seemed that my choice to be a lesbian—even though it was the right one for me—had cost me a relationship with my parents.

I turned my attention to my son and myself. Since I was no longer trying to squeeze into a pre-existing mold, I was able to pour all my energy into creating a wonderful new life: I love teaching, so now I teach at an Arizona community college; I love writing, so now I write; I love the outdoors, so I backpack in the red rock canyons of Utah and Arizona, I soak in the hot springs in the Jemez mountains of New Mexico, and I kayak off the coast of Maine. The more I follow my heart, the more I love my life: I am stronger, healthier, and happier than I ever could have been as a military wife. And as time goes by, I think my parents can see that being a lesbian is the right choice for me. My mother addressed her last letter to both me and my partner—a sign to me that everything's going to be all right.

Marjory Nelson, 1951.

Marjory Nelson, right, with friends, 1990.

Becoming

MARJORY NELSON

On my 19th birthday, I married an ex-Marine. It was 1947 and women were being pushed out of all the good jobs they'd held during World War II. The colleges, now flooded with returning GIs, declared that women were taking up all the men's places. I dropped out.

All my creative energy went into fixing up my home, cooking, sewing, cleaning, and caring for my husband and three children. In the 1950's, women were expected to live only for our families. My women friends and I supported each other in doing that. Since I believed that my unhappiness was my own fault, I kept on smiling, and worked to be *well adjusted*, the catch phrase of that era.

In 1960, the pieces of myself I had tried to hold together came unglued. After years of sheer hell, reading Betty Friedan helped me understand the pressures I was under to give up my life for my family. At 36, torn between my children's and my needs, I somehow found the courage to go back to school. It was one of the most difficult decisions of my life. When a university 200 miles away offered me a three-year fellowship, I left my adolescent children with their father and set off for a new life. After 25 years of marriage, my husband and I divorced.

For two summers I went to North Carolina to work as an organizer with anti-racist groups. I went to Washington, D.C., and lived for a year at one of the communal houses of the National Woman's Party lobbying to pass the Equal Rights Amendment; I taught Women's Studies at Antioch College, then at the University of New York at Buffalo.

I was meeting many lesbians and developing insight into how deeply the patriarchy had reached into my psyche, my language, even my body. I was angry. I remembered when I was three years old the boys in our neighborhood took me into their clubhouse, took off my clothes, terrorized, and sexually molested me. My three older brothers would gang up on me, tie me up, terrorize me, and threaten to kill me. My parents didn't want to hear about it.

I yearned to find a woman my own age with a similar background for mutual support and understanding. When I did, we set up a sort of marriage, but one that was very different from my first. The trust between Polly and me enabled each of us to take unprecedented risks. We sold our worldly goods, bought a motor home, and traveled around the country doing political work.

Settling in San Francisco, I became part of a collective organizing a center for women over 40. I freelanced as a writer and organizer, and worked in a women's bookstore. Menopause brought huge fibroid tumors, pain, and bleeding so severe that doctors recommended a hysterectomy. I went to an alternative healer who taught me to visualize, to meditate, and to take responsibility for my body. This new commitment to health led me to examine and end a lifetime of obsessive dieting. Allowing my body to be my natural fat self (all three of my father's sisters were fat), was perhaps one of my most difficult challenges. The fat lesbians of the Fat Underground gave me courage. I started swimming daily, walking, and eating wisely. I ran a group called Fat, Female, and Forty.

Was becoming a lesbian essential to my journey of self discovery? Absolutely, especially occurring as it did within social movements that taught me to question everything, not only my own oppression as a woman, but my own privilege, too. I continue to heal, studying my craft of therapy, doing intense inner work of my own; I'm writing, painting, gardening, and doing yoga. Who else but a fat old lesbian would do her yoga on the beach? Last year I made a beautiful quilt for my first granddaughter and now it's time to make another.

For me, being a lesbian is not only about sex or personal growth, but also about community, about struggle and building new, multicultural institutions. I look forward to years as a radical old feminist dyke. I am becoming myself.

Ann D. Kwong, 1985.

Revelation

Ann D. Kwong

I met Ellen in karate class on the south side of Chicago in January of 1986. She had graduated from college the year before and was a white belt. I was five years older, a purple belt, married to an OB-GYN resident, and finishing up my Ph.D. After graduation, I went off the pill and back to karate, aspiring to motherhood and a brown belt. I had to go to karate classes on the north side of Chicago at the main dojo. Oftentimes, I would give Ellen and other students a ride in my car; Ellen and I became fast friends. At that time, Ellen was not only doing karate, but crew, applying to medical school, and working as a technician in a lab.

The movie *Desert Hearts* had just come out and Ellen recommended that I go see it. I did. With my husband, Jon. Then I went two more times. By myself. I asked Ellen why she recommended it and she shared that she was struggling with feelings of attraction to a woman and wondered what I thought about it. I told her I thought it was perfectly normal for people to be attracted to others of the same sex, avoiding all implications that statement had for me.

Over the course of that summer, Ellen and I began to spend more and more time together, sometimes with Jon for a walk or dinner. Once in a while all three of us would drive up to Horizons, the Chicago Gay and Lesbian Center, where Jon and I would wait in a Mexican diner around the corner while Ellen talked with someone about coming out.

As Ellen and I continued to talk, I began to realize that I was growing jealous of this unknown woman she was attracted to. Jon mentioned to me that he thought it was possible that Ellen was attracted to me! I couldn't believe it. I was sure it was someone else, and I didn't know what to do with my jealousy. At the same time, I was having doubts about getting pregnant, but I didn't want to rock the boat by going back on the pill.

While I was testing for my brown belt in karate, I noticed that I was feeling unusually tired. I thought I had the flu. The flu lingered for several weeks with accompanying nausea and vomiting. At this point, Jon, took a urine sample from me, ostensibly to test for a urinary tract infection. I didn't have the flu at all. I was pregnant and scared as hell. I realized that I was now responsible for another human being who was completely dependent on me.

I felt I could no longer evade the questions I had about my life and my relationship with my husband. For a long time, I had felt something was wrong with me and with our marriage. I did not want the doubts and questions that I had about myself to be conveyed to my child. It seemed to me that I had nine months to identify and resolve the reasons for my doubts.

Meanwhile, Ellen and I were still spending a lot of time together talking and walking each other back and forth to our separate apartments along with my entourage of three dogs and a cat. I began to feel nervous and uncomfortable spending a lot of time with Ellen and then going home to Jon.

One weekend, after Jon had left to visit some friends for a week, Ellen and I had a talk. She told me I was the woman she had been in love with for the last four months. Much later, I found out that Ellen fully expected me to turn her down, and that she had only confessed her attraction to me on the advice of an older lesbian who had recommended it as the fastest way to get over an unrealistic and impossible attraction to a married woman.

Instead of rejecting Ellen, I kissed her. One thing led to another, and we spent the entire week in each others's arms. I floated around in a state of limerance—that new relationship euphoria—going weak in the knees whenever I recalled our nights together. I also developed painful tension headaches when I contemplated what this turn of events might mean for my relationship with Jon.

One unalterable fact was that from the first night Ellen and I spent together, it felt absolutely good and right to me. Yes, I was scared, and my head told me it was the "wrong thing to do." But with my body, heart and my soul, it felt so right to be with Ellen that in the end I couldn't give her up for all the "right things" the rest of the world heaps upon straight marriages. When I was with Ellen, I understood what had felt wrong and what had been missing. I was simply a gay person trying to be straight.

Up to that point, I had been attributing the tensions in our marriage to cultural and social differences around public and private displays of affection. Jon was an American-born son of Caucasian parents and I was an American-born daughter of foreign-born Chinese parents. I thought I didn't like to kiss Jon because my parents, like a lot of traditional Chinese, never kissed or displayed any affection towards each other in public or at home in the presence of their children. But I wanted to kiss Ellen all the time, everywhere, and every chance I got!

When Jon returned from his trip a week later, I told him about Ellen immediately. At this point, I didn't want to leave him, and I didn't want to leave Ellen. I didn't want to hurt anyone, and I felt like I was being forced to choose between the right and left halves of my body. I couldn't do it. At the very beginning, Jon was supportive and understanding. He wanted me to stay with him and also encouraged me to explore my relationship with Ellen. Later on, when he realized that my attachment to Ellen was not going to disappear, he was deeply hurt, and there were times when he threatened me, and I was afraid. But what kept me in limbo for so long was not my fear of what Jon might do to me if I chose to leave him. It was not wanting to leave and hurt him. Leaving my marriage went against everything I had been taught.

I was raised in a deeply religious family in a suburb of Chicago with no television, no phonograph, and the constant drone of the Moody Bible Institute on the radio. As the eldest child of post-World War II immigrant Chinese parents, I was caught in a clash between the American culture around me and the peculiar time warp of class and culture that each set of immigrants codifies in stone for their generation. My brothers, sisters and I didn't have a choice about doing well academically. From grade school on, we knew that we had to go to college and become engineers or doctors. I was not allowed to go to parties in high school and was told I could go out with Chinese boys when I was close to a decent marriagable age—30. When my girlfriends brought their boyfriends to the house, my mother would throw them off our front step.

The first time I brought Jon home to meet my family, I made sure there would be a lot of other guests around to restrain my mother. When we started living together two years before we were married, my mother was convinced I was going to hell on account of it. She pressured me to marry but I resisted. For as long as I could remember, I had never wanted to get married. When I was young, I collected stamps, tadpoles, and butterflies and told people I was going to be a hermit and live in the Andes mountains.

The only way I finally agreed to get married was to convince myself that marriage was a joke, a piece of paper which really didn't change anything. Jon and I were married in September of 1982 in Cook County Circuit Court by Judge Lucia Thomas. We had no family members or witnesses present; we didn't even have wedding rings. The judge could hardly tear herself away from reading the *Chicago Sun Times* as she asked us if we "really wanted to be together 'til death do us part' and all that jazz." I had met my match—I couldn't believe how jaded she was, and she was the judge! To conclude the ceremony, she wound up a music box which played half of Mendelssohn's Wedding March before it broke down. I felt sorry for the excited bride and groom in the large Mexican wedding party in the waiting room.

I didn't think anything would change now that we were married. But I was wrong. My mother was ecstatic that I was no longer living in sin, and my father was relieved that her complaints were over. Total strangers and professors in our departments at school began acknowledging us as a couple.

I threw myself into work as my belly grew over the next few months. In fact, my bag of waters broke one Sunday, a week before my due date, while I was working in the lab. Jon stayed with me the whole night, but Ellen could not come—she was was not a "family member." I really missed her. By the time morning came, I was exhausted from labor. When Grace was born I was able to hold her right away. When they took her away to weigh her, she started to cry, but I called out to her, and the minute she heard my voice from a distance, she stopped. If I stopped soothing her with my voice, she would cry again. My heart melted. Later that day, everyone came to visit at once: Jon, my parents, my brother and sister, Ellen, my Ph.D. advisor, and the therapist that Jon and I had been seeing. I didn't try to explain to anyone what all these different people meant to me and why they were there.

When I decided to leave my marriage, I felt like I was crossing a bridge to a shore that I could not clearly see. Nothing prepared me for the journey. I was raised to only consider my duty and responsibility to my family and society. My personal desires and feelings were supposed to conform to the greater good of my relationship. But in choosing to leave my marriage so that I could be happy with Ellen, and if not her, then with another woman, I was throwing all that I was taught to the wind.

Just days after my divorce was final, I took a job in a New York City lab, where most of my colleagues were men from Korea, Japan, and China who were married and had wives who waited on them hand and foot. I was amazed at how some of these men expected their wives and children to just pick up and move with them from place to place. Usually their wives spoke very little English and were trapped in their apartments, unable to go out without their husbands' escort. The husbands spent most of their time in the company of the other men in the lab, working, drinking, and smoking, while their wives and children waited for them at home. It was appalling to me how much sacrifice was taken for granted.

I found a babysitter, and within the next month, my ex-husband Jon moved to New York City to begin a fellowship program and to be near our daughter, Grace. I did not take it for granted that Ellen would come to live with me. So when she applied to transfer her last two years of medical school to New York City so that we could be together, I believed this was as close to going to the Justice of the Peace as we were ever going to get.

In the past few years, our lives have settled down. Jon and I are committed to living near enough to each other so that Grace has one school and two homes. We have a schedule which is reliable, yet flexible. We split both the week and the weekend, share the same babysitter, and Jon, Ellen, and I talk face-to-face about how things are going. One of my favorite memories is attending a Christmas Eve concert at a gay and lesbian church (Metropolitan Community Church of NYC) and sitting in the audience with Jon and my brother while Ellen and Grace sang in the choir.

While overall our arrangement is fairly amiable, there are still a lot of unresolved tensions. Jon has been in relationships with a number of women. Most of them have been comfortable with Grace, Ellen, and me. But I always worry that a new wife will try to turn my daughter against me and persuade her father to seek full custody. Ellen and I are also considering the possibility of having another child, and we worry about how that might upset the balance in our relationship with Jon. Because of my involvement with Asian Lesbians of the East Coast and our attendance at MCC-NYC, my daughter knows a lot of other committed gay and lesbian couples and some of their children. In this way, I hope that she is learning to be proud of who we are and to know our family is not alone.

Bettye Marvel with her childen, 1974.

Bettye Marvel with her current partner, 1991.

Love Song

BETTYE MARVEL

Bettye Marvel is the Co-Chair of the Gay and Lesbian Speakers Bureau in Mt. Vernon, Indiana.

I met my husband-to-be at the local Southern Baptist Church. He became a deacon in the church, and me a deacon's wife. We had four wonderful children together. I participated in all the church's women's groups and played recreational softball and volleyball in the women's league. It was through sports that I met the woman who brought me out. She was also married with four children. My first sexual experience with her was like someone turning on all the lights. All the love songs finally made sense. I knew I could no longer live a pretend life.

The following months were a mixture of joy in having found my true identity and anguish at having to explain it to my husband and parents. No one from church would speak to me or visit me anymore. I was ostracized by the church leadership and removed from my Sunday school and mission study teaching positions. My husband and parents thought I'd gone insane and made an appointment for me to see a doctor. I didn't go! The fact that all these events transpired in a small midwestern town of 7,000, where I had grown up and everyone knew my business, added to the exasperation. Still, I held firm, and continued to be strong in my spiritual self. Thankfully, God doesn't restrict fellowship and prayer to a building.

Ten years and two months after my divorce, I met my partner, Chris. We experience life together with a fervor and desire I never dreamed possible. All of my children love my partner and accept her as family, thanking her for making their mother happy. I have been blessed with five grandchildren...so far. Our life is not without worries, but we face everything together and love lesbian life. I'm so glad I didn't die wondering.

Sharon Paloma, left.

...at age six.

The Not-So-Tall Tale of Cowbutch Joh

SHARON 'JOH' PALOMA

Throughout my childhood I was called a tomboy. This was a common term tagged onto any girl who enjoyed climbing trees, playing football, or doing what adults thought only little boys should do. Being raised in Texas, it goes without saying that this tomboy was also a cowboy, or "cowbutch" as I call myself now.

On almost any occasion you could find me in blue jeans, cowboy hat and boots. My spurs would be jingling, my cap guns snapping; I was Roy Rogers fighting off the bad guys and rescuing the defenseless. I had a neighborhood boyfriend who loved to dress up in old dresses and pretend he was Dale Evans. What a sight we were! "Dale" would cook dinner and take care of our baby doll while I rode off into the sunset. The days seemed endless in our make-believe world. We were probably the happiest "married couple" on the block.

My old spurs now hang in my study and a few sweet memories remain in my mind, but far too many memories are locked away in some deep place where I hide my shame and my pain.

From the outside, one would assume that I had a normal family. Yet, beneath the facade were fractured and disjointed parents raising very wounded children. My father was painfully passive and had no involvement in my life. My mother was extremely volatile and bitter; rage ruled our household.

Starting in my elementary school years, my mother would point out "queers" and begin extended graphic descriptions of how perverted and vile they were. She loathed homosexuals; her words went beyond the usual homophobic ones I heard in other places. As a young child, full of tenderness and compassion, I did not know how to deal with such hatred.

At the age of 15, I was a counselor-in-training at a summer camp. Harriet, my head counselor, was the first person to help me overcome my great fear of water. I had failed my beginner's swimming class two summers in a row. But with the day-to-day help and encouragement from Harriet, I passed my senior lifesaving course and became a certified lifeguard. My letters home were full of pride in my swimming and praise for Harriet. Then one Sunday afternoon, while talking on the phone, my mother proceeded to tell me that she knew I was sexually involved with Harriet. With anger and vulgarity, she demanded that I pack my car and immediately drive home. My mother said that as soon as I got home, she would take me to a doctor who would run tests to prove I was having sex with another woman. The conversation devastated me, not only because I had not yet experienced any sexual stirrings, but also because the accusations were so vile.

Harriet found me sobbing and shoving my clothes into a suitcase. I told her about the conversation with my mother. She was shocked and outraged. She told me she was driving to Ft. Worth to confront my mother. This terrified me; no one had ever confronted my mother. Later that evening Harriet returned, saying, "Joh, I've talked to your mother and everything is straightened out. She said you could stay."

Only a small part of me was relieved. The rest of me was experiencing a private emotional breakdown. My mother never apologized for her false accusations nor for the cruelty she had inflicted upon me.

By the time I was 17, I had become acutely aware of my attraction to women. But it wasn't until I entered my freshman year at Texas Woman's University that I had my first sexual encounter. Toni and I were both 18, both freshmen, and both virgins. It was an exhilarating time for me, but also a very frightening one. I had now become what my mother loathed. I lived with a constant sense of danger.

During spring break, Toni and I were separated for three weeks. She vowed to write me every day. When I returned to campus I found my mailbox crammed full. I spent most of the day reading her very personal and endearing letters. I stored them in shoe boxes and hid them in the bottom of my closet.

One afternoon while I was in class, my mother came to school with some change-of-season clothes. She searched through my closet, discovering and confiscating my love letters. That evening she burst into my room in a violent state and began striking my face and calling me the vilest of names. It didn't take me long to realize she had discovered Toni's letters. My mother continued raging, insisting that we get in her car and find the women Toni had mentioned in her letters. Fortunately, Toni wasn't on campus.

The next few hours were terrifying! While driving around, my mother would ask me questions, and each time I answered, she would strike my face with the back of her hand. We would pull up in front of various dorms and I would give her the impression I was going to find my gay friends. Actually, I would leave a message for them to stay away, that my mother was on a rampage. My mother was unsuccessful in finding any lesbians. By the time she left me at my dorm, my face was swollen and bloody; I was completely traumatized. I staggered up two flights of stairs to my room, not knowing what awaited me.

The following day marked the beginning of my imprisonment. My mother had wasted no time in conferring with the president of the university, using my letters as evidence. Sitting in the president's office with my battered face and jagged nerves, I was told that if I cooperated by giving full names of all the lesbians I knew on campus, my punishment would be lessened. I told them I could not do that.

The university president, my dormitory mother, and my own mother were furious and decided to isolate me from everyone on campus as well as all activities. They were hoping the restrictions would force me to give them names. For over three months, I was only allowed to attend regularly scheduled classes and was given a thirty-minute block of time to eat each meal. For the rest of the time I was to be in my room. My dorm mother would call me throughout the day, making sure I was there. I even had to notify her when I was taking a shower. Since my roommate had dropped out of school, I was completely isolated. I could go nowhere, talk to no one, and do absolutely nothing other than attend classes. No one on campus dared speak to me for fear of being brought into this nightmare. The authorities of this school were able to pull this off without a hitch. Everyone waited to see how long it would take before I broke.

Prior to this time, the entire student body had been preparing for the biggest yearly event: the school plays. Each class would write an original play which would be fully choreographed and costumed. I was ecstatic because the play I had written had been selected by my freshman class. Before my box of letters had been discovered, I had been very active in directing my play. Afterwards, I was not allowed to participate in any way. On the night of the performance, my dormitory was virtually empty. As I sat alone on my window ledge, I heard laughter and applause coming from the auditorium. Not only was I barred from seeing my play in full dress rehearsal, I was not allowed to be present when they announced that, for the first time in history, our freshman class had won second place. When the semester ended, I was abruptly taken home. Throughout the ordeal, I had remained silent. My silence protected those I cared for and stood up against injustice.

During the fall my mother insisted that I attend Texas Christian University and live at home. I was to be obedient, and of course, heterosexual. Since survival demanded that I live a dual life, I had to date young men while being gay in the shadows. I would often lie about where I was going and would stash a change of clothes at a gay friend's apartment. I'd leave my house under the pretense of meeting one of my straight friends for dinner and a show. I would then change clothes and spend the evening at a gay bar or party, being very happy to be a dyke. The unhappy times were the straight dates, when men would pick me up at my home and actually take me out. Living such a dual life was exhausting and degrading, but necessary if I wanted to survive.

The next year I was able to escape to the University of New Mexico. My mother's sister lived in Albuquerque and I had always been close to her. My mother and aunt thought that if I left Texas I could "get my life together." It was in Albuquerque that I went headlong into homosexuality. I loved my newfound freedom and distance from my mother. However, while at UNM, my mother insisted I attend weekly sessions with the local shrink. My first visit set the stage for all other sessions. He began by saying, "Joh, your mother tells me you have a problem with homosexuality." I told him I had no problem with homosexuality and refused to discuss that subject with him. He then asked, "What do you have a problem with?" I replied, "My mother!" From that point on, my mother and our relationship became the focus of our sessions. When the psychiatrist had to personally deal with my mother and her irate letters, he began to understand my "problem." It was then that he advised me: "The safest thing for you is to get out of town. Don't let your mother know where you are going." He believed she was capable of following through on her threat: "I gave you life and I have the right to take it."

For the next five years my parents heard not a word from me. My mother hired a private investigator to find me, but I was able to stay one step ahead of him. I became nomadic, not only in my travels but also in my relationships with women. I began an eight-year entanglement with drugs, especially hallucinogens. Many people have asked me, "Why the drugs and so many women?" The way I explain it is that I had been so controlled and thwarted in my development that I had no healthy resources for dealing with the real world. In truth, I really don't know all that plummeted me into such a lifestyle, but I look back on those years and weep for the loss of myself and of the creative potential of my young life.

In 1971, I jumped from "the frying pan into the fire"; I let myself be swept up into the Jesus Movement. I flew into the arms of God and wrapped myself in the church. When I was in the 6th grade, a teacher had asked me, "Joh, do you have a father? All I hear you talk about is your mother." I replied, "Yes, I have a father, but my mother is 'my mother, my father, and my god.'" My mother owned me, controlled me, and conditioned my responses to life. In 1971, I transferred that power over to a Protestant God, the only one big enough to take my mother's place. It was at this time that I also reconnected with my family and tried to reconcile with my mother.

The church, like my mother, was quick to condemn homosexuals. I had no defense against the word of God, and I let myself believe homosexuality was a vile sickness. Since my heart's desire was to please God, I had no other choice than to try to annihilate my lesbian soul. I realize now that no one can kill any part of themselves; they can only shove it deep inside. I also realize homosexuality is neither perverted nor sick, but at the time, I believed I should "die to my old lifestyle" in order to be received by God.

During this dismal time a wonderful thing happened. One evening, while waiting for the church service to begin, I was browsing through ads in a Christian newspaper. One caught my attention: "Steve and Gypsy, The LIGHT —a Christian coffeehouse, Gold Beach, Oregon."

I was enchanted with this woman's name. I said out loud, "I've got to meet Gypsy." Within two days I was packed and heading down the road. It took me four days to make the long trip, but within minutes of arriving in Gold Beach, I came face-to-face with the gentle 18-year-old woman named Gypsy. It was as though I'd known her all my life. Gypsy and I readily formed a friendship. From the beginning, our days were full of laughter.

I lived with this small Christian community for only three months. Then, my nomadic feet began itching and I decided to move back to Albuquerque. I left Gypsy on June 11th, her 19th birthday. I was 27. I don't know why I left. I think it was hard to let myself be happy for any length of time. As I said good-bye to Gypsy, sorrow flooded me. Yet, even then I knew our friendship was strong and that we'd see each other again.

Five months after arriving back in Albuquerque, I married a man I had known for seven weeks. We had met at church, and the only thing we had in common was our hippie past. He desperately wanted to be married; I desperately wanted to be "normal." So we set the date and tied the knot in the presence of our parents. I soon realized the knot was a noose and that I had placed myself in a miserable situation. Yet the same scriptures that told me God abhorred homosexuals, told me God detested divorce. I had no place to go. I believed I had to remain married for the rest of my life. In resigning myself to become a perfect Christian wife, I piled tragedy upon tragedy. My husband had also come from a very fractured past; we hid our marital problems from our families as well as our church friends. Everyone thought we were happily married. People thought I was a little gloomy and despondent, but told me every couple had their ups and downs.

When I first got married, my mother was skeptical, but after five years of marriage and three children, she was convinced I was now a "healthy, normal woman." Our mother-daughter relationship was still wrought with problems; she still tried to control me, and my children. But the warfare around homosexuality had ended, and that was a relief. I did not realize the high price I would pay for severely suppressing who I was.

My children also paid a price. They saw me as a victim, wounded and unhappy. Although I loved them dearly, I could not give them the things they needed for a healthy childhood; I did not have those things inside myself to give.

After several years of living as a heterosexual with a husband I could not love and my lesbian self buried under guilt, my body finally reacted in a violent way. I was diagnosed as having Systemic Lupus. This disease demanded that I avoid sunlight, fatigue and stress. As the disease raged through my body, I waited to see if any major organs would be affected. At one point, I was so ill my husband and I were discussing my funeral.

Although this was a very difficult time for me, it was also a time of forced retreat. Lupus made me let go of my grip on life and my great need to be the perfect wife. Like my days in college, I found myself in confinement, but this time in a creative one. It was during these years I began to reclaim my lost self, to slowly raise the coffin lid and see if there was any life in my lesbian soul.

Throughout this time, Gypsy and I had remained the best of friends. When she was pregnant with her first child, she and her husband moved to Albuquerque just to be near me and have me be with her during the birthing. On November 25, 1973, I helped the midwife deliver Sarah Angelina. Six months later I gave birth to my firstborn, Joshua. Gypsy and I shared motherhood in a marvelous way. We'd sit for hours, nursing our babies, lost in conversation.

The following year, Gypsy and Steve moved back to Oregon. It was always hard for us to leave each other. Throughout the years, we'd travel across the country to visit. With each wonderful visit came a sorrowful good-bye. We finally decided that once we'd raised our children and buried our husbands, we would rock on the porch together and never have to say good-bye again. It was a future we both waited for, a dream we clung to.

In 1989, amazing things began to happen, all of which were a direct result of my four-year bout with Systemic Lupus. During those years of restriction and isolation, I had begun to understand and heal from the early abuses that had brought me to such a place. After struggling so long for emotional health and balance, I emerged as a whole person, eager to get on with the life I wanted and no longer the life others expected me to live.

The first incredible news of that year was that my doctors told me my Systemic Lupus was in remission and no major organs had been affected. This good diagnosis was a catalyst for the rest of my major decisions, one of which was to return to college and become a Respiratory Therapist.

Everything exploded like a brilliant sunrise. Nothing could hold me under nor hold me back. At long last I was able to throw off the pretense of heterosexuality and embrace my lesbian self, vowing never to betray her again. By 1991 I was divorced, raising my three children, and working in a local hospital as a Respiratory Therapist.

These times were like straddling a rocket, heading for the moon—everything was happening so fast. A metamorphosis had taken place. I had taken control of my life; I had learned to love and nurture myself. I had fallen in love with my lesbian self for the very first time. I found that part of me to be beautiful, warm and compassionate. It was good to be "out." Many call it "coming out of the closet." For me, "closet" it was not; "dungeon" would be more fitting. I had emerged as an "out and fully visible" lesbian, and Gypsy was hearing all about it.

My story doesn't end here. As I began to explore my lesbian self I realized I had been carrying Gypsy in my heart as my lover, and that my love for her far exceeded that of a friend. Once I openly acknowledged this, I was flooded with passion for her. I wrestled with these feelings for weeks. Gypsy was my "straight" friend. Questions bombarded me: How could I tell her I loved her and longed to share my life with her? Would my declaration of love destroy our friendship? My struggle was severe. I finally threw caution and common sense out the door and relied solely on my intuitive heart. I had to let Gypsy know how I felt.

On April 2, 1991, with great trepidation, I made a monumental phone call. "Gypsy, I want you to sit down, there's something I need to tell you." My heart was racing. "Honey, I love you. I've always loved you! I want to spend the rest of my life with you." All I could hear from Gypsy was "Un-huh" and "Yes. Un-huh." I thought to myself "Oh no, she doesn't feel the same way," but I continued.

When I finished gushing, Gypsy said, "I love you, too, Joh. I've always loved you!" Months earlier Gypsy had realized the depth of her love and her longing to be with me. She had chosen to remain silent, knowing how important it was for me to have the freedom to follow my own heart without any outside influences. To her joy and mine, my phone call simply affirmed what we had already known.

Over the next few weeks we spent countless hours on the phone. We exchanged volumes of love letters and began to work through the obstacles that lay ahead. She was in Oregon, I was in Texas, and the miles that separated us seemed impossible to span. Missing her and wanting her became unbearable. I phoned and asked, "Will you meet me in Albuquerque and marry me?" Her reply was, "Yes, YES!"

On May 13th, my plane landed in Albuquerque. Gypsy had arrived the night before and was waiting for me at the airport. It was wonderful seeing her. It seemed to take forever to make our way to the hotel room (20 years to be exact), but once there, the rest of the world fell away. Four days later, we came out in search of food. As we feasted on enchiladas and sopapillas in Old Town, we listened to a flamenco guitarist singing a beautiful song, "La Paloma." Paloma—the dove—stayed with us and became our last name.

Three years have now passed. Gypsy and cowbutch 'Joh' are "porch rocking and rolling" women. Our ex-husbands? We wish them well. Our children have bonded and are thriving in a home full of love.

You may ask, "What of your mother?" Three years ago I wrote her a long "coming out" letter, telling her about my relationship with Gypsy, and in it trying to relieve her fears. She disowned and disinherited me. A year and a half ago, I spent four days at her hospital bedside. As she lay dying, she was still unable to reconcile with me. Her first question, after not having seen me for several years and wanting nothing to do with me, was "Why are you here?" I replied, "Because I love you." While she could not accept me, she did allow me to bathe her and turn her pain-racked body every twenty minutes. She died one week after I left. I hope she has finally found peace.

It's no longer hard to let myself be happy; it's no longer necessary for Gypsy and me to say those hard goodbyes. We are living in Ashland, Oregon, happy and thriving!

Mardi Richmond on her wedding day and now.

After the Accident

MARDI RICHMOND

I can't talk about my marriage without talking about getting loaded; I fell in love with Mikke, in part, because of our mutual need to get high. Not a day of my married life went by that was not focused on getting stoned, drunk, or in some other way plastered. Besides, both Mikke and getting loaded represented the same things in my life. Both were about growing up, learning to live, finding comfort, escaping pain and, sometimes, having fun. And both were about silences. I can't talk about what happened in my marriage, the breakup and coming out as a lesbian without talking about getting clean and sober and breaking silences.

My life has always had silences; deep dark family secrets hidden in the attic. Secrets like incest, addiction, abuse and suicide. Growing up I found a whole different set of secrets that were my very own and that stayed locked, not in the attic, but in my own private closet.

In the fifth grade, Angela was one of those secrets. Angela, who was in my class, told all of her friends that any girl who touched another girl was a lezzie. One night at a slumber party, Angela reached out in the dark and held my hand. The next day I wrote "I Love Angela" on a stick and tied it to my bike with string. When some of the neighborhood kids swiped the stick and read the words, they were very quiet. I think that was scarier than if I had been teased.

By the time sixth grade rolled around and I got a serious crush on Melinda, I knew I had better be more careful. So when I realized I couldn't talk to her without stumbling over my words and turning bright red, the way kids do when they have crushes, I stopped talking. But I didn't just stop talking to her—that would give me away. I stopped talking to everyone. When a friend would come up and say something to me, I would simply smile. My sixth grade teacher, Mrs. Pierce, tried the hardest to get me to talk, but I just smiled at her, too. Soon everyone was calling me "Smiley," and I didn't have to worry about anyone discovering my secret. One of the things I learned that year was that the more I practiced, the better I got at keeping things to myself.

In the seventh grade I discovered a new tool for maintaining my silence: getting high. Pot, reds, and Boone's Farm Strawberry Mountain Wine—they worked so well that soon my secrets were even hidden from me.

When I met Mikke in the summer between eighth and ninth grade, I knew I had found a kindred spirit. Mikke used to ride a little Honda 125 through the back trails to my house. We would go for rides into the woods and smoke joints. Sometimes we would go to his house and drink the beers his mom bought and pretended to never notice missing. I fell in love with Mikke then, with a boy who would play poker for beer and climb trees to get high in the highest spot. Later, in high school, we would drive into the hills in his van, get high and make love. We grew—going from children, to teenagers, to semi-adult lovers—together.

Today, looking back, I can see that he got high for many of the same reasons I did: to hide from pain, confusion and his own silences. Then, all I saw was a boy who liked to play hard, get loaded, escape.

I learned to love Mikke the way childhood friends love each other. We sometimes talked for hours, but we never really talked about what was hard or scary. We lived by our family code of "don't talk."

The closest I came to telling Mikke about my feelings for other girls was in high school. Mikke and I had been having a hard time. I had just had an abortion. I was scared, very scared, of sex. I did not want to get pregnant again. Mikke was scared, too. Instead of talking about our fears, we were trying new drugs, searching for a better escape.

Then Jane came to our school. She was the daughter of a military man, always moving. This was her third school that year. Instead of Mikke and I hanging out with each other, we both started hanging out with her. Jane and I spent long hours after school lying on my bed, talking and talking. We didn't even get high. I don't remember what we talked about, but I do remember her brown eyes gazing deeply into mine and one afternoon when we just held each other. Soon, the feelings that I had hidden behind drugs rose to the surface.

I might have told Mikke I was falling in love with Jane, except he told me first. Actually, he didn't tell me he was in love with her, only that he had made love to her. I was crushed. Jealous. Furious. I felt completely betrayed, not because my boyfriend slept with my girlfriend, but because my girlfriend hadn't slept with me. The worst part about it was that Jane and I never had a chance to talk about it. Within a week, her dad got transferred and I never even saw her again.

Mikke and I came together through that pain. I knew I couldn't keep loving Mikke if I had those feelings for Jane. Yet Mikke was there, loving and warm. Jane was gone. His guilt and my lost love, never named, but very much there, brought us even closer.

What I didn't know then was that the part of me that woke up with Jane, slowly started dying when I drew closer to Mikke. I drank more beer, smoked more pot, and popped more pills, trying to help kill off the piece of myself that I kept in the closet. That's how it is with silences: they lead to death.

When we were eighteen, Mikke moved away to college. I stayed home to work and attend the local community college. We wrote each other and we talked on the phone. He had a new connection for speed and sent me some to sell locally. I was dating a new boy. Then I went to visit Mikke at the University of Oregon.

He was miserable, lonely and unhappy. It drizzled nonstop in Oregon and he claimed the gray was going to kill him. I was unhappy, too. My new boyfriend had just told me he wanted to do something with me besides get high. He wanted to talk about what he was feeling, what I was feeling. He wanted to plan our future. Mikke and I spent the week on his dorm room bed getting high and fucking. We decided then to get married.

We moved to Santa Cruz, Mikke transferred schools and I started working. We lived together for a while first, found we were compatible in our habits, and liked to do some of the same things. The years passed by quickly, and soon we decided to make our life together official. Our wedding followed.

Being married to Mikke was okay. Good in many ways.

I was comfortable then—we would get high, never missing a day. Still, something never was quite right. Maybe it was because some part of me was attracted to women. But in all honesty, I was also attracted to Mikke. Maybe it was because we never really talked and what we hid kept growing. Maybe it was because I was getting tired of spending my life stoned. I wanted more. I wanted to feel.

I tried to stop using many times. I would get glimpses of my life passing me by. I wanted to die, and I would think: maybe if I stopped getting high, maybe then things would get better. I started hating myself for getting wasted, but no matter how many times I tried, I couldn't stop. Instead, I did what I knew so well: drank a beer, smoked a joint, made love with Mikke, didn't feel.

I didn't see how desperate I was to get clean and sober until after the accident. Mikke and I had been married less than a year when it happened, but I remember it vividly.

I stood looking at a pile of metal. My car, once a white Volkswagen bug, lay skewered on a fence post by the side of the road. One side of the roof was crumpled down to the red vinyl of the seat cushion, both front fenders were creased, and the rest of the car was, well, simply unrecognizable. My hands started shaking; tears welled up in my eyes.

"Jesus," said the cop standing next to me. "You should have died in that one."

She was right. The 4x4 fence post sat right where my head should have been. Somehow, in spite of the seat belt, my body slammed against the steering wheel, throwing my head forward. The post stuck through the driver's window and stopped near the headrest of the passenger seat.

I stared in disbelief at my narrowly escaped metal grave wondering how this had happened. I knew I was tired when I left for work that morning, and the roads were slick from the first rain of the season. But how could a bee flying in through the window and into my face cause a near death?

I would not have been surprised if this had happened a few days earlier when I had been blasted, stoned out of my mind, just about every time I drove. But for three days I hadn't had as much as a beer after work or a puff at bedtime. For three horrendous, twenty-four-hour days, I hadn't taken anything. I also hadn't slept. I'd barely eaten. And my hands were just beginning to stop shaking.

The cops were real nice to me that morning. They called my husband and when the phone did not rouse him from his deep sleep, the cop who first arrived on the scene sent a patrol car up to the house to get him out of bed. I still wonder what it was like for Mikke to wake up to a pounding on the door, stumble out of bed and through the dimly lit house, and see a police officer's face in the front door window. I wonder if he worried about the bong on the table or the roaches in the ashtray or the twenty-five sensemilla plants growing beneath lights under the house. I wonder if the cops would have treated me differently if I had smoked my usual joint that morning.

When Mikke finally pulled up to the scene of the accident almost an hour later and jumped out of his red four-wheel drive Toyota, his words echoed the police officer's. "Holy shit," he said. "I can't believe you lived through that!"

I couldn't believe people kept saying that to me.

Mikke took me home, up the mile-and-a-half hill that I had driven down that morning. "Shit," I thought, "now I'm late for work." I went into the kitchen to call my boss and tell him why I was late. He said, take the day off. I said okay.

When I walked back into the living room, Mikke and Tom, our housemate, sat on the couch. Tom had just finish rolling a joint from the newly dried harvest. Mikke lit it up and handed it to me. I handed it back.

"I'm trying to quit, remember?" I said with anger welling up in my voice.

"I know you're trying to quit," he said with equal anger. "But you almost died. My wife almost died and I need to get high. I thought you might need to get high, too."

I did need to get high, but I didn't want to get high. Instead, I wanted to tell Mikke how scared I was, how afraid I had been. I wanted to hear how glad he was that I was alive, that I didn't die. I wanted to crawl in his arms and cry about my life and my car and how hard it was not to get loaded when I was feeling so much. But I didn't say anything. I just sat back on the couch and watched Mikke and Tom pass the joint.

That night we decided to go to the county fair. The GoGo's were playing and I had been looking forward to seeing them all week long. When we got there, I held the seats at the bleachers while Mikke and Tom went to get the 24-ounce cups of Coors beer from the concession stand. They came back with three cups.

"We got an extra one just in case you change your mind," Tom said. "If you don't want it I'll drink 'em both."

"I don't think I want it, Tom," I said.

"Maybe just a couple of sips?" Mikke said, holding out the cup he had been drinking from.

Maybe just one sip, I thought. Then I shook my head no.

"Aw, come on," he said, pushing the cup to my lips. I took a sip. It tasted good. Then I took another.

"Hey, that one's mine," said Mikke, grabbing back his cup. "Yours is sitting right next to you." He motioned to the full cup of beer sitting beside me on the bleacher.

I picked up the cup and took another sip. Then another. Then a gulp. Soon I had gulped down all twenty-four ounces. The warmth of the beer crept slowly up my spine.

"See, I told you, you just needed to get high," Mikke said.

I leaned back and propped my elbows on the bleacher behind me, realizing I couldn't live like this. I didn't want to live like this. But I couldn't not live like this. Then I thought about what it would have been like if my head were where it should have been when that 4x4 jammed through the window of my car. Mikke is right, I thought. So was that cop. I should have died in that crash.

The more I wanted to quit getting loaded, the more I wanted to die each time I drank a beer or puffed on a joint. After the accident I knew I couldn't stay clean while I was with Mikke. And that if I continued along like I was, I would die. Possibly in a car crash, maybe from the drugs, probably because I couldn't live with myself any longer.

But the change didn't happen all of a sudden. I didn't wake up the next morning and swear off drugs and alcohol and get on with my life. Leaving Mikke took a while. Getting clean and sober took even longer.

What I did do was stop getting high quite as much. I traded in the drugs for a straight diet of alcohol. I made some new friends, women friends, who did not get high. These were the first women I had gotten to know and been close to since Jane. And yes, they were lesbians.

But it wasn't until I met Mel that things really began to snowball. She worked as a checker in the market near where I worked. I would go into the store every day at lunch, buy my yogurt and banana, and head down to the ocean to eat and watch the waves. She started talking to me one day about a shirt I was wearing. "Support Women in the Trades," my shirt said. "Where can I get a shirt like that?" she asked.

We started talking that day, flirting a little when I went to buy my lunch. I started thinking of other reasons to stop in at the market as well. I needed beer after work. We were low on dog food. Finally, one day, I worked up enough nerve to ask her to have lunch with me. She countered by suggesting dinner.

Later on, at dinner, Mel asked me if I was happy in my marriage. It seemed like such a funny question to me. No one had ever asked me that before. I had never even asked myself. Somehow, the word "no" came out before I even had time to think. I could no longer keep quiet.

Still, I probably wouldn't have mentioned my crush on Mel to Mikke except that when I saw her my heart beat faster and each time I talked to her I stuttered and my face turned bright red. Every time Mel touched me, just a slight touch of her hand on my back or a brush of our shoulders, my body jolted. Surges of energy ran up my spine; desire filled every inch of me. I had never had these feelings in all of my twenty-two years and I wanted to keep feeling them. It was like a light turning on inside, a new awareness, a new hope. I also knew that if I could have these kinds of feelings for someone other than Mikke, something wasn't quite right in our relationship. Still, I secretly hoped that if I told him, it would take the power out of my crush. And that maybe I could find those feelings with him.

But Mikke had a different reaction. "I can't compete with a woman," he said when I tried to talk with him. He told me to go away and figure out what my feelings were all about. When I moved out of our house, I wasn't sure I wanted to leave, but as soon as I left, I knew I was where I needed to be.

It has been ten years since our divorce was final, but ten years feels like a lot more than a decade. It seems like a lifetime ago.

My life did not instantly change when I left Mikke. I spent the first six months struggling to live without drugs and alcohol. The second six months, finally clean and sober, I spent in agonizing loneliness. I no longer had my childhood sweetheart. I no longer had the booze or the drugs to numb my heartaches. I wanted to die then even more than when I was using.

Learning to live and love and speak out came slowly and with practice. My role models came from the women who surrounded me. I watched these recovering women struggle to live with courage, dignity and strength. I began mimicking them until I found my own strength, hidden deep inside.

Silences no longer have much place in my life. I opened the door just a little by telling Mel that I was unhappy in my marriage and then by telling Mikke that I had feelings for a woman. Once that door opened a crack, the family secrets hidden away in the attic, as well as my own, left locked in a closet, came tumbling out. Today, I cannot tolerate the discomfort or the pain of secrets. Fortunately, I no longer have to.

On the surface, my life today is not so very different from my life ten years ago as a young wedded wife. Again, I wear a wedding band and live with my life partner in a little house. A Toyota truck still sits in my driveway and a dog still sleeps by my bed. Aside from the fact that my partner is now a woman, my life appears very much the same.

But the differences run deep, down through the core of my being. Today, I have friends as well as a lover. I have built enough self-esteem not only to stay sober, but to return to school, to change careers, to co-parent a little boy. I wake up every day and smile at the woman next to me without having to light a joint first. I have discovered new directions and new dreams; dreams I didn't even know existed.

A friend of mine asked me recently if I thought I could take all these changes, all the growth and honesty, and share it today with a man. I thought about this question long and hard. I have had attractions to men, even since identifying as a lesbian. Sometimes, when I have felt the weight of hatred—after a carload of young men has driven by my lover and me and yelled, "What you need is a good fuck;" after I was denied recognition as a parent because I was not the "real" mom; after my lover and I were turned down for insurance because we were not legally married—I wish for a life without the tensions of discrimination.

Could I today maintain all of my life changes if I were again with a man? Could I be happy today with a man? Could I stay clean and sober? Maybe. Probably. But I can't help asking myself another question: Why would I want to? After experiencing the joy of loving a woman, of holding her in my arms, of stroking her breasts, of feeling her strength, love and desire match my own, after having lived as a woman-loving woman, I can't imagine why I would want to live any other way.

Living with Her

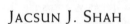

JACSUN J. SHAH

Before I lived with her
I was forever dragging around
my furniture, seeking
the perfect arrangement.
Always, the rooms of my house
like the cells in my body
seemed empty. Or too full,
sharp edges everywhere.
Squared-off days squeezed against each other
in blocks of months, held
in the tin fist of marriage.

Now, living with her, everything fits.
Each room I enter is a body that envelops me.
Each day fans out, then folds us
into its warm pouch of night,
and the round months garland us
with cool moonflowers.

Living with her,
I lean into the curves of wonder.

Ordinary Lives

KAREN TAKATA

It was something like buying clothes, always searching through the racks, but for what I wasn't sure. I'd tried on different styles and colors. Some things were okay, some definitely not. Finally I found it; the right outfit, the perfect fit. My discovery put everything in place and I felt great relief. I didn't have to look anymore.

The outfit that took so long to find was not jeans or skirts. It was about being a lesbian, a matter which surprised me. After all, I was married with two children. The fact that there was a lot of love in my life concealed my confusion, my constant sense of displacement. I was happy to be a mother and happy to be loved. I had the kind of marriage that gave me space. My husband and I were good friends: we liked and respected one another. We were busy with our own lives and shared our home like housemates. Our strongest shared interest was our love for our children.

Love for my children. That is where my discovery got costly. How important was it to me? How much was I willing to pay? I agonized over these questions for a long time. Watching my happy, secure five- and seven-year-olds, I wondered, "Could I play it straight for them? And for how long? Ten years? Twenty? Or the rest of my life?" I remembered something I'd once read about secrets; it takes energy to keep a secret. Secrets are like corks held under water by constant pressure. When we keep a secret life, when we are false in our relationships, we pay a price of some kind. I knew I could not keep this life hidden from my children. I had tried hard to teach them the importance of honesty. Withholding the truth is said to be the same as telling a lie. This was the price I was not willing to pay: lying to my children. It was time to get honest. It was time to put on my new outfit and come out.

I don't think coming out is ever easy. I was fortunate, living in a lesbian-friendly town. I'd been surrounded by the lesbian community, and though I was only semi-conscious of it during my married life, I was very grateful to have its support as I came out. It was surprisingly easy to suddenly call myself a lesbian. What was hard was finding a way to connect to the community. I felt very alone as an older, married mother with young children, and as a Japanese-American.

Some of my lesbian friends were older, some were married, some had children. Those who were my age, however, had been out for years. Those who were married to long-time partners had conceived their children by donor insemination. And none of them was Japanese. In fact, as I searched for my place within the community, I found no Japanese-American lesbians anywhere. I was a minority within a minority. I began a quest to find Japanese women with similar experiences because finding these women, I hoped, would validate my experiences, helping me to understand where I had been, and where I now was.

I began by reading. My first lesbian book was a collection of personal accounts of the coming out experience. These were stories full of familiar feelings and fears but for most of these women, coming out came much earlier in their lives and not one of them was Japanese.

I picked up lesbian anthologies and first checked out the lists of contributors. I soon realized I was not likely to find much published by Japanese-American lesbians. Then one day a few years ago, standing sandwiched between shelves of gay and lesbian books, I remembered the Japanese-American Citizens' League, the J.A.C.L. (at the time, I was amused at the thought that J.A.C.L. could also stand for Japanese American Closeted Lesbians).

The J.A.C.L. is a national organization which provided us with the collective confidence to be proud Americans. To the post-war Japanese-Americans, reclaiming honor and pride was important. To be "good citizens" was important. The J.A.C.L. was valuable, especially for the first generation of immigrants and the second generation of American-born citizens. The third generation, my *sansei* generation, has also benefitted from the J.A.C.L. We have been encouraged to celebrate the many aspects of Japan's culture, keeping it alive, and passing it on to our children. But for many sansei that also meant continuing the effort to always be "good citizens," and carrying the guilt if we weren't. The unspoken expectations placed upon the sansei were to assimilate and blend into white society. Be successful, but in a quiet, polite way. We were never to bring disgrace or shame to our families who had suffered so much already. The cultural expectations were hard to ignore, so I tried living the life prescribed for success and happiness. I got married.

When I came out to my family and friends, they were surprised. I must have been convincing in the roles I had tried to play. But then again, perhaps they saw what they wanted to see. I tried my best, which was all my parents ever really asked of me. That I could not fulfill their hopes and dreams brought me a lot of pain and still does.

My family weathered the disappointment and disgrace fairly well simply by getting on with their lives. They busied themselves with ordinary concerns as if trying to appear, once again, just like everyone else. I got on with my own life, no longer ordinary. I entered a whole new world. Finding other Japanese lesbians eventually took on less significance. I came to realize I had some things in common with all kinds of women; that all of us carry our unique stories and few of us ever see the heartbreak that lies beneath ordinary lives.

With the support and reassurance of good friends I ventured out into the lesbian world. In my head the old familiar voices of convention and doubt nagged at me, but when I finally stopped caring what other people thought, I became fearless.

I had always been a shy and private person, but realized that coming out was coming out. So with my newfound courage overriding the fear, I ventured off alone to lesbian softball and basketball games, concerts, tea parties, dinner parties, and campouts. Surrounded by so many lesbians, I studied the social dynamics. I remember simultaneous feelings of exhilaration and terror. I remember feeling invisible, as if I were not even there; or if I was seen at all, perceived as an imposter. At the time I wished for a girlfriend to hold my hand and walk me through this unfamiliar territory. Now, I'm so grateful I was alone. The passage was not always easy, but uncomplicated by another's needs, my transition was truly mine. Close friends, kind words, unexpected smiles, and a steady voice from my heart, kept me clear in my purpose. Yes, I was a stranger to all this, but this was now my place. Occasionally, while waiting at a stoplight on the way to work or cheering from the sidelines at a soccer game or sorting clean laundry into four neat piles, I find myself surprised. Surprised to have come this far, to be where I am, living as I am now.

And just where am I now? I'm still in the same town, in fact, the same neighborhood. I am proud and pleased to be living a very ordinary life, much like everyone else.

My son and daughter, now eleven and nine, have become great supporters and close confidantes. Their compassion, curiosity, eagerness to learn and ability to understand continue to amaze me. We talk through any problems that come along, we ask one another for opinions and advice, we share each other's triumphs. As I watch them grow into caring, capable people, I, too, grow in my own ability to be more honorable, to be a good person and to be a good citizen. My children challenge me now, as my parents did before, to try my best always.

Added to the richness of my family is the friendship and love of an extraordinary woman. Her kindness and generosity of heart won not only my trust and love, but that of my children as well. She came into our lives three years ago. At some undesignated point along the way, hidden between the many ups and downs, we became a family. On Mother's Day, my son made his other mom a bookmark with "Laurie is Cool" in colorful letters. When asked one day by friends why she likes purple popsicles, my daughter answered, "Because that's the first popsicle I had with Laurie." And Laurie is always the first to pull out her wallet to show friends photos of her kids.

Now and then I go out to a nearby beach and stand at the edge of the water line. Eventually the water crosses the line and, without moving a step, I find myself standing in water, feeling the sand shifting beneath. Change. Moment by moment, everything changes.

My own changes occurred the same way. Realizing the need for change took a long time. Deciding to make the change took a long time. But once I was committed, once I'd crossed the line, it was just a matter of taking one day at a time. Day by day I left one life for another.

There are those great moments when, in the middle of whatever I'm doing, my mind freezes an image. It's like God or a higher power putting a picture before me saying "Look at this." These pictures are usually good pictures, ones of blessings for which I'm thankful, ones that bring me joy. A recent one came at my daughter's baseball game: My daughter up at bat with Laurie as assistant coach pitching to her; my son and former husband helping in the dugout; and my former mother-in-law cheering with me from the crowded bleachers. It was simply a picture of kids and families having a good time. But beyond that, it said to me that my life is good, things can work out, and love is the most important thing.

Once we recognize what it is we are feeling, we recognize we can feel deeply, love deeply, can feel joy, then we will demand that all parts of our lives produce that kind of joy.

—Audre Lorde

Sharon Knox-Manley, right.

...third from left, with her children and former husband, 1988.

Large Family Logistics

SHARON KNOX-MANLEY

I'm a 46-year-old woman married for 27 years. I have four grown children, ages 27, 25, 24, and 21, and seven grandchildren.

It all started with a long-time friend, Nancy, returning to her native hometown of Biddeford, Maine with daughter in tow, leaving her husband and re-entering my life with her new lover, Pam—an out lesbian. Although Nancy's new love was not yet relocating, she visited on weekends and holidays. This gave Pam and me time to develop a friendship.

While Nancy seemed to be experimenting with having a real live lesbian wrapped around her finger, the newness soon wore off for her. Months down the line, Nancy and Pam split up, leaving Pam a much crushed and hurt person. Knowing Pam and her sensitivity, I offered her a shoulder to cry on, someone to talk to or write to. My husband, like most men I guess, urged me to get closer to this lady, explaining that he wanted to see the ultimate male fantasy: two women being sexual together. Little did he know I was falling in love with Pam. This was mid-January through February, 1991.

In early April, Pam's firm had relocated to northern Maine, and she was put in charge. With much encouragement from my hubby dear, I offered to spend a week helping her move and settle in. Because I had developed an unbearable attraction to Pam, my emotions were mixed.

The time came—Pam picked me up and off we went with a U-Haul full of furniture. The move was strenuous, as we were two ladies juggling the furniture around. After two days, the house was finally set up. How hard and well we worked together. As we sat back on that Saturday evening, looking over our accomplishment, drinking a few brews and talking away into the night, we felt very close. It was the beginning of what I thought was going to be an affair.

We made love that evening for the first of many times. It lasted all night with the two of us wrapped in each others' arms welcoming the sunrise. I was in awe of the feelings I had for this beautiful, gentle lover. Thinking it was a thank you for my support and help in moving, I was grateful for the experience of lesbian love and knew it probably would come to an end when my husband came to pick me up the following weekend. How I dreaded going home. I wanted this new love to stay with me. Our loving was wonderful that entire week. I cried when she was away at work knowing my days with her were coming to an end.

Before my husband was to arrive, Pam and I slept together for what I thought would be the last time. Not so, since with our consent, my husband finally got to witness "two women making love." Now that I look back, I know I believed that if we let him watch, he would allow our get-togethers to continue.

Which they did for a few months. Pam travelled three hours every Friday to spend weekends at our house and three hours every Sunday to return home. By this time, I had to admit to myself that we were both in love. By mid-July my husband and I decided to move in with Pam, to enlarge her home to accommodate all three of us. Sound strange? Believe me, it was. It worked for a very short time. Trying to maintain my life with Pam and knowing I was fast pulling apart from my husband was so stressful, we all agreed something had to give. It was around this time I realized I was becoming a totally different person, a lesbian. After attending "Women's Week" in Provincetown, Massachusetts, there was no longer any doubt in my mind.

November came. Before the holidays, I decided to start a coming out process. Pam and I had moved into a room in the house together. My husband was no longer witnessing our lovemaking and was preparing for his exit. He was angry but he also understood. There were fights but also apologies—he kept asking me to stay with him once I got over this phase. I don't think he realized I was serious until I signed the divorce papers.

As for me, there were letters to write. First, my sister and brother. With a flood of relief, I read a letter from my sister in the return mail. Yes, she said, she had figured as much by the visit the summer before—Pam and I were that obvious. Yes, she thought the world of Pam, and yes indeed, she wanted my happiness above all in life. Somewhat slower to respond, my brother eventually became Pam's best friend. Then, a letter to my parents—and the dreaded return mail. But a phone call came first to confirm my letter. After a long swallow and what seemed an eternity of holding my breath, my mother told me how very much she and Dad loved me, loved Pam; how they'd never, in 27 years, seen me as happy as I'd been in the last few months. A few days later, a letter from my mother came for me to read whenever I have any doubts. I told her thank you—fighting back my tears of joy. This is the closest I've been to my family in years.

My marriage had been difficult, but I'd always told myself to keep it together for the kids. They thought we had the ideal marriage, and I knew they would be surprised to hear of anything changing. I wrote four letters to my children, and after much soul-searching, decided to mail them. In between mailing and their delivery, I felt I had done a terrible wrong, that I needed to tell them face-to-face. So Pam and I dropped everything to drive to my children's homes to intercept those four letters.

One daughter, a couple of hours away, I had told by accident over the phone. So she was stop number one. I tried to explain how finding out this way wasn't planned, how much I loved her, her husband, and especially my grand-babies. How I was indeed still her mom and a grammy and how nothing would change that. With a lot of crying, we realized there would be difficult times, but as long as we could talk, there was a chance.

My oldest daughter lived four and a half hours away. By the time we arrived, she was in bed. After getting her up, I proceeded to explain my love for Pam, but was quickly hushed up by her screaming and bodily threatening of Pam. Before leaving, I told her she had a letter in the mail, to please take the time to read it, and that I'd be in touch. By this time, after speaking with two of my four children, I was totally drained. We decided to stop at a motel, try and get some rest, and rebuild my strength.

Morning came. I intercepted my son's letter, held onto it, and decided to return when he was home from work. In the meantime, I went to visit my youngest daughter. I'll never forget the look on her face as I walked into her apartment. She was holding onto her newborn son with my letter clenched in her hand. Her sobbing came straight from her soul. As I reached to take hold of my grandson, she pulled away. I talked long, hard and fast. As she started to calm down, she gave me my grandson to hold. We sat and talked some more. We left with good feelings, and she seemed reassured that her dad and mom were both still her parents, living in separate places, but there for her always. On July 18, 1992, she was married at our house with Pam as her maid of honor. This was a highlight in our lives.

Now, to return to my son. Since he was still living with us when my hus-band and I moved to join Pam, and overheard some of our arguments and con-versations, I'm sure he knew something was up. I talked to him quietly. He took the news and told me that it wasn't something you wanted to hear from your parents but that he did understand. I left the letter with him to read in case he needed more answers. He was married June 28, 1992. His father was his best man; Pam and I sat proudly smiling on his wedding day.

In late July, 1992, I filed for a divorce, ending all ties of marriage. Pam and I needed to go on in our commitment to one another. So we exchanged rings and began contemplating a baby of our own. We both knew rough times would be ahead but that as long as we continued to talk and be open with each other and our families, life would continue to be good for us. Pam's family accepted me completely. They visit often and include me in all family functions. It's a nice feeling.

I have days when I still cry for all those I've hurt or confused—my husband, my children, my grandchildren, and especially my mother and father-in-law. We saw each other at my son's wedding and although my father-in-law was somewhat cool, my mother-in-law, teary-eyed, gave me a sincere hug. That was also a beginning.

Time has gone on, very gracefully. All my children have fully embraced Pam; she is a much respected part of the family. Pam and I were happily married at "The Wedding" during the March on Washington, April 25, 1993. We share a log cabin overlooking nine acres in the woods. We are very active in various projects in our small town and, as its "token" lesbians, we are doing our part to make our neighborhood our home. I order lesbian books from our little local bookstore, and they place my orders without a blink—they've even agreed to stock Maine's *Community Pride Reporter* alongside the other small monthly newsletters for all to peruse. A baby of our own did not happen so we're content being grandparents to "our" children. I'm Grammy and Pam is Gammy Woo-Woo. Our life is full of love and happiness—and a deep feeling of family, friends, and community.

M en have always been afraid that women could get along without them.

—Margaret Mead

Margaret Randall, 1986.

...with her son and former husband, 1962.

Theories of Relativity

Margaret Randall

When I came out to myself and those I love, I was 49 years old. Still legally married to my third husband. Mother of a son and three daughters who had by then given me four grandchildren (now I have six). I had also recently returned to the United States after 23 years in Latin America—Mexico, Cuba, Nicaragua—and I was fighting the U.S. government that had ordered me deported due to the critical nature of my writing. I was in the middle of menopause and also in the midst of a process of retrieval of incest memories. A complicated time.

Recognizing the lesbian in me was and wasn't complicated. Finding my place in a community of women had provided my greatest comfort: joyful, like breathing effortlessly after a wracking cough or gasp for air. From there to the understanding that I loved women—in that deeper more erotic sense—seemed a natural progression.

I remember around that time driving with an old friend; we were returning from dinner in a nearby city. Somewhere in the middle of an offhand phrase, she said: "Well, when you come out as a lesbian..." To my circle of women friends, it must have seemed a given. A week or two after that remark, I had a female lover.

This was how it felt inside: easy, right. On the outside there *was* complexity. My immigration case required, at all costs, my avoiding publicly coming out. The McCarran-Walter Immigration and Nationality Act under which I was being charged listed "sexual deviancy" as one of its exclusionary clauses. Having committed myself to the freedom of dissent battle, I knew I needed to keep public attention centered there. For three years the lesbian community nationwide did an amazing job of keeping a secret almost everybody knew!

The need for secrecy wasn't so easy for my partner and me. When the pressures threatened to make us crazy, we'd meet with one of my immigration lawyers for comforting advice. A sunny breakfast at Washington's old Taberna Cafe: over hash browns and black coffee Michael would reach across the patio table and grasp our hands: "Take it to the edge," he was fond of telling us, "be who you are. Just try not to walk into an INS office with your arms around one another..."

My husband, from whom I was already estranged, had been a friend for years before we became intimate. The political consideration that kept me from being completely honest with him, as well as with a few other good friends, held me in its own painful web. It would take years to come to terms with each of these lies by omission.

My son and his family were living in Paris at the time. Much later he confessed that the more sophisticated milieu made my revelation easier than it might have been had they remained in Cuba. At the time he simply held me close—in the Albuquerque airport as we took leave of one another—and said: "You've always been so out there about who you are and what you believe; I know how difficult it must be for you to keep silent about such an important part of yourself; and I just want you to know that when the time comes that you can go public, your kids will be right there with you." Dear, dear Gregory, rushing, as had long been his custom, to speak for everyone.

Ana, my youngest, was 14 at the time. She traveled to the U.S. when I returned, settling for a while with her father in New York. She was probably the most culturally familiar with my new "lifestyle." She was also jealous, as in: any partner my mother has is going to take her attention away from me. We all struggled through a few years of adjustment, having less to do with my lesbianism than with Ana's own complex change of place and my propensity for serial monogamy.

Sarah, then in her early twenties and still living in Cuba, took my lesbianism on as she does everything that comes her way. If this was important to her mother, by god she would educate herself about the culture. On a visit to Albuquerque just after I'd begun living with my first woman lover, she checked out the bars, the softball games, even a woman's dance. It was love, support, embarrassment, bravado, and anguish tossed into a single pot.

And then there was Ximena. My middle daughter has always been the odd one out: somehow different, less easy in her skin, more tentative, her considerable talents diluted by bouts of dependency upon others. She was already living in Mexico City and struggling with important changes of her own. When I told Ximena I'm a lesbian, her immediate response was to tell me she was uncomfortable. "Can we see a therapist together?" she wanted to know; stipulating he be straight, male, and Spanish-speaking.

It was during that hour session with a terrific Chicano psychotherapist that I was confronted with the questions I believe may be at the core of many young people's confusion around the issue. What does it mean when women who have thought themselves heterosexual come out as lesbians? Is homosexuality biologically or socially determined? Do we exist on a continuum rather arbitrarily divided into separate sexual categories? If homosexuality were an acceptable social option, wouldn't many more women gravitate towards one another?

My daughter's version of these questions was defined by her own distraught feelings: Does this mean you never loved my daddy? How does this affect my own sexuality? Will I become a lesbian too? What will people say? I knew it was her fearless honesty as well as our love that enabled Ximena to be so candid during that hour with me and a stranger. Questions and answers were clear. I don't believe much remained hidden. And of course it still took us years to work through so profound a shift.

I'm not a lesbian who remembers being excited by girls as a child, or falling for my high school gym teacher. Oh, I can bring up a few female-to-female erotic moments if I search the years. But I grew up pretty well socialized into white, middle-class, and fully-gendered expectations: a longing to be cheerleader and homecoming queen (neither of which proved within my reach), crushes on the captain of the football team and later the "egghead" who wanted to be a writer just like me; and finally the very heterosexual camp-follower woman's role in the New York Beat scene of the late 1950's.

I married the first time when I was barely eighteen: a spoiled and troubled rich boy with whom I lived for almost four years. After our divorce, I went to New York where I began to take myself seriously as a writer. But not as a woman. There, as a single mother, I gave birth to my son. Change, in the body and the heart. But for whatever combination of complex cultural reasons, it was easier for me to learn to respect my incipient craft than my achingly misused body.

Then there was Latin America, and with it my involvement in a succession of revolutionary movements for social change. I married again, lived with several men without benefit of legalization, had three daughters. I began to have lesbian friends, particularly among some of the women from the United States who came to visit us in Cuba or Nicaragua. At first we didn't talk about our sexuality. Wrong. We talked about the smallest incidents in my heterosexual liaisons and not at all about their lesbian lovers.

I remember one dear friend in particular with whom I shared a hotel room at a Cuban conference in 1968. We had known one another for years. I must have understood, or at least suspected that she was gay. Yet the topic never surfaced. She was undoubtedly careful not to broach it; I wasn't sensitive enough to do so. We have talked about this since, of course, laughing and sometimes crying about the missed cues, the silences.

But back home, in the early 1970's, waves of politically active women were beginning to choose other women as their sexual partners. Sexism, inside as well as outside the movement, pushed women to options other than heterosexual marriage. Out lesbianism was suddenly a part of our public reality. Lesbians had been lesbians all along, of course, silently or not so silently living their lives. We now know what a rich and varied language they developed in which to communicate with one another—thank you, Joan Nestle; thank you, Lillian Faderman; thank you, Elizabeth Kennedy and Madeline Davis, for preserving the stories. At the time, however, lesbians remained largely hidden from the mainstream community.

But these women of the '70s, these feminists as they engaged with their new sexual selves, provided the language we (who did not yet know we were lesbians) needed; and a community that made alternatives possible. Now we could speak about identity, choice, a continuum. The new writings were filled with words and concepts like heterosexism, compulsory heterosexuality, homophobia, the fact that "choice" itself is often not a choice. Thank you, Adrienne Rich. Thank you, Audre Lorde,

I remember occasionally wondering why I wasn't a lesbian, and sometimes wishing I was. Feeling a certain envy. Certain that my identity was set—in a mold I had never before questioned. Looking back, I link much of that failure to question to the fact that I was so deeply involved with political movements in which individual questioning of any kind was considered bourgeois, self-indulgent, unacceptable. We were, after all, trying to change society. Nothing less. And from a position of overwhelming weakness when compared with our enemy. Every bit of personal energy was needed in the struggle: collective in nature... and thoroughly controlled by men.

Little did we know that we would never change society until we understood who we were inside—and made room within our political causes for all our human needs.

When I began to crumble beneath the weight of so many years of broken energy—personal as well as political—I was living in Nicaragua. It was 1983. I had moved to that country three years earlier with Ana, who was then ten. Later we were joined by Ximena when she graduated from her Cuban high school. I had left my last male partner behind in Cuba, a dear poet and musician who remains a good friend. And for the past few years I had lived with my youngest daughters, indulged in the occasional short-term affair with a male comrade, but mostly immersed myself in a struggle in which coupling was the least of anyone's concerns.

The U.S.-sponsored Contra war was heating up. I and everyone I knew worked eighteen-hour days. The political situation was becoming more and more difficult. As had been true during my Beat period in New York City—though for very different reasons—one-night stands became the norm; it was easier to cede to the compulsion of the moment when you didn't know how long you or anyone else might be alive. I began to understand that I was very very tired.

Several moments stand out as beacons or signposts along my rapid downward spiral towards full-fledged emotional exhaustion. A Salvadoran woman *comandante*, the second in command of that country's Farabundo Martí National Liberation Movement (FMLN), was murdered in Managua. She was stabbed more than eighty times while she slept in what she had supposed was a safe house. I never knew Comandante Ana María, or Nélida de Montes (her real name). But the savage image of her death affected me profoundly.

Then there was my suddenly revived ability to cry. A volatile weeper, I had been unable to shed tears since more than eight years earlier when I'd received the news of a close friend's death. Also a Salvadoran, Roque Dalton was a great poet. His children and mine had grown up together in Cuba. Roque and I had joined forces on all sorts of meaningful projects. When in May of 1975 he was murdered by a fanatical member of his own revolutionary organization, I cried for days—then felt myself run dry.

In May of 1983, I suddenly cried again.

These were the initial outer symptoms of an inner shift. I needed to come home, to my body as well as to my place, my roots, my need to write.

Leaving can be problematic when you're in the midst of a war and must abandon your comrades. My continued presence in Managua, however, was clearly of little use to anyone—least of all myself. I was scared all the time. I rarely slept, lying awake at night with one hand on the old wooden stock of my .38 caliber Colt and Wesson. The more than forty books I'd produced to that point—most of them written between eleven p.m. and three in the morning— were superficial, I thought, in direct relation to the ways in which I had had to fit them around "more pressing" work.

What *was* the pressing work of my life? At 47, I needed to find out. What was my evolving identity? I needed to know the answers to these questions, although it would be a while before I understood I was on a larger quest. My Nicaraguan comrades were, to a person, supportive of my journey. They urged me to go home. And I did.

Even now, a decade later and in the more settled philosophical practice of questioning one's lifetime choices, I sometimes find myself in conversation about lesbian identity. Is it choice? No, of course not. Given an equality of social options (which we all know do not yet exist), it is logical to assume that as many women would relate primarily to other women as engage primarily with men.

I know butch lesbians, and some who are not so butch, who maintain they have always been gay. Socialization may have sidetracked them for more or less of their lives, but they have always loved women—and known that. I believe them. I also have friends who say they have moved along the continuum, in one direction or the other, through several more or less clearly defined identities. I believe them too. I think about my own life and have a harder time coming up with answers.

When attempting to draw lines, the categories homosexual, bisexual, and heterosexual are a pretty impoverished lot. We must acknowledge the androgynous, transsexual, transgendered, asexual, celibate by choice, and those who leap to the successive—or simultaneous—calls of more than a single sexual identity.

And what do we really answer if we delineate six rather than three such categories? It's imperative, I believe, to understand as well that these identities are not *only* sexual, in most cases not even primarily so. They are about freedom from patriarchal structures and attitudes. They are about companionship, commitment, family values, creativity, passionate living and personal fulfillment.

For myself, for whatever reasons, I lived as a heterosexual woman for 48 years. Older and wiser, I have been a lesbian for the past ten.

Until such time as I more fully understand where the lines of heterosexual orientation, ability to know myself, social expectations, courage, and choice converge in my single experience, I will say: for many years I considered myself a heterosexual woman. I married and lived unmarried but coupled with men. I had children, in and out of marriage. A few of the men with whom I lived remain friends. This has everything to do with how we see the world, ourselves and one another; nothing to do with my sexual identity. The father of one of my daughters once said he didn't want her to spend too much time with me; she might be influenced by my lesbianism. I understood that then, as I do now, as having everything to do with his world vision, nothing to do with mine.

Now I am a lesbian, close to 60, happier and more fulfilled with every passing year. I love and am loved in ways I never dreamed possible. How much of this has to do with Barbara and I being women and how much with the maturity that comes with living, I cannot say. It doesn't seem important to me. Except when I'm fighting—as I often am—for gay rights.

All that is good and commendable now existing would continue to exist if all marriage laws were repealed tomorrow...I have an inalienable constitutional and natural right to love whom I may, to love for as long or as short a period as I can, and to change that love every day if I please!

—Victoria Woodhull, 1871

Joanne Warobick, 1982 and present.

Not in My Wildest Dreams

JOANNE WAROBICK

Our wedding was formal, in the tradition of the groom's Greek Orthodox family. As a non-Greek, I was accused of every scandal from "women's lib," to "giving the Evil Eye" at large family gatherings. And as things turned out, these would probably be remembered as the least of my "sins." As unconventional as it was for us to attempt our mixed-heritage marriage, and as often as Steve assured me that the wedding was up to us, once we agreed to a church ceremony, the plans were out of our hands.

I guess I first realized something wasn't right the day my mother accompanied me to buy my wedding dress. It was winter, 1982. We were on the bus headed for the bargain basement of Dey's Department Store in downtown Syracuse. I made my mother decide on the gown. Then, going home, I began sobbing uncontrollably. My mother sat next to me shaking her head and muttering "This is not good. This is not good."

When the big day came, I did as much as I could to make it my own. This included hosting a women-only champagne brunch from noon until three. In the pictures my friends had the biggest smiles and held on to each other much of the time. Unfortunately, the champagne couldn't touch my own anxiety.

The wedding ceremony was at five. I went home in time to take a shower and put on the white gown. I was still at home when the formal bouquets arrived. This had been the ultimate compromise, in my estimation. I had a very large flower garden and had suggested we make bouquets from flowers I had grown. My future mother-in-law was appalled at the idea. At the last minute, while everyone else was busy worrying about their make-up and hair, I was inspired to run out into my garden. There was a torrential downpour. I pulled up clumps and clumps of forget-me-nots and tried to push them in on top of the florist's bouquet. The result was wild. I had clumps of mud and weeds down the front of my dress by the time I marched down the aisle.

All day long I had been coaching myself to find some way to feel real, to feel passion about what I was doing. The entire event was entrenched in tradition. As often as I told myself, "This is how every bride feels," I also heard my wild self answer, "You are not meant for this, and you know it." It was a conflict that I was to become very familiar with over the course of my married life. It was a conflict that would eventually consume all of my time and energy as I involved Steve in long drawn out discussions about how I felt "different." And as much as his artistic and unconventional side longed to understand this, he had made an implicit and unalterable allegiance to go along with what was expected. At all costs, there were appearances to be kept up, and that was the true nature of his commitment to me.

Possibly the height of unreality for me on that wedding day was the moment when the entire congregation turned to wait for the bride. That was me, standing next to my father. He had been extremely uninvolved up until that point. When I whispered to him that I was not going to wear my veil, he did not ask why. He just helped me push it back off of my face. With my earthy bouquet in one arm, and the other on the arm of patriarchy, I set off. Before us spread a sea of shocked and disapproving faces. Unknowingly, I had spit in the old "Evil Eye" of tradition one more time. By neglecting to keep the veil over my face, I was proclaiming my indecency. In other words, my virginity was as muddied as the bouquet I'd thrown together from my garden.

Over the next two years, I spent much of my time feeling unsettled and lonely. No matter how angry and dissatisfied I knew I was, I told myself the problem was with my attitude. I tried to believe that in time I would grow to understand my role as a married woman. However, it seemed that I was missing something that had not yet been invented. I was involved with my own travels, dreams, friendships, while Steve occupied his time with work and plans for remodeling the house. I knew other couples were planning for their futures and starting their families. The freedom I bragged about in our relationship was much more truthfully a lack of intimacy.

One Friday night, after we'd been married two and a half years, we met with Steve's parents at a quiet restaurant for dinner. The conversation turned to our vacation plans and I excitedly told them about my intentions of spending an entire month in Santa Cruz, California, with a friend who lived there now. My father-in-law proposed a toast, "To the kids. And may this be the last of the separate vacations. And may my son put his bowling ball to good use and tie his wife down with it."

I felt sick to my stomach and horrified. I flashed on a childhood memory of the day my mother spent disposing of my father's bowling ball collection. He insisted on saving old bowling balls, and lined them up to border her flower beds. On this day, I followed her, amazed, as she carried them down to the swamp and rolled them under, one by one. It was not until this moment in the restaurant that I understood the depth of my mother's silence and anger. Fortunately, the silence afterwards was broken as Steve spoke. "Dad," he said very slowly, "I wouldn't want a wife that I had to tie down."

I woke the next morning from bad dreams and began writing to myself in my journal: "Okay. Here goes. After two years of biding my time, I am ready to leave." By noon, I had my husband's attention. He understood that I had to go away, even if it was for a trial separation. However, he was, as usual, concerned that I carry through with the plans we had that night. I thought about it and felt so energized by my decision, I agreed to play wife "one more night."

That evening, we had a surprise party planned for Steve's best friend's wife, Melanie. The plan was to meet at their house before she got home from work. Everyone arrived on time, crowding into the kitchen towards the back of the house. We had either underestimated attendance or overestimated the size of their kitchen, because there was barely room to breathe. Or maybe I was holding my breath because I found myself standing in the dark next to Melanie's sister, Erin. We waited and waited for Melanie's arrival. She was over an hour late in coming home. In the meantime, I had a chance to get to know her notorious lesbian sister, and I must say, I didn't mind the wait one bit.

I had listened to Melanie's side of things for so long that frankly, I had grown tired of imagining how Erin's choice to love women, and to fly a purple flag from her attic apartment when she was sixteen, could have been the downfall of the entire family. Erin and I had met one other time just weeks before my wedding. I liked her immediately and felt sad when it was time to leave that day. I had the strongest feeling that in leaving I had missed out on something. Every Saturday that first summer I was married I had driven by her house hoping to get a glimpse of her washing and waxing her infamous foreign black sportscar. When I did see her, I never had the courage to stop. Instead, I would drive faster and feel confused about my sudden shyness. I was reminding myself of this, as I admired her in a gray silk shirt and thin red leather tie. I made a silent vow of fearlessness. Then I began to enjoy the chance to stand too close, talking and laughing in the dark, crowded kitchen. By the time the lights went on and everyone yelled "SURPRISE!" I knew that Melanie's birthday was the least of that night's surprises.

I was suddenly determined not to let Erin get away again without making some plan to see her. When she asked if I wanted to sit down, we found a quiet place on the stairs in the hallway. We were sitting so close our thighs were touching. I didn't move away. Her mother suddenly appeared to be very interested in seeking me out to talk about Steve. She'd had her eye on us all night. I kept pretending I couldn't hear a word she was saying over the music. And then Steve showed up to see where I'd gone. Erin whispered in my ear, "Sometime I think you'd enjoy meeting some of my friends. We could go dancing."

And I answered, "Let's go."

"Right now? Tonight?!"

"Yes," I whispered back, then out loud I told Steve we were leaving. He said he thought he'd leave with us. I looked him in the eye and said, "You can't come. It's women only."

I had lived in Syracuse my entire life, but after I left the party that night with Erin, it never looked the same again. There were bars in places on the north-side I had assumed were empty warehouses; doorways appeared and doors opened because Erin knew where to knock. It was as if there was an invisible world within the old one.

That night we went directly to The Laurel Tree, an industrial northeast inner-city women's bar. Once we were inside, and I saw women dancing and talking and drinking together, I began to feel extremely powerful. Suddenly, it no longer mattered if I figured everything out in my mind. I was fully happy to be right where I was. Erin and I sat together, very close, and talked for a long, long time. She straddled the bench we sat on and faced me. I thought I felt her arms around me, or was I wishing it? I looked discreetly around the bar to see what other women were doing. I fully believed I was about to invent something new. I grew silent, and Erin reached to pull me closer. Then I turned my face to hers, and thought to myself: *if you kiss her, everything will change.*

I felt lost in time, and acutely aware of my heart racing. I knew in that split second I would dare to take that risk. I also had the strangest thought that over half of the world's population was female, and I had already spent twenty-seven years missing out on loving women. My mouth found hers, soft and sure. I was aching with hunger for her softness. In that moment, the rest of the world fell away. There was no longer any right or wrong, just my head resting against her chest. Later, we slow-danced, and I felt like I was floating. As the lights came on in the bar, I suddenly remembered we had forgotten to return to the party. We left the bar and rushed back.

It was nearly three a.m. when I walked into the house. The party was still going strong. Erin's sister, my old "friend," flew across the room and screeched, "Did she take you to that GAY bar??" The whole place was silent. I heard the porch door slam behind me as Erin left. It was all up to me now, I thought. I looked out at every person there and said, "Yes."

Considering how much I felt that first night we were together, it all seemed like a dream in the context of the life I had known. The next day was agoniz-ing, as I tried to act like nothing had changed. I phoned Erin's house and her mother told me she had "gone out with Chris." I felt such hopelessness, and believed the night before had probably meant nothing to her. Erin was proba-bly the type that spent every Saturday with some new sweetheart. I realized I knew very little about her.

By the time I got off work the next day, I had convinced myself that Erin was going to be a new friend and nothing more. I decided I would invite her over as I would any friend. And I made sure Steve was going to be out.

Erin's mother answered the phone again. This time she asked who was call-ing. When I told her, "Joanne," her voice took on the same incriminating tone that I'd heard in Melanie's voice the other night. There was also disbelief in the way she asked, *"Steve's Joanne?"*

I swallowed hard and asked again for Erin. This time she let Erin know she had a phone call. We made plans to see each other the next evening after work.

I answered the door with a dishtowel in my hand. I started shaking all over when I saw her. She was carrying a beautiful bouquet of flowers which she handed to me. The scent of freesia was heady in mid-winter, their colors exotic. As I wondered if it was appropriate for me to be accepting them, I saw the inviting smile of the woman who was offering them to me. I responded by walking quickly into the kitchen, pulling a big rocking chair into the doorway, and telling her, "You can watch me. I have to do the dishes."

I thought I was being casual and doing a good job of hiding my real feelings. Then I started breaking glasses. For some reason, I couldn't hold on to them. I started to laugh nervously and turned to grin at her. She was already halfway across the kitchen, moving towards me. She smiled and wrapped her ams around me, whispering, "You didn't really invite me over here to watch you break glasses, did you?"

My hands were still in the soapy warm water when she started kissing me. That was the end of the dishwashing that night. I looked up and out the window to see my ninety-year-old neighbor, Maude, doing her dishes and staring at us. We left the house to find some privacy and ended up at another bar. We spent the next few hours making out in a dark corner.

When Steve saw the flowers the next day, he asked me where they had come from. I told him Erin had brought them, and I felt my heart pounding. He laughed and said jokingly, "I better watch out. I may have some competition."

I hated the self-assurance in his laugh. I boldly told him that I didn't think it was funny. He stormed out of the room.

That was only the first confrontation in the months of confrontations to follow. These times were the happiest, the most difficult, and most sexual of my life. It took just three weeks after meeting Erin for me to find a place of my own. As luck would have it, the only place I could afford was a tiny studio over a Greek deli.

Never before had I been so alone going through such changes. Several months later I found a copy of Del Martin and Phyllis Lyon's classic *Lesbian/Woman* in a used bookstore. I was in the vulnerable place of not wanting Erin to know how lost I felt, yet I was also trying to understand the new life that had chosen me. So I carried the book in a paper bag to the park near the deli, and I read it in one afternoon. Then, on my way home, I threw it in a dumpster.

Erin and I moved to the West Coast after that first summer. Being a storyteller at heart, I'm tempted to stop here where I'm emphasizing the joy and romance. However, as with any truth-telling, there are many subplots woven into my coming out. These others reveal a darker picture of that time. They reveal the complexities of ending one relationship in betrayal and beginning another one with my loss unexamined. I suddenly found myself torn between preserving a way of life that was comfortable and supportive of everything I had ever known about myself, and having to leave it all behind to find out who I might become.

In spite of the emptiness I felt being married, Steve and I had also shared much tenderness and all the responsibilities of having a home. We had a large extended family and support in our community of friends, neighbors, and co-workers. It took a tremendous amount of courage for me to risk the loss of all of that on the unknown. After sorting through this for years now, I am able to acknowledge my sadness at leaving, and my sorrow for having to break the commitment I had with Steve.

Carrying these burdens into my new life with Erin, I was shocked and disappointed to find the sexist underbelly of our passion for each other. I joked about this ironic twist of fate at the time, even calling her a "male-chauvinist dyke," for with Erin, in some respects, I assumed even more of the roles of a traditional wife. Steve and I had shared all of the cooking, cleaning, and laundry. I found myself doing all of these chores for Erin! We rationalized that she couldn't do them well, and I guess I went along with it assuming there had to be some radical element in this, just by virtue of my lesbianism.

Where Steve and I had never raised our voices once in our years together, Erin and I fought often, with yelling, door-slamming, and brooding silence afterwards. Nothing was simple. It has taken me many years to realize how deeply my relationship with Erin was affected by isolation and lack of support from others. My wildest dreams ended up including much more than just passion for my new lover. I had to learn, often the hard way, that I was at the beginning of a deeper discovery: a passion for being fully myself.

Letter to My First Lover

MORGAN GRAYCE WILLOW

You are not my first
lover, though I have called
you that, since the men
don't count. And Pat?
Well, she and I were friends
who happened
to sleep together.
Besides, I only made love
to her, never
the other way
around. So, I count
from you, Jeffie,
the first woman
I wanted to turn
myself over to.

If I'd made a better co-
dependent, it might
have worked. But I felt so
inadequate those nights
you leaned over
the toilet, puking up
vodka. I hadn't enough
training in taking care of
drunks. Plus,
I was a lot smaller
than you. All I could do
was help you to bed.
If you were out
cold, I couldn't move
you at all.

Now I know
this is a good
thing, failing
as an alcoholic's co.
But then, I thought
I'd failed
as a lesbian.
                Such an
attractive bar dyke
you were, in your black
leather jacket, your
bleached-blond-James-
Dean hair, the rim of gold
around that one tooth. I'd
make you smile just
to see it.

But you were afraid
of my body. Pat and I,
a couple of heterosexual
girls, were just playing
around. She never stopped
me from exploring all
her skin, from the line
of hair to her pink
toenails on deep-chocolate
feet. Never stopped me
from going down
on her.
                Never stopped
the kind of touch
I wanted from you
those nights you cradled
me in one arm, reached
with your other, bypassing
the whole hungry
rest of me.
                I was not allowed
to touch you
at all.

I was confused.
Those were the early
seventies. All the dykes
we knew talked about nothing
but who was the butch,
who the femme, how many orgasms
they had, how many nights
a week.
          Meanwhile, I counted
all the sex of our entire
relationship on
one hand.

          So, Jeffie,
I left you. Concluded
sex wasn't
what it was cracked up
to be and entered
a long underworld
as a married woman.
He was a guy-next-door
type. A pal. No stairway
to sexual heaven,
but I needed
a friend.

Every now and then—when
there weren't other women
in my life—I sent
clouds of apology out
to you, Jeffie, my first
dyke, for going straight
after being your lover.

I hadn't meant for that
to happen. I was excited
to come out. But
I just didn't
get the rules.
          Besides, the world
held out prizes

for going straight, like
medical insurance, joint tax
returns, and a place
at the family table.

        I have a vision
of you now, Jeffie,
after treatment. You are
stradling a chair
in a smoke-filled room,
both in and out
of the circle. Your hair
is still short, no
bleach. The grey makes
you look more like who you
really are. You smell
of English leather, as always,
when I walk up to you
after the meeting. I say:
Look. It wasn't all a waste.
I'm a dyke after all. I know
my way around my body,
and my lover's too.
        I just wanted
to let you know that
my heart, old worn
jacket that she is, still
has this one sleeve
where only your arm
fits through.

When Colleen first came to live with me, my son drew a picture of her with a beard. Even though we were securely closeted, he knew. When he graduated from high school, he invited Colleen. He said that our being lesbians had opened doors for him, that he was able to have a more expanded view of life possibilities.

—Marica Schwemer

Zandra Johnson-Rolón, right with her partner.

From Straight Marriage
to Lesbian Marriage

Dr. Zandra Johnson-Rolón

I was born Zandra Zoila Rolón on June 2, 1956 in a small city called Brownsville in the southernmost tip of Texas. I was the firstborn in a line of firstborns on both my mother's and father's sides, and I inherited many people's expectations.

My mother and father were very attractive and somewhat middle-class within their Latino community. They were fairly restricted by their culture in what they could do or be. In most Latino families, there was an order to things that one was expected to follow, simply because everyone else had done it in that certain way. This mostly had to do with race and culture. My grandparents had experienced discrimination and exclusion due to their race, so the more we "blended in" and did not "make trouble" the better for all of us. This is what my mother was taught and tried to teach me.

The indoctrination started early. Both of my parents were photographers, so *looks* were very important. From a young age I was groomed to be attractive to the opposite sex and learned well the art of being a nice southern girl. I was given every indication that my future depended on my poise and beauty. It seemed that not being attractive would somehow doom me. I was involved in many beauty contests. Many!!! And though I've become a doctor, I'm convinced that my mother is still somewhat disappointed that I didn't become an actress or a model.

Being Latina in a family rich in matriarchal leadership, I saw the women surrounding me doing everything from raising families to running businesses to fixing anything that was broken. This provided a great opportunity for me to be a tomboy. I had permission to learn how to build things as well as run a household. Education after high school was not discouraged but neither was it pushed. I was told I had to do the best with what God had given me—meaning my looks and my personality. It was a rude awakening when I discovered that looks could only get you so far.

I got married at age 21 to a very strong and dashing man from Wilmington, Delaware who came from a family with their own expectations for their son and his new wife. This was an interracial and interfaith marriage. Larry was white and Jewish. He also insisted that "things look right." We had to have the right clothes, the newest cars, and impressive jobs. We had to be seen in the right places with the right people. I now look back and realize that our entire relationship was based on how we were perceived by our friends and families.

As destructive as this relationship came to be for me, it also allowed me the room for self-discovery. It was during my marriage to Larry that I began to pay attention to my own needs and develop my strengths as a woman. The world was going through important social changes, learning new terms such as Women's Lib, ERA, and Civil Rights. I was going through my own "social changes." I began my college education, and had my childhood "tapes" challenged in the classroom. Over time I became brave enough to contemplate alternative lifestyles and the politics surrounding such lifestyles. My new values and political perspectives became a great threat to Larry, to my marriage, and soon to the rest of my family. However, as these relationships grew shaky, I was being nurtured by women, finding solace in their friendships and later in their love.

Women were teaching me the importance of having a mind and taking a stand in life and the importance of strength in numbers. I was discovering my inner beauty through their eyes and not through the eyes of the world I once called home. Suddenly, I began to discover that neither men nor society found women with opinions attractive. I was labeled "angry and aggressive" and a threat to the structure of the family. All of a sudden, I was told I wanted too much out of life, that I was too demanding, too inquisitive, and too challenging.

Divorce was traumatic and painful and at the same time very liberating. I was made to feel that the demise of the marriage was my fault. This came more from Larry's family, but there was disappointment mixed with an implied "I told you so" from my family as well. I truly grieved over the loss of this relationship, which I had tried hard to make work. Now I think I was more in love with the concept of marriage than with the man I married. My concept of marriage was of a harmonious union where two people respected, supported and loved each other. I was often told that my image was a fairytale picture and not reality, that my expectations were too high and that I needed to be thankful that I had a "good man" at all. Yet I had come to learn that *being* the right person was more important than *having* the right person.

After several relationships—a few with men but mostly with women—I met Deborah and I came out. I really came out with a vengeance! I was out, loud, and proud! I think of Deborah as my wife, a woman to whom I've been married for almost thirteen years. It has been through my relationship with Deborah that I have grown to appreciate and understand what marriage is supposed to be about. I never could have imagined the level of intimacy and security I would feel when I met my true mate. I remember my mother once asking me if I had met my twin in Deborah. At the time I believed I had. But after years passed, I became aware that what I'd found in Deborah was my match—the one who can match me in my intensity and my passion for life. This match, I realize, is the secret to a successful relationship.

There are many things about a straight marriage that I miss, things that straight couples take for granted, such as showing affection in public. I don't like that I have to be aware of my surroundings before I reach over to kiss my partner. It doesn't often stop me from kissing her, but there is a moment of hesitation that was never there before. I often do show affection in front of people. I think this has to do with my family being a very "touchy-feely" Latin bunch; hiding my feelings has never been part of my experience.

I also miss the acceptance I had from my family when I was with a member of the opposite sex whether the relationship was a good one or not. My mother encouraged me to do all I could to save my marriage with Larry even though she knew that the relationship was abusive. Problems in my relationships with women were treated as positive signs—my mother hoped that maybe, just maybe, if I broke up with one of the women I was dating, I would "come to my senses." Since coming out as a lesbian I have found no support in my family in my times of great need.

Another aspect of being with women that is difficult is that Deborah and I have celebrated thirteen anniversaries since the beginning of our relationship and it's only been in the past two years that we have received acknowledgment in any form from our families. We have had two formal commitment ceremonies; Deborah's father and my gay uncle came to the first, and my brother and sister, with their families, came to the second. Mind you, both Deborah and I come from *very large* families and invited everyone. We received anniversary cards from my sister and niece. Aside from this handful of family members, no one else came or even sent a card of congratulations. Deborah and I, on the other hand, have never missed one family wedding. Absence of family members at our ceremonies would have been considered rude and disrespectful if we were a straight couple. My family drove all the way from Texas to Wilmington, Delaware for my wedding to a man they didn't even like.

On a more positive note, having gone through our commitment ceremonies has given our relationship validity and strength and has shown our families that our commitment is more important than their acceptance. Both Deborah and I, at different times, have had to be willing to let go of our families of origin in order to create our own family. For me, this has always been very hard and lonely because I love my family. However, I've had to challenge their old ways of thinking and demand a level of respect that my relationship deserves.

Deborah, who has never been married to a man, believes it's harder for lesbians who have been married and known the privileges of straight life to exchange those liberties for a lifestyle of struggle and disrespect. And while I have lost some privileges to a lifestyle of protest and demonstrations, one where we have to rally for basic rights, it is also a lifestyle where we become the teachers of human respect and dignity. I often say that living as a fully out lesbian is not for the meek. It takes a lot of daily courage to live with dignity. However, after all the rallies and meetings, we pack up our courage and go home to the partners, lovers, mates and spouses who love us, support us and encourage us to do our work the next day. In spite of all this, my only regret is that I didn't come out sooner!

Something [Judy Grahn's] poem unlocked in me was the audacity of loving women, the audacity of claiming a stigmatized desire, the audacity to resist the temptations to abandon or betray or deny "all of our lovers"—those of whatever sex, color, class with whom we need to make common cause and who need us. "A Woman Is Talking to Death" was a boundary-breaking poem for me: it exploded both desire and politics.

—Adrienne Rich,
What is Found There: Notebooks on Poetry and Politics

Deborah Abbott, 1978 and today.

The Wildness Inside

DEBORAH ABBOTT

"The only thing that matched the wildness I felt inside when I wrote was kissing a woman."

Natalie Goldberg

I'll never forget the look on my mother's face as my brand-new husband, Christian, backed our pea-green Fiat down the driveway at the close of our wedding reception. It was not a look of shock exactly—she was smiling a little and faintly waving. Yet something in the way her mouth fell open suggested that inside she was having a vague yet powerful premonition, the kind my Baba Nellie from the old country used to have all the time.

Christian kept backing down the steep driveway and I kept waving. So did my best friend, Rachel, who was sitting behind me in the backseat. The three of us were headed down the Big Sur coast to Esalen, a retreat center by day and a free public hot tub by night. Christian and I had invited our guests to join us for a midnight soak; in the end, Rachel was the only one to come along. As my mother disappeared from sight and I let my hand drop into my lap, I had a feeling—my own undefined premonition perhaps—that the look on her face had something to do with the fact that Rachel was joining Christian and me on our one-night honeymoon.

To me, it was the most natural thing in the world, it was the *best* of both worlds: having my handsome husband beside me and my dearest woman friend behind me, loosening my braid and brushing out my long thick hair.

As Christian drove down the winding coast and Rachel stroked out my tangles, I considered another possibility. That I had misinterpreted my mother's look; that really it had been a half-concealed mixture of relief and surprise. Surprise that I was marrying at all. Not because I had never shown much interest in boys, but because boys had never been interested in dating me.

I was not date material, nor a logical candidate for marriage. No matter that I was pretty—Sears had selected my graduation photo for their displays. And that I could look in the mirror and recognize my own beauty: large hazel eyes, broad angular Yugoslav face, long wavy hair, full breasts, and a "nice figure." Yet there had always been the problem of my leg. Albeit only one "bad leg," but one was enough. I had had polio when I was two. I wore a brace. I limped.

I had grown up in Monterey with one sister, no brothers, in a small adobe house on a rutted dead end road lined with a dozen other houses—all filled with girls. Susie's brother Larry didn't count since he was years older and always inside practicing the piano. And fathers didn't really count either; mine was a cuddly 6'4" teddy bear who bounced me on his knees and told corny jokes just like my grandfather and worked a lot of overtime climbing poles for Ma Bell—especially during storms. My mother was the one to contend with. She was strong and smart and often angry, telling me over and over through the years that she "wasn't cut out to be married and have kids." She loved my father, though she couldn't show it, yet was constantly admonishing him about one thing or another. She'd shake her head and confide in me "Men—they're just a bunch of big babies. I might as well have three kids."

I played with girls. I built Lincoln Log cabins with my girlfriends and hideouts in the woods. We put on carnivals and haunted houses for my little sister and her girlfriends. I played marbles and Chinese jumprope with girls. And Wagon Train, Rawhide, Annie Oakley, and the Lone Ranger—brandishing cap guns and shouting "Head 'em up, move 'em out" to imaginary herds of cattle. And occasionally we played with dolls. The only boys I knew lived on the next road down the canyon. One of them did something "dirty" to my friend Sadie that she cried about when I asked. Another one who wanted to join our club was willing to close his eyes and eat our initiation "cookie"—which was made of mud and had a fat earthworm in the middle. We laughed at him when he opened his eyes, spitting brown goo; even if he'd swallowed, we would not have let him join.

Until I met Hilary in French class in eighth grade, I'd had many girlfriends, but never a *best* friend. Hilary and I immediately clicked. We were both smart—smart alecks, my father would say. We made fun of our teacher, Monsieur Lacon, practically to his face. He tried to trip us up by calling on us to conjugate verbs, but we always knew the answer, which frustrated him to death. Hilary and I spent all our free time together. We sent each other poems, gave each other little gifts. When I went off to Shriner's Hospital for operations on my leg, Hilary wrote to me every day for months.

When I returned home, Hilary had developed a crush on a very pretty, very shy boy named William. She and William had a romantic relationship which went as far as walks on the beach, hand-holding and a kiss or two. As soon as Hilary started dating, I began a surreptitious affair with her older brother. The secretiveness of it—I never told Hilary—made it exciting.

Hilary and William broke up a few months later; I made a move on William and within two weeks had gotten him down on my bedroom floor.

The next fall, I went off to the university in Santa Cruz, not much of a leap from my home in Monterey. Hilary's brother was already at UCSC; Hilary and I had visited him there once. No one in my family had gone to college, so knowing even one person at a school so close by made the transition a little less terrifying to me.

Although William remained my official boyfriend for my first three years at UCSC, I didn't see him very much. I missed Hilary badly. We wrote, we called each other, she visited often. Whenever she came to Santa Cruz, we slept in my single bed and showered together in the morning. I remember a dorm-mate once looking shocked as Hilary and I emerged from the same stall. Despite these intimacies, it never occurred to me to have sex with Hilary; I never remember feeling aroused. My first two lovers had been Hilary's brother and ex-boyfriend; perhaps this was the closest I could come to acting out my desires.

One winter, Hilary began getting close to another woman. I was jealous and privately incensed. Throughout December I watched Hilary sewing her new friend an elaborate wool hat. On Christmas Eve, at my family's house, I opened her gift to me: a set of mugs with a sticker on the bottom reading, "seconds." I borrowed my mother's car and drove recklessly across town, left the mugs on Hilary's doorstep and drove home sobbing.

Hilary and I didn't really drift apart, we broke up—though we never would have called it that. I felt terribly hurt and rejected. Hilary had begun dating a doctor's son. I was made painfully aware that my parents weren't cultured or educated, that the only books in the house were glossy volumes of *Condensed Reader's Digest*. And that I was Yugoslav peasant stock: big-boned with strong hands, smart but exposing my lack of refinement at every turn. My mother had always called Hilary's parents snobs, my father dubbed them highfalutin'; though I had defended Hilary and her family, even sided with them, in the end I felt as shamed as my parents had.

A couple months after I stopped seeing Hilary, I moved out of the dorms into a little cottage a few blocks from the beach. One day I looked out the window and saw a young woman wave at me and flash an irresistible smile. It turned out she was my next-door neighbor, a student at the university, too. As with Hilary, Rachel and I formed an immediate, intense bond. We started spending evenings together, taking turns making dinner. We both left May Day baskets on each other's doorsteps that first spring; I often came home to cards and bouquets.

Rachel graduated in June and returned to Los Angeles. She promptly met a man, married him, and soon after discovered he was a drinker and a compulsive gambler. Realizing the terrible mistake she'd made, she left him and returned to Santa Cruz. We found an apartment together. I had broken up with William; Rachel was on the rebound and was dating several men, including three Richards at one time. I was often home in the evenings, missing her company and fielding her calls. I began feeling enormously resentful of all the men coming in and out of our small apartment. One night one of the Richards phoned. "Let her know Dick called," he said with an assurance that told me Rachel had not told *him* about all the others. I responded, my voice laced with sarcasm: "Well, which DICK is this?"

Christian, one of Rachel's men friends from the city, came to visit one weekend. Rachel breezed in with a man on her arm, gave Christian a hug and hello, and shortly after disappeared into her bedroom with the new hunk. I took it on to entertain Christian. He was good-looking in a soft way, more feminine than masculine in manner. He was playful and wooed me with his country blues guitar. By the end of the weekend, Christian was off the couch and in my bed. I was no longer alone in my room listening to Rachel getting turned on by some new man or another. I had my own.

Five units and a senior essay short of graduating with a major in biology and a minor in creative writing, I moved to San Francisco to be with Christian. Within a few months I was pregnant. While this was not a planned pregnancy—at least not consciously—making a baby was a next step that seemed so much clearer to me than getting an M.D. or an M.F.A. Everything in my family and cultural backgrounds had prepared me to be a mother; nothing had prepared me to be a doctor or writer.

Christian and I decided to get married to appease our parents who were mortified that I was "PG" and unwed. We were married in one of the mission chapels in Monterey. When the Father met with us to discuss our ceremony, he pointed out the side room where the shotgun weddings took place. Behind his back, I patted my already bulging belly, looked at Christian and winked. We were married at the altar; Christian strummed his guitar and sang "If I were a carpenter, and you were a lady, Would you marry me anyway, would you have my baby?"

I refused to wear white, to wear a veil, or have my father give me away. I walked down the aisle with a parent on each arm; Christian walked beside me on his mother's. I wrote the vows, omitting any reference to "man and wife," or "serve and obey." I stressed in more than one passage "only so long as we shall nourish and support each other,"—"til death do ye part" made me feel instantly claustrophobic. Tucked into the wedding announcements was a prominent notice that by no means was I becoming Mrs. Christian Moore. I was, and always would be, Ms. Deborah Abbott.

Matthew was born a few months after the wedding. Rachel was at his birth at our home in San Francisco, holding me through the long hours of contractions. Rachel and I had been staying close with letter writing and phoning. Still, I missed her so badly, I convinced Christian to move back to Santa Cruz a couple of months after Matthew was born.

Just as we were settling into life in Santa Cruz, Rachel went off to her high school reunion, met a man there, married him and moved back to Los Angeles. I was devastated, though I wasn't able to say so, either to Rachel or myself. Rachel was clearly as important to me as my husband, yet we could never acknowledge that; we had no hold on each other, no language or tradition to validate our special relationship. While I was inwardly grieving my loss and was angry to be abandoned, outwardly I was supportive of Rachel's marriage, even though after meeting her husband, I privately concluded he was an arrogant jerk.

Rachel became pregnant soon after her wedding and it wasn't long before she realized this husband was mistake #2. He was heavily involved in an EST-like program which he claimed would make him a better husband and father. An hour after their son's birth, he was gone to a weekend retreat.

By the time Matthew was six months old, I was going stir-crazy being a stay-at-home mother. I had been working since I was twelve and hated being dependent on Christian, whose earnings as a library clerk were modest, and whose appetite for steel-bodied guitars swallowed up what little extra money there was. My hunger was for women; I was lonely. With Rachel gone, I was spending days with my young son and evenings with Christian. There was nothing *wrong* with Christian's company—we were companionable enough—but there *was* something missing. I was never compelled to stay up talking with Christian; whenever Rachel came to visit, we would routinely watch the sun come up, and bleary-eyed yet sated from the richness of our conversation, laugh and finally sleep.

In January of 1978, I sat on the floor of the Santa Cruz Women's Health Collective office, Matthew at my breast, attending an orientation meeting. I had been a functional feminist all of my life—my mother wore the pants in the family and my father's mother, Inez, whom I visited most weekends, was a big, indomitable woman. From them, I had inherited a fundamental belief that I was powerful, I wasn't to put up with any mistreatment, and that I was somewhat superior to men. Still, I was relatively unaware of the women's movement. I got rapidly politicized at the collective and before long, was calling myself a socialist feminist. Within a few months, I left behind a series of secretarial jobs in doctors' offices—male doctors, naturally—and moved into an all-women's healthcare environment where, at the age of 23, I was editing a nationally distributed newsletter, teaching natural birth control classes, assisting in medical exams, and training volunteers for the hotline. I was also conscious, for the first time in my life, that I was making friends with lesbians.

The only lesbian I had ever known of was my Aunt Mary who lived in San Francisco. When I had spent those long months at Shriner's Hospital recovering from various orthopedic surgeries, Mary had been my most faithful visitor. When I was little I remember being intrigued with Mary: she always wore pants with a big noisy bunch of keys clipped to her belt loop, she swore a lot and, most conspicuously, she had no husband. She was different from my other aunts, who always talked about recipes and kids. And, there was the ever-present Jean, her "room-mate."

Even after briefly staying with Aunt Mary years later, I never considered I might be lesbian. Mary gave me a tour of San Francisco's gay bars one night. They were smoky and dark, women with tattoos, hair slicked back and cigarettes dangling from their lips, leaned over pool tables; they looked me up and down in such a brazen manner that I was alarmed.

Yet it was less than a year later that I found myself in bed with my best friend. Rachel had driven up from Los Angeles for the weekend; Christian was out of town at a musical gig. It was late afternoon. I was sprawled out on the queen-sized bed nursing Matthew to sleep. Rachel was beside me. As the room filled with a warm golden light, Rachel and I lay whispering. Matthew finally slept. I carried him off to his crib and returned to the bed to find Rachel softly crying. I held her against me, and in a moment of tenderness, began kissing her hair, her forehead, her cheeks. With tears still falling, she offered me her lips, and I kissed them, too. She kissed me back, this time passionately. And then somehow, we were undressing each other and making love.

Nothing prepared me for that moment; I could never have predicted it. I was astonished that we had crossed that line of intimacy we must have been at the edge of, unknowingly, for years. I was also completely overcome by how powerfully I had been aroused by our lovemaking. I was generally satisfied with my sexual relationship with Christian and other male lovers before him, yet with Rachel, was astounded at the depth of my response. For days after Rachel returned to L.A., I would lock myself in the bathroom, simply touch myself and come. The memory of Rachel's soft skin, luscious breasts, intoxicating sex smells and wet interiors made me crazy with longing for more. The fact of our lovemaking seemed like a dream or a fluke coming out of nowhere, never to return. I had no sense I could make it happen again. For days, thinking I had had my once-in-a-lifetime sexual experience with a woman, I felt terrible regret that I hadn't been brave enough to go down on Rachel, to taste the wetness I had touched. I wept at the lost possibility as I walked around the house in a stupor of arousal and amazement—bowled over with the awareness that I had made love with a woman and that it was the most incredible erotic experience of my life.

Afterwards, Rachel and I wrote long letters and talked on the telephone for hours, sorting out what had just happened between us. We laughed when I described making love with her like having longed for the rich sweetness of ice cream in a land of popsicles only to discover the ice cream shop right around the corner!

I realized that for my entire life I had loved girls, loved women, and that it had simply never occurred to me to consider women as lovers. I had brought my sexual self to men, collected it afterwards and returned to my women's community. Falling into Rachel's arms was a revelation, acutely personal and profound, which shook my body and psyche with the force of worlds colliding.

Rachel and I made love a few more times, then decided to stop. We were both married, had infant sons, were living hundreds of miles away from each other, and were not able—emotionally or economically—to make any big changes in our lives. We were afraid that a lover relationship—which in our experience with men had proven to be precarious—would jeopardize the decade-long friendship we had so carefully cultivated and come to count on. And there were other fears we could not name.

I hated keeping my sexual involvement with Rachel a secret from Christian, though we had established an "open marriage" and he had had an affair of his own. I ended up telling Christian about Rachel one night when he was entertaining the idea of inviting Rachel to join us in a ménage à trois. That we had left him out of his fantasy, that I had beaten him to it—had already made love with Rachel—angered him. That I had chosen a *woman* lover was devastating. In Christian's mind, not only had I forsaken him as my exclusive sex partner, I had spurned his gender as well. Despite countless couple therapy sessions, Christian could not get beyond his feelings of rejection and betrayal.

Christian and I separated two long years later. In the meantime, I had gotten pregnant and we had a second son. Christian had also had a series of affairs. When he told me that one of his lovers was pregnant, I finally kicked him out. Though I was tremendously relieved to be out of the marriage, I was anguished that I had left my boys with a "broken family."

Yet from the beginning, Christian and I had parented equally. While I nursed the babies in the night, he would be at the other end changing diapers. As we separated, we worked out a co-parenting plan: half a week with the boys, half a week without. While there were plenty of stressful adjustments for our sons in suddenly having two homes, there were also benefits for them in having the tension and fighting resolved. Christian and I stayed in contact daily, mostly over the phone, discussing everything from which preschool we thought would be best, to the whereabouts of the missing brown shoe. It became clear to me after only a few weeks of our separation that what had ended was Christian's and my relationship as a couple; our relationship as co-parents was by no means over and, in fact, would be a lifelong connection.

One of the things I did in that first week of the breakup was apply for a small loan to buy myself an electric typewriter. I lied on the application, told the credit union I was buying a used car; I was afraid they'd never approve a typewriter. This was a powerful act for me. In the seven years Christian and I had been together, he had acquired countless guitars and a vast blues record collection. I had never gotten myself a typewriter, which was as much a tool of my craft as musical instruments were of his. While time to write *was* scarce with my job and two small boys, even in the time I did have, nothing besides a few poems had emerged in all those years.

It's difficult to understand or articulate this creative silence even now, fifteen years later. From the beginning, I had resisted becoming "Christian's wife" and had corrected relatives when they attempted to define me in that way. I had been criticized by family members throughout the years for "making Christian do women's work" even though Christian had been committed to doing his share. I had maintained and developed many supportive friendships with women during my marriage; in fact, these were my primary relationships. My feminism had found deep roots in my work with the health collective. And yet … in some insidious way, I had surrendered my creative life. Buying that typewriter was an essential act of reclaiming some of what had been lost.

In the next few years I found myself in places I would never have been had I stayed married. Parenting half-time was liberating for me, and I sometimes felt guilty admitting I had the best of both worlds: time with my children—which I looked forward to and mostly enjoyed; time apart from them and their many demands—time with myself.

During my no-kid days, I was joyous. I had to be accountable to no one for the first time in years. It was thrilling to simply be in my house, to putter around the kitchen making food I liked—which the boys would have turned their noses up at—to clean things up and know they'd stay that way for the next few days, to have a conversation with a friend on the phone and know there would be no interruptions. Years after the divorce, I still cherish being alone in my home, and even the most mundane tasks give me pleasure.

For a short while after Christian and I broke up, I entertained the notion that I might be bi. I did some socializing in heterosexual hangouts and quickly realized that, as frustrated as I'd become with Christian, Christian was an exceptional man. He was essentially kind, intrinsically honest, called himself a feminist along with me, and had a poorly developed male ego. I found men on the straight dating scene who thought nothing of talking about themselves the whole evening, had little understanding of my issues once I did get a word in, and mostly wanted to get in my pants. I never did let any of them in my pants and, within a few weeks, ended the chapter in the book of bisexuality.

While I had become clear that men were out of the picture for me, I had no idea how to date women. I established my first real lesbian relationship through a friend who introduced me to Natalie. Natalie was sweet and very shy; I made all the moves, she eagerly responded. What I most remember of our years together was how well we connected in all the little ways. I was nurtured as I had never been by any man—soup at my bedside when I was sick, love notes in the mail, long hours of listening and being listened to, lovemaking which seemed to last forever and was exquisitely responsive to my needs.

What didn't work in my relationship with Natalie, and in many of the ones with women to come, was trying to mix my lovers with my sons. Natalie had a strong separatist streak and considered men pigs—categorically. My boys, to her, were just "little men," oppressors in training. Whenever she was around the boys, any of their behaviors which could be faintly construed as aggressive, became evidence of their imminent rapist status. I hadn't wanted to create family with Natalie and the boys—my sons had sufficient family with Christian and me—yet I hadn't planned to keep my two worlds absolutely divided. I struggled with my lover's animosity, feeling protective of my sons. I knew that the way Natalie responded to them was sometimes destructive, and I kept them apart as much as possible. Despite my commitment to nonsexist childrearing, I recognized that my boys' behaviors *were* sometimes aggressive and I privately worried about how that aggressiveness would manifest itself when they were grown. But with Natalie there was no way to voice my concerns and get any constructive support. What amazed me, angered me, and eventually made me laugh with the irony of it all was that after we broke up, Natalie became involved with—a man!

One of the gifts of my first lesbian relationship was that I developed the self-confidence and skills to finish my bachelor's degree and apply to graduate school. I had been working full-time at the collective and then in a child nutrition program, barely making enough to pay my rent and feed my kids. In my marriage, I had given most of my time and attention to Christian and my sons. In my lesbian relationship, I got nurtured back. The infusion of energy in my direction was enough to push me over a barrier which had seemed extraordinarily high. While I had never questioned my intellectual capacity, my family had never been able to give me the tools I needed to move on.

I met my next lover, Kate, as she interviewed me for an article she was writing for a local newspaper. I was one of a handful of women with disabilities whose life stories she was gathering. When she arrived at my house I had just come back from swimming—another piece of myself I had reclaimed since the divorce—and was still dripping wet. Kate had grown up on the water, loved to row and sail; after the interview, she took me out on the bay. We soon became involved.

With Kate, my physical world expanded enormously. This was a profound opening for me since I had all but abandoned my body years before, trying to hide my disability as best I could in allegiance to mainstreaming pressures around me. Besides rowing, Kate taught me to boogie board, backpack and ride a tandem bike; we were outside exploring much of the time. Kate also managed, by virtue of her sensitivity and her own vulnerability, to touch and help heal some of my deepest childhood wounds. Something long guarded cracked open; I was flooded with passion, a wildness emerged. I wrote a plethora of poems, made love with Kate in ways that left me liberated and empowered.

In the end, Kate's moodiness became traumatizing to me. As a child, I had been punished with the "silent treatment" and had been left alone in hospitals too often; I couldn't handle Kate's erratic coming close and pulling back. When she withdrew for the last time, I was heartbroken, believing that all the doors she had opened for me, she'd closed behind her.

But eventually I found new bike buddies, camping partners. I learned to sea kayak and went off and got trained to be a whitewater river guide, as Kate had encouraged me to do. I came to claim my jock identity. And once my heart mended, I could appreciate the gifts Kate left. They were huge gifts; once unwrapped, what I found inside was me: like Natalie, Kate returned to me parts of my self, treasures long buried.

The next relationship I had was with Val. Val and I had little in common besides being river runners for the same company, being Scorpios, and loving sex. Our relationship was purely sexual. In the beginning, I would spend hours fussing over a meal before Val arrived. She'd look at the pot bubbling on the stove, the table I'd so carefully set, look me in the eye and say "That's not what I came here for. I came here for you." And off she'd drag me to the bedroom for the rest of the weekend. What Val helped me understand was that I didn't have to *do* anything, didn't have to take care of her in any way to get what I wanted. And with Val, all I wanted was sex.

Sex just kept getting better and better in my relationships with women, unbelievably thrilling. With men there had always been the unspoken assumption that intercourse was the "real thing," that any action before was foreplay, a pesky chore—kind of like warming up the engine on a cold morning so the car won't stall—to get me wet enough or willing to be entered. With a male lover I had rarely succumbed to the missionary position, but even on top felt this terrible pressure to please him and try to get myself off before *he* got off, which was usually way too soon.

With women, it has been utterly amazing to be penetrated by a hand that fills me as much as I can handle, for as long as I can take it, and to be orally stimulated at the same time. *And* to give my lover all of that, too. With lesbian lovers, there has never been any clear starting or stopping point to sex. Orgasms aren't always the pie in the sky—though undeniably the memory of them has made me drive hours in the rain in the middle of the night to get one more. Women's ways of teasing, the nuances of their seductions have been intricate, and infinitely more refined than any I've ever experienced with male lovers—capable of arousing me to coming before I have even a stitch of clothing off. Tenderness after—even in casual affairs—has almost always been there with women lovers, so that no matter how wild the fucking, sex has felt like lovemaking to me. I have loved all the positions, the possibilities, the absence of prescribed roles. As Rita Mae Brown says, "Once you know what women are like, men get kind of boring. I'm not trying to put them down, I mean I like them sometimes as people, but sexually they're dull."

Fifteen years after coming out, I'm deeply content with my lesbian life: half of the time I'm with my sons, who seem to be weathering the storms of adolescence so far; the other half with myself in all of the ways I like to be in the world.

I've been single for the past year. Dating is still mysterious to me. I'm aware that, because of my disability, I never got to practice when I was a teenager; I feel awkward and ignorant about how dating's supposed to go. As bold as I am in many ways—I'm quite comfortable reading my erotic stories to an auditorium full of women—I'm shy about making sexual overtures. I'm also aware that while lesbians are at the forefront of examining the "isms," there's still a gap between our theories and practices. It's painful to know and to publicly state that to many lesbians, because of my leg, my brace and my limp, I'm simply not date material—best friend material, but not a candidate for romance—no different from my experience with the boys in high school.

Still, I'm quite content these days in my own good company. "I'd rather be a free spirit and paddle my own canoe," as Louisa May Alcott claimed. And I *am* paddling my kayak, rowing my raft down rivers whenever I get the chance. I love tending the plants on my doorstep, rubbing my cat's soft belly, feeding the birds; sitting with a friend at my kitchen table, curling up in bed with a heap of books, a cup of coffee, a poem I'm working on. As much as I love being in an intimate relationship, as much as I miss nasty sex and tender arms, I'm somewhat weary of "issues" and compromises. Having accommodated to the needs of my children for the last 17 years, I have little desire to do more of that, for now.

Rachel is still my closest friend; we just celebrated 23 years of loving each other and being in each other's lives. Our sons are best friends. For my 40th birthday I invited 40 friends to my party. It was enormously reassuring to look around the room and realize that no matter what challenges may be ahead, I have created a large network of women who are family to me and who will be there to offer support.

It is clear to me, too, that little of this would have been posssible had I stayed married. In my marriage I grew *in spite of* my relationship with Christian; in virtually all of my lesbian relationships I have grown *because* of the women who've loved me and I have loved.

I am extraordinarily grateful that Rachel and I fell into bed with each other that late summer day. While I may have continued on as a heterosexual with some contentment, I would never have experienced the deeply engaged and fully connected life I have as a lesbian. Life as a straight woman was often more comfortable, more predictable, and certainly more acceptable to my family and the world at large. Yet living as a lesbian is incomparably rich, more complex and nourishing. Perhaps having grown up with a permanent, visible disability, knowing I'd never fit in, made the costs of coming out as a lesbian easier for me to deal with than for many women. When I first told my mother I was a lesbian, she exclaimed "But it's not normal!" What I answered was: "Having polio isn't normal either, Mom, and you taught me I was okay, that people's attitudes were the problem." My mother had no comeback.

As much as I've embraced myself as a woman with a disability, as glad as I've come to be of my Yugoslav peasant stock sensibilities, I've become proud of being a formerly married lesbian. Whether I'm in or out of a lesbian relationship, whether I've got an ex-husband in my past or not, I'm a life member of the lesbian community. Formerly married lesbians are an integral part of an amazing culture of lesbians, with a wildness inside that could not, after all, be tamed.

A Lesbian Love Letter

JOANNA KADI

This is the letter I wish someone had written for me when I was a young woman.

Dear Sister:

There are stories I must tell you. Stories with knowledge and words and feelings that must be passed on. Many times our stories to each other have not been shared as they were meant to be but rather they have been cut short, interrupted in the flow of one generation to another. What does it mean to be a lesbian of color? What are the stories around this improbable/probable happening? Improbable because in a sexist, racist, and heterosexist society it is not likely we would find our way through the maze of external and internal oppression to come home to this. Probable because it is oh so likely we would love each other/our selves this much. As I reflect on the lack of stories offered to me as I grew up, I want to write this letter to a young woman of color and reach backward in time and offer it to myself as well. I want to pass on what I know as a working-class, Arab half-breed queer girl. And while my personal stories intersect with a larger framework, it is crucial to remember I speak only for myself, not for whole groups of people.

When I came out as a lesbian, both pairs of lips opened. My words inched their way forward, the stories stirred and began to move. This fulfilled their purpose, because stories must be shared with others.

My words came to the surface slowly. To write that sentence now does not and never can capture the unbelievable slowness of the process. It began 13 years ago when I began meeting lesbian feminists. At the time I lived with my abusive husband. With him, I went for days without speaking. Once on a week-long car trip together, I said nothing save monosyllabic responses to his infrequent questions. He never noticed.

This dream, which I had several months before leaving, sums up my marriage: Mesmerized, I watch my parents-in-law. Mrs. H. tries to placate her husband. As is often the case, he is furious and she wants to diffuse the anger before he lashes out at her. She tiptoes through various pieces of conversation, hoping one pleasant snippet will engage him, distract the beast, hold the anger at bay.

Fear permeates every part of her. I view my present and my future. I try to scream: "This is what it's like! This is exactly what it's like!" But I cannot speak. The heavy white gauze that has been growing in my throat these past years is so thick that words cannot find their way through or around it. Not only am I unable to speak, I am beginning to suffocate. Soon I will die.

I did not die. I watched a film in which women are tortured, mutilated, and killed for the sake of men's orgasms. I changed my future and became politically active in the movement to end violence against women and my activist colleagues noticed my silences. I experienced this as strange and bizarre but I liked it. Women noticed, they urged me to talk, they exposed me to the excitement and wonder of feminist politics in the early 1980s: women's culture, women's organizing, global sisterhood.

And women's writing. The stories by Cherríe Moraga, Gloria Anzaldúa, Chrystos, resonated in my bones. The words of warrior-poet Audre Lorde held particular importance. She wrote: "The white fathers told us: I think therefore I am. The Black mother within each of us — the poet — whispers in our dreams: I feel, therefore I can be free."

"I feel, therefore I can be free." When I first read this sentence, it grabbed at me with an urgent force and I understood (part of) its meaning immediately. Because when I came out I began to feel. Alive and in love for the first time. Not only with my lover, Jan, but with my people. These feelings were new and different because prior to this I rarely felt. As is common with oppressed people, I had no time to; survival claimed my time. For example, I had not felt the trauma of my husband's temper nor his invasion of my body while living with him. I shoved the pain down, moving mechanically through our house so I could get through to the next day.

Feminism made it impossible for me to continue repressing my feelings. Working to end violence against women, understanding the extent of the brutality with which so many of us live, beginning to consciously remember the brutality I lived with from infancy on, pulled me into anger, grief, and critical feminist analysis. It also pulled me toward a passionate love of women and a desire to make my life with women. I left my husband after six years of abuse/six years of marriage.

During those first years as a dyke, I found "heterosexual privilege" a hard concept to understand. Silencing, rape, and assault hadn't felt like privilege to me. I now understand how public support of heterosexual relationship contrasts sharply with public harassment and assault of lesbian couples, and how this impacts daily living. I still believe public support doesn't make up for the violations so many heterosexual women experience within the institution of marriage.

And there are more complications. Because this is the letter I wish someone had written for me when I was a young woman, I must tell the whole truth and not gloss over the pain-full parts, the dissonance I experienced early on among certain women, the stark reality that women hold privilege carelessly and abuse power thoughtlessly. Many lesbians know nothing about working-class oppression and choose not to learn, many treat their lovers as badly as my husband treated me and choose not to change, many know nothing about Arabs and choose to remain uninformed.

As a member of these oppressed groups, I had to make conscious choices about my life, particularly as I moved through the residue from years of sexist, racist, and classist oppression. How could I truly love Arabs without feeling, comprehending, and letting go of the self-hatred forced on me by my white oppressors who taught me that we are dirty? How could I truly love women without feeling, comprehending, and letting go of the self-hatred forced on me by my male oppressors — my father being the first, with many men following his lead — who taught me that women are "only good for one thing?" And how could I truly love working-poor and working-class people without feeling, comprehending, and letting go of the self-hatred forced on me by my wealthy oppressors who taught me that we are stupid?

My coming out process, easy in some ways, tremendously difficult in others, opened many doors. It affected much more than my sexual identity. My racial and class identities were strengthened and affirmed. I was able to understand and move through past experiences that had shaped my life. And I got in touch with my true desires — for justice for poor people, for liberation from imperialism, for my lover Jan.

These are some of the stories I must tell you, stories with knowledge and words and feelings that must be passed on. They are part of the larger framework of stories now being offered up by so many powerful women, the ones already mentioned, Kate Rushin, Makeda Silvera, V. K. Aruna, MiOk Song Bruining, Beth Brant—the list goes on and on. These stories can be shared as they were meant to be, so they can flow from one generation to another. This will cause many things to happen. One is to help ensure that young women of color know a simple and powerful fact: lesbians of color exist. Growing up, I did not know this. I was 22 when I discovered lesbians existed, 25 when I came out to my self. It's highly improbable that I would have learned this earlier, and it's highly probable that once this simple and powerful fact presented itself, I would realize where I belong. How can we not love each other/our selves this much?

Esther O'Donald on her wedding day and on her own.

I Still Believe in Marriage

ESTHER O'DONALD

I believe wholeheartedly in the concepts of monogamy and marriage and in creating traditional and non-traditional family units, whether heterosexual or gay. My interpretation is that in this blending, a lifelong mutual support system develops, where members play, love, work and live for the family's benefit. My heterosexual marriage was nothing like that.

The story of why, how and who I married began when I was five."There's a new little neighbor girl for you to play with," my mother explained. "And a brother two years older than you. He can be your boyfriend and take care of you when you go to school." The lesson was taught again and again during my childhood: I had to have a man to protect me or I couldn't get by.

My mother believed it, too, in fact she was constantly on the lookout for the perfect match for me. In kindergarten, a painfully shy Roger became "Hot Rod" because my mother had seen the movie *Rebel Without a Cause*. In first grade, Sir John walked Lady Esther to school, arranged and chaperoned by Mom. She even coached him in his role by encouraging him to bring me little gifts and pick flowers for me along the way.

By the time I reached second grade, I had learned the lesson: men were important, powerful and essential to my survival if for no other reason than they provided the necessities of life. Anything humanly possible would have to be done to keep them from leaving. No price was too high. Is it any wonder I always wanted to be the daddy when we played house? Or that I got in BIG trouble when I tried to kiss my best friend Barbara goodbye as I went off "to work?"

My mother had three children, all illegitimate, all due to ignorance of birth control and her search for validation and protection by having a man in her life. It was the only way she knew.

For women in our family, there have been generations of abuse and addiction, of incest and rape. "Don't rock the boat!" was their means of survival. And then it happened to me. My mother's advice after I'd been raped twice at the age of nine by one of her boyfriends was "If it happens again, go to the bathroom and pee as fast as you can." My grandmother championed my cause, calling the authorities and filing charges—but not without letting me know very clearly that I had ruined my mother's life by allowing such a thing to happen.

Allowing it to happen? It took me almost 30 years to understand the damage caused by that guilt.

The family didn't rally around me. My mother withdrew, unable to cope with what had happened, and I spent much of my adolescence living alone or with my married sister until I ended up in a foster home at the age of 15. The bastard who raped me spent six months in an "honor camp."

As a teenager I longed for fences, for boundaries and rules, for a world where everything was black and white and not the endless shades of gray I had always experienced in my chaotic homes. It's no wonder I yielded to my foster parents' will and became a Mormon like them. Now there were fences everywhere, with a new one popping up every time I traipsed too close to the boundary between acceptable behavior and what I felt in my heart.

The security of the Mormon Church gave me a cocoon to hide in. For the first time in my life, I had a place where I fit in, a ready-made circle of friends. The patriarchal order of the church reinforced everything I'd ever been taught—Man/Master, Woman/Slave. It's a simple enough concept (one even a woman can understand). In 1969, girls still went to college to get their M.R.S. degrees, and Brigham Young University (BYU) was affectionately called B-Y-Woo by those looking for that all-important mate. By popular opinion, life didn't start until you were married, and I was determined to be the first in my crowd to get a life.

I married just eight months out of high school for all the usual reasons: to leave an unhappy home, wear an expensive dress, and be the center of attention...and because it was expected. My husband, Mark, had been told when he returned from being a missionary for the church that he should marry within six months. He was at three months and counting when we met. On our second date, the conversation centered on marriage: "So, when do we get married?" he asked. "I don't care, sometime after Christmas," I replied.

We were married one day short of Mark's six-month deadline, in the Los Angeles Temple with all the appropriate Mormon hoopla, for "time and all eternity." Eternity is an awfully long time for a marriage labeled "platonic" from the onset by its inhabitants. The prospect of spending eternity married to my husband grew more and more frightening, like a child's monster looming in a darkened closet. It took almost 16 years before I felt brave enough to open the door and let the bogeyman out.

By joining the Mormon Church, I gave up the need to think for myself and discovered a husband who was more than willing to tell me what my opinions were. If someone asked what I thought about a political issue, even something as clear-cut as Watergate, I went totally blank and was unable to respond.

For the first ten years of my marriage, I was the perfect Mormon housewife. I canned, froze, pickled and dehydrated everything that didn't move faster than I did. My house may not have always been spotless but the pantry was always full, and there was always at least a two-year supply of wheat, honey, powdered milk, beans and rice in the garage. We had everything a model Mormon family should, except for children. All of my clothes, most of my husband's shirts and every crumb of our baked goods were homemade. I taught Sunday School and led the choir, holding as many as six church "callings" at one time. Oh yes, and I worked full time.

As I innocently formed warmer bonds with my women friends than I had ever felt with my husband, my sleep became filled with wonderful dreams of rescuing them from the men they were married to and spiriting them off to a colony of amazing, capable, happy women. In my dreams, though, no one ever came to rescue me. I would deliver the women and see that they were well settled in, but I always went home to make dinner. I didn't have a clue what the dreams meant but they would come back every time I felt especially close to someone.

It wasn't until Sonia Johnson spoke up for the Equal Rights Amendment and was excommunicated from the church that I gave real thought to a political issue of any kind. The church put out the word that all members were to vote against the ERA and that anyone publicly dissenting was not only in danger of falling out of favor with the church but with "God Himself." Oh, I dissented, but silently, questioning for the first time every edict of the church and every direction given by my husband.

Perhaps to save face or to quell a groundswell of opposition from the membership, the church started leadership training classes for its women. I was asked to teach the classes in our congregation and, with no texts to aid teachers, I got to write my own material. The opportunity to research so much herstory gave me a pride I'd never known, and the simple act of preparing my lessons gave me license to think thoughts I'd never dared entertain.

As my horizons expanded, I began to see a glimmer of what life could be like - but not in the church the way it was and certainly not in my marriage. I couched my fledgling feelings for women in my silently growing feminism, still not identifying them for what they were, and hoped someday I'd be brave enough to live my own life—whatever that might be. Every night I prayed my husband would die so I could get out of the marriage. I could not yet even consider divorce.

It's important to note that my husband was not an ogre nor was he physically abusive. He just wasn't someone you'd like to spend your life with, much less eternity. In fact, he even helped with the housework and enjoyed fixing meals on a semi-regular basis. He took great pride in the fact that *his* wife could cook and quilt with the best of them. Any kudos I received for my abilities were quickly translated into a pat on the back for him and elevated his status among his peers. He volunteered my services regularly for everything from making last-minute posters for events to cooking a Mexican dinner for 250 people with no help from anyone. Usually, I never heard a word of thanks or appreciation for the work I'd done, just an off-handed "so-and-so-liked-the-whatever," and that usually came when he needed me to do another project.

Whenever we went to a church function, Mark deposited me at my seat and then went off to socialize. I remember a $50 per couple fundraiser where I spent the entire evening sitting alone. He took his plate with him and mingled with friends until it was time to go home. When I confronted him, saying I felt foolish sitting alone, he said I should have asked him to stay if it was important to me.

You're probably asking yourself why I didn't take my plate and do the same, why I allowed myself to act the victim. The easiest answer is that I hadn't met myself yet. I was so painfully shy as a result of my childhood and of being overshadowed for so many years by this man, that I honestly didn't feel I had anything to offer by way of conversation. In fact, it took more than three years of teaching leadership classes for me to integrate what I'd been teaching into my own life. It took a full frontal attack to my feminism to make me realize I was living an awful lie.

In 1984, we moved to Montana looking for work and Mark fell in with a group of men who decided it was their mission to defend the valley from attack, though we were not in any particular danger. Prior to Mark's involvement with the group, these vigilantes had tried unsuccessfully to murder a local judge for being too liberal. More recently, a member of the group had made connection with the Aryan Nations stronghold in northern Idaho and everyone was planning a weekend trip there to join up.

Mark emptied our checking account to finance his journey. When I confronted him about taking all our money, his response was that he needed it since one of the brothers couldn't afford the trip. It did no good to remind him that he was unemployed and we needed the money ourselves.

About two weeks after their trip, I returned home from work one day to find Mark sitting on the porch of our home, grinning from ear to ear, eager to show me how he had redecorated the den. What I saw made my blood run cold. On one wall hung a huge Confederate flag. The opposite wall contained a rack of literature for distribution, pins, patches and other Aryan Nations' paraphernalia he'd collected while in Idaho. "Isn't it great?" he asked. I couldn't even respond. Then he opened the closet. Inside he had arranged all of his guns and ammunition to show them off "to their best advantage" to whomever he planned to invite into this sanctuary. I later learned he had made arrangements for some of his Idaho friends to come and visit at our home.

It was definitely time to go, but I didn't feel I could just pack up and leave the marriage. I still had a lot of self-examination to do and needed toughening up around the edges. As time progressed, Mark noticed the changes and even commented once that he didn't know if he liked me anymore. I didn't care.

My safe place in what had become an enemy camp was inside my mind, and I went there often to regroup. I began reading everything I could get my hands on: newspapers, feminist publications, self-help books. Opinions grew inside me and I gradually exposed them to sunlight, one by one, until the sound of my own voice didn't frighten me anymore.

One morning, while in the shower, I finally saw everything clearly. Mark had been unemployed for over a year and I had been paying all our bills on my meager income. If I could support both of us on what I was making, I could darn sure support myself. By nightfall, I had a Post Office Box (number 1492, my voyage into uncharted territory), and had leased a home of my own from an understanding landlord willing to wait until payday for the rent.

Within six months of the day Mark joined the Aryan Nations, I was settled in my own place, and divorce proceedings had begun. His last words to me as he left the state were, "You're going to die here, you know. You haven't got what it takes to last a winter in Montana without a man." I lasted two years (easily) and would have stayed forever, but I needed to return to California, partly because my mother was dying, and partly because I felt an urgency to be among people who thought and felt as I did. It was years after my mother's death before I learned how easily I could have found those people in Montana.

About a year after my divorce, someone asked me what I would really like to do for a living if I could do anything. I replied that I'd like to lobby for women's issues in Washington, D.C. My reply not only surprised the person asking the question but shocked me as well. That was my first inkling that I was ready for the next step, that I was strong enough to fight for what I believed in.

Even at that, it took almost five years beyond my divorce for me to get up the courage to come out to myself. I'd joke that in my next life I was going to love only women. At 40, I decided it was time for my next life to begin.

Although I've identified myself as a lesbian only for a relatively short time, there is no doubt in my mind that my choice is correct. There's something empowering about choosing a life that strains against tradition and committing yourself to the ensuing struggle. It almost seems there should be some type of formal ceremony for lesbians when they first come out, where we all gather around, celebrate and bestow our blessings on the new warrior to give her courage for what lies ahead.

I brought a truckload of traditional values with me when I became a lesbian, many of which may seem a little out of place compared to what you usually find in the gay community. My goal of a simple life in the country, white picket fence and all, sounds just like it always did with one major exception—I know now that I want to share the rest of my days with a wonderful, capable, strong and loving woman. No man could fill the role I'm casting. In a world where partners seem to come and go at the drop of a hat, I consider myself truly lucky to have found a woman who shares my values, dreams, and sense of commitment. Four months after our first date, we decided we wanted to celebrate our coupling with vows and a ceremony.

As we prepared for our lesbian wedding, I realized how strongly I believe in a lifetime commitment—one where I can truly feel happy and content. Frankly, I've been called naïve by a few of my lesbian friends, including one woman who boasts of having been "married" 27 times.

We encountered some interesting challenges, though, in planning for the wedding—issues that aren't faced by couples organizing opposite sex ceremonies. Our goal was a very traditional type of wedding that incorporated the best of heterosexual customs, eliminating anything that might be construed as servile. We needed to find a church (we wanted a traditional chapel) and minister willing to marry us without imposing rigid limits. One church was willing to perform the ceremony as long as we didn't use the words marriage or wedding, but we found that negative attitude more than a little stifling. Other churches blanched at the idea. After much searching, we finally found the perfect church and minister but we were well aware of how much easier the process would have been if we had been a "normal" couple.

When we went into our local bank to establish a joint personal checking account, the scene was nothing short of comical. The new accounts representative was determined that since we were two women opening a joint account, we must be starting a business together. The idea of a business evidently made it easier for her to understand why we would share the same address and telephone. At one point, the branch manager came over to observe the transaction with some degree of interest. Repeatedly during our exchange, we were asked about the business. Finally, in frustration, we said that we didn't know yet what type of business it was going to be and left the bank.

It was difficult not being able to be publicly giddy about planning the wedding. If we were a straight couple, we would have been able to happily proclaim our intentions in any store in town. Instead, shopping for rings and invitations became an act of supreme diplomacy and our joy remained hidden in furtive glances and sisterly touches.

Being out as a lesbian is difficult—being out as a lesbian couple intent on marrying created a lot of controversy in our lives. Everyone had their own ideas about marriage, it seemed. Straight friends asked us why bother since it wasn't legal. To many lesbian friends, the term "married" only meant "living together until it doesn't work anymore," and this scenario didn't match the depth of commitment we had for our coupling.

Comparing my life now with my years in a heterosexual marriage isn't easy. There simply is no comparison. Perhaps it is sufficient to say that my life then was one of lies because it wasn't safe to tell the truth—about anything. I lived in constant fear of making my husband angry. I juggled finances since there was never enough money, and never let him know we couldn't afford his extravagances. Now, my lover and I talk freely about our finances and it feels not only comfortable but oh-so-right to plan together. There's never enough money, of course, but we both know where we stand.

The old me worried constantly about what everyone else thought and never had the confidence to stand with her decisions on the rare occasions she made any. Now I am out all the time, at home and at work—and I've even been accused of being opinionated and hardheaded. What a change!

Although my family has handled my lesbianism well, many friends have not. My former best friend says I'm going through a phase and hopes I'll come to my senses soon. My partner and I have returned to put down roots in Montana, where I mistakenly thought the friends I left behind would embrace us and welcome us home. For every friend lost, though, many more have come along. The gay, lesbian and bisexual community in Montana is not only alive and well, but significant in number.

There have been interesting questions as friends see me grow happier and more self-assured. One woman approached me at a meeting and said, "I don't know what's different in your life to make you so happy but I'll do anything it takes to join you." I explained that she'd have to start by leaving her husband and finding a strong and beautiful woman lover. She nearly choked on her lunch before she realized that laughing was a healthy response. We're still good friends.

I've even been asked why I would risk my "standing in the community for a life of hedonism." No one can understand how meaningless that "risk" is unless they've made this change. My life is honest now—and balanced. Whatever ingredients were missing in my relationship with my husband, I have in *abundance* in my lesbian marriage.

Tina Buttry

Family portrait, 1985.

Full Circle:
An Interview

WITH ELTEASER "TINA" J. BUTTRY

This interview was conducted by Ellen in the summer of 1994 after Tina heard about this book from her partner, Gale Edeawo, and decided to contribute. Dredging up these old memories was difficult but rewarding as she put the puzzle pieces of her life together for the first time.

Ellen: What was it like for you growing up?

Tina: I can immediately remember a balmy southern night. About six boys and one girl—me—sitting on my porch steps. Most of my preadolescent years were spent in this circle. I was the leader of this group. There was never any verbal vote, it was an understanding we all shared. This was not my doing, it was how they chose to honor me. These were my buddies.

Since I was not allowed away from the porch after dark, we sat on the stairs leading up to my house. Our neighborhood was once the antebellum aristocratic white section of Savannah. The houses were large, beautiful wooden structures, which had since been divided into duplexes. Some of the streets were made of cobblestone, others were covered with soft black dirt and served as our football fields.

For many years, these boys were my closest friends and support system. But when I got to be a teenager things got uncomfortable. I was oblivious to the taboos regarding social interactions with boys. The women in my community were well aware of how close I was to my male friends and began saying things like, "The boys won't like you when you grow up." and "Let the boys win sometimes." I had been allowed to roam the neighborhood. I was self-assured, independent and fun-loving.

I never knew what transpired in the conversations between my mother and these other women, but restrictions were soon imposed on me. I obviously made the women nervous with my freedom. The messages from these women confused me. Why were they saying these things? Since they were telling me I was different and should show different behavior, I joined the girls' crochet circle. But when a football game started, the guys would come and get me and off I'd go. The more I excused myself from the crochet circle, the more confused and ashamed I became. I felt torn; I could hear the women's words and my heart's desire pulling me in opposite directions. The women and girls did not like the real me. I started to hate myself. I stayed in pain throughout my adolescent years. Eventually, I was not asked to sit with the girls. Something was very wrong and it had to do with who I was.

Ellen: So there was lots of pressure to conform?

Tina: Savannah was a town where class structure was rigidly enforced—a legacy from the pre-Civil War days. The Blacks in my town adhered to the antiquated class codes of dress and conduct. People who deviated from this structure were severely punished. An exile status would be invoked, and with it came the loss of all black community ties. That might include loss of membership in a professional or social organization, loss of career, and even the loss of friends and sometimes family.

Therefore, the gay culture in Savannah was very closeted. The women and men who chose to participate in this lifestyle often dated the opposite sex or even married to shield themselves from suspicion.

Ellen: How were you introduced to lesbians?

Tina: I was living with my godmother, Casey, around the time I entered college. After a while I started to put two and two together. I understood all the unusual behavior in our house, like the times Angela came over in the middle of the night and slept in Casey's bed, the physical closeness Cynthia and Casey shared, and the time I was along while Casey bought special lingerie, just for Barbara to wear when she came over for the evening. It all made sense.

Once I knew their secrets, I was invited to the parties. There was never any explanation about this lifestyle. I learned as I went along. When we went to parties, we dressed. There was no mistaking what gender we represented. I was very careful to portray myself as butch, because being butch put me in power, or so I thought. The rule was: the butches are in charge.

Once I went to one of the parties and there stood my third-grade teacher, who also had been my Girl Scout leader. I asked her to dance and felt like I was in heaven. I think I was in shock that I could finally touch this woman. But I didn't consider myself lesbian. I went to the parties because Casey went. I was very comfortable with these women and enjoyed the closeness and conversations. Yet, I felt no attraction toward any of them nor a need to declare my status. They would say: "You're a lesbian and you don't even know it." They were right, but what they recognized, I didn't. Their label didn't turn me into a lesbian.

Being part of that group allowed me to meet other lesbians my age, young women in their late teens and early twenties. There was a naturalness to our being together; our being different was never discussed. Around my second year in college I was approached by Rena, a very aggressive young girl with an olive complexion and a mole just above her lip which accented her beauty. She was seventeen; I was nineteen. We started spending time together, and I fell in love with her. And, for the first time, I felt sexual attraction for a woman.

Rena was cute and playful. When I spent the night at her house, she would attack me lustily with her parents in the next room! I always felt guilty, mainly because her mother was so nice to me and treated me well. Once we were having Sunday dinner with her parents and a member of her mother's church. The conversation took a huge swing and ended on "funny people." The woman said, "I can spot them anywhere." Rena placed her hand in my lap and started rubbing my upper thigh. "Anywhere?" Rena said in an inquiring voice. "I can spot them a mile away," the woman reiterated. Rena turned to me and said, "Boy she must be good." The woman echoed, "Sure 'nuff baby." Later, Rena and I repeated her comments and laughed and laughed.

Although Rena and I dated steadily, we both had boyfriends. When Rena announced that she was interested in sleeping with hers, I told her I couldn't be a part of her life. She was adamant, and so was I. We separated after almost two years. We continued to see each other at parties and always remained friendly.

Ellen: What happened after that?

Tina: Months later I was introduced to R.L. by a mutual friend, and he eventually asked me to go on a date with him. This was the start of something big. He captured me with his boyish charm and his ability to talk about how frightened he had been when he was in, "The NAM"—his name for Vietnam. He was a tender, gentle and emotionally steady person, no highs or lows. By January, 1968, we were an item. There was no great transition, from loving Rena to loving R.L. I had loved them both, each in their own time.

Soon after my college graduation, R.L. asked me to marry him. This proposal came on the tailend of a trip I had made to New York. I was there visiting some lesbian friends who had moved from Savannah and were trying to convince me to join them. Our conversation had centered on Savannah's punitive, straight community and their newfound freedom: to live together, raise their children in privacy, away from prying judgmental eyes. They did seem to have more freedom, but I was not yet brave or strong enough to try to live in both worlds. I still wanted a family, which in my mind included children and a father.

Ellen: How was married life?

Tina: Everything fit together. I was teaching and R.L. worked in the aerospace industry. Then one evening, R.L. received a call from a man who had attended my alma mater. The voice said, "Your wife likes women and I thought you should know." The caller went on, "I'm just trying to do my duty," then hung up. R.L. looked puzzled, set the phone down very slowly. His eyes welled with tears. He relayed the conversation. "Is there any truth to what the caller said?" I spoke very candidly about my relationship with Rena. I told R.L. I had left the lifestyle for fear of being exposed, told him I loved him and wanted to be a part of a family.

I realized the shock this must have created for him and suggested that he take time and space to think. I told him if he found this too much to accept, we could separate or even divorce. I also let him know that this information could not come up in our marriage as a means of manipulation. He insisted that I stay, but the next three days were hell. I thought I would lose my mind. Many terrifying questions raced through my head. I wondered, what would I tell my parents? Would I lose my job if word got around to the school board? Could R.L. and I continue to love each other or better still, would he still love me?

I had given R.L. the power to decide our fate. After days of deep thought, he returned with what felt like a verdict. He told me he was comfortable with my history and that it should not affect our love for each other.

While Rena did show up in my dreams, from that moment on I literally never looked at another woman. Since I thought R.L. was always watching me to see my reaction to other women, if I saw an attractive woman, I developed a habit of looking in the opposite direction. I didn't want R.L. to feel insecure in any way. Feeling I owed him something for his pain, I secretly vowed to never mention Rena's name in our relationship. Over the years we had two wonderful children, Kenera and Rob, moved to the San Fernando Valley, and experienced the ups, downs, and doldrums of married life. At one point we got so entrenched in our roles—I was the family utility person, taking the kids everywhere, R.L. had his career as a computer programmer, and I became the isolated, depressed housewife, which eventually caused me to seek therapy. But our love for the children kept us together as a family. After some time in therapy, and with a renewed sense of self, I mentioned to my therapist who knew of my past that I thought I was a lesbian. "I know," was her reply. I was shocked and angry. I felt betrayed. I wondered who else knew and hadn't spoken up.

My natural self was on the rise again. What a dilemma—I couldn't tell my husband. I felt the pain of attempting to bury myself again. The numbness and the depression wouldn't come as easily as it had in the past. I reminded myself of the commitment I had made to this family. I vowed I would honor that commitment. The question was: How to stay in the marriage and remain alive and true to myself?

Ellen: How did you handle the situation?

Tina: About a year after my self-disclosure, R.L. was diagnosed with lung and bone cancer. My world as I had known it immediately changed. For six months the two of us went in and out of denial. I was angry with the doctors—that they hadn't detected the excess calcium in his blood during his routine physical, angry with R.L. for getting sick, angry at the military for spraying him with Agent Orange. I was fearful of taking care of a very ill man.

We shared numerous tender moments, many hours of crying together. There was no room to understand what was happening to him and to us. The cancer, an unwelcomed guest in our midst, ravished his body. Yet R.L. kept his mind. He didn't fight against his death; he flowed as he always had, with dignity and grace. We lived each day to its fullest and allowed friends and family to participate. There were many memorable moments during those six months, but the most endearing was when our friends of twenty-two years, John and Jeanette, made it financially possible for R.L., Rob and me to fly to Florida for Kenera's graduation. They also went along to help care for R.L. During the ceremony, the college president asked that all the parents of the graduates stand up. R.L. grabbed the arms of his wheelchair and, with his legs and arms shaking, pushed himself up to a half-standing position. Proud tears fell—ours and his. He had wanted more than anything to see his daughter graduate.

After our return to L.A., R.L. lost all interest in day-to-day matters. He passed away quietly six months to the day of his diagnosis. Services were held in Los Angeles and in Savannah. We had been together 24 years. The grieving period was almost unbearable, but I kept going in some kind of fog.

After nearly a year, I renewed discussions with a friend and my therapist about my lesbian feelings. Loneliness propelled me out of the house to seek the lesbian community. One day I hit the women's bookstores. I approached a clerk who gave me a magazine, *The Lesbian News*. She looked me straight in the eyes and handed it to me, saying, "This is the Lesbian Bible. It will get you where you want to go and tell you what you need to know. Read it." Next stop was the bars, where I went hoping to better understand what this life was all about. I met a few people and had lots of good times. I wanted to meet black lesbians, and where I lived that was next to impossible.

I don't know what I envisioned, but it was not there waiting to embrace me and say, "welcome back." Out of desperation I went to a lesbian discussion group, twenty miles away, on a rainy night, using directions I had obtained over the phone. I was so incoherent when I walked into that room that I didn't even see the woman who had invited me to the meeting. It seemed like fate that spoke those pretty words of Lord Byron: "Love is to man's life, a thing apart. Tis' woman's whole existence." Those words, spoken aloud, brought me back to consciousness.

I had once told some friends that I'd marry the first lover I met who could read poetry to me. I didn't expect it to be a woman. I looked around the room to connect a face with that poetic voice, and my eyes fell upon this black woman. I rushed up to her at the break and introduced myself. We exchanged names and numbers. I was never so happy to see a black woman in all my life. I expressed my desire to find the black lesbian community. Her response was: "You have met the right sister."

Ellen: Did you go out with her?

To be a wife and to be dependent on a man, either economically or emotionally or both, is to concede that a woman cannot stand on her own feet, that she must derive her status as a person from the achievements of another, that her connection with the wider world is always mediated by a man. To be divorced or to be a lesbian is to confront the world on one's own, to know that one's accomplishments are of one's own making, and to be fully adult and human.

—Ellen Lewin, *Lesbian Mothers*

Robin Finley, 1961 and today.

From Lesbian Life to Wedded Life and Back Again

ROBIN FINLEY

My journey has resembled a bumpy boomerang ride. I came out in the early '70s, walked down the aisle in the late '80s, and slogged through divorce court in the '90s. There were truly happy moments and devastatingly troubled days in each decade. I have shed my skin for the last time and feel I am now ready to live the life to which I was born.

My youth was spent in Texas where little girls were taught to twirl the baton, though I preferred to take up a toy rifle and re-enact the final days of the Alamo. Somehow I sensed that I would not join my peers as a majorette in life's parade, but I never dreamed how different I was from them. Education became my substitute for being. As a straight-A student I was able to throw myself into schoolwork to keep social life at a safe distance. I had no real interest in relationships and treated high school like a long business appointment. The main objective in my life was to please my parents for whom I was the biggest source of life's satisfaction. I celebrated high school graduation by taking a cross-country trip with my mother in a brand new Plymouth Duster.

Sophomore year of college brought me the remarkable experience of falling crazily for a woman who demonstrated devotional depth by presenting me with her cherished childhood volume of *Winnie the Pooh*. I was shocked by the realization that I was a lesbian, but so overwhelmed with positive emotion that I went with it—all the way to Canada where we transferred our lives to a new university. It was the beginning of eight years of hiding reality from my parents, rarely assigning pronouns to the important people in my life, being generally vague about everything, and thus leaving my parents' dreams intact.

My mother was an unusually militant homophobe. She sensed my devotion to certain "friends" and in turn developed rabid dislike for each of them. Finally, bolstered by the strength of a three-year relationship and great pressure in the gay world to come out, I admitted the truth to my parents. It happened innocently during a weekend visit. My mother was expressing disgust at the homosexual world, placing special emphasis on its sexual activities. She asked what was meant as a rhetorical question, "How can they do that?" Instinctively I replied, "Out of love." That was the confirmation she needed, "My god! You're one of them!" She nearly drowned in hysteria for a solid year. I flew to my parents' home on consecutive weekends, futilely attempting to console them. My mother's sobbing was violent. Family pictures were torn to pieces and thrown into the lake behind the house. My father was quietly and utterly crushed.

Still, I felt strength in my resolve to stand up for my relationship. I was with someone whom I'd fallen in love with before we ever met. She was a gifted photographer. I had seen a collection of her large-format portraits of women which were so exquisitely sensitive that I felt an instant attraction to the artist. We met and indeed fell in love. She introduced me to New York City, and our life was full of the excitement of too much culture.

Over the months following the initial confrontation with my parents, this secure relationship began to crumble, as my lover felt responsible for whatever part she played in my family's dramatic breakdown. Shortly thereafter, while vacationing with friends, I witnessed her in the arms of one of my oldest acquaintances. I learned their affair had been going on over a year.

From there my life continued alone except for adopting a dog to replace the one who left with my lover. I struggled to rebuild something with my parents— a less formidable challenge since I was single again and thus unassigned.

As was my pattern, I escaped to academia where graduate studies substituted easily for reality. I converted every available hour of my life into course credits and netted a degree in record time. Suddenly, during an unguarded moment of leisure time, I met the world's sweetest man in the neighborhood dog-walking park. We embarked on a tender friendship, crying over the women who had done us wrong (*both* of our ex's had dumped us for other women!). Incredibly, ten years after my first relationship with a woman, I fell in love with a man.

We developed a very active and supportive life together. We even rendezvoused with my parents for family vacations. In time my mother ceased to ask for reassurance that everything was "really in place."

Life offered unprecedented momentum. The openness and freedom I discovered in the heterosexual world was amazing. Suddenly I could tell everyone at work what *he* and I did over the weekend. *He* and I alternated families for holiday visits. *He* and I bought a house together. *He* and I could meet for drinks in brightly-lit places which seemed airy compared to the anonymous and smoky atmosphere of most gay bars. *He* and I had a life that everyone openly supported—even my lesbian friends who were somewhat bewildered but willing to condone anything if it meant my happiness. I even let myself wear baseball caps while riding in his convertible without thinking my dyke visibility index was too high. His family embraced me warmly—especially on the heels of the terrible experience with *that woman* before me. His sister offered herself as the sister I never had.

I was known at work as the only staff member who was *happily married*, even though we had yet to tie the knot. I often thought he was one in a billion—the one man I could trust, happily sharing my life without longing for the years spent with women. People often seemed surprised when they met my husband after knowing me for some time—occasionally confiding that they expected to meet a tall, athletic, Nordic type. Instead they were met with a curly-haired, gentle man of slight physique who quietly got a haircut the day after an absent-minded store clerk glanced our way and asked, "Can I help you ladies?"

People loved to visit our home, often commenting on the lightness of the place. He filled it with music and green plants. I filled it with humor and the latest piece of mechanical art I had made. His male dog and my male dog were bored with any struggle for dominance. It was all very unthreatening.

Then, after three blissful years, we committed holy matrimony. That was the turning point in our lives. Before, we had the utmost idealism about our relationship and discussed every little decision in detail. With marriage, assumptions became the rule, and blatant sexism reared its head: If I worked late, I was a workaholic. If he worked late, he was just meeting the demands of his job. It was too draining for him to spend three-day weekends with my family, yet we drove to a nearby college almost every weekend to visit his brother. He greeted the news of the biggest promotion in my career with the comment, "Now, I'll never see you." I found myself increasingly assigned to the roomful of under-stimulated wives at couples' gatherings.

Our backyard fence became the symbol of domestic discord. The first year we lived in the house, when my work schedule was lighter than his, I undertook to build a beautiful wooden fence around our backyard to keep the dogs at home. As my project grew, requiring that I pour concrete and custom cut cedar fencing, I sensed that I somehow embarrassed my husband by doing "men's" work. Visitors to the yard automatically complimented him on the craftsman-ship. I finished half of the yard and decided to put the rest on hold until we could complete the project together. Somehow it was never worked back into our priorities, and I grew to resent him more and more as I stood guard every time the dogs were outside, or waded into a rainy yard to untangle the rope used to keep my dog from exploring the neighborhood.

Once it occurred to me that I felt what I imagined a child with a terminal brain tumor might encounter at Disney World. Wonderful things were placed in front of me, but I experienced them with shallow, transitory enjoyment, real-izing that I was slowly dying, and that decisions were increasingly being made for me by people who knew best. The worst part was that I did not recognize these growing problems. Somewhere along the way, I lost myself to the rela-tionship, the lifestyle. I put aside my feelings because I wanted to belong to that world so much. All of my energy went to keep on spinning the plates of het-erosexual life. My only refuge became gardening projects—an acceptably fem-inine form of manual labor.

Incredibly, during these years, I began to experience strong flashbacks from my childhood when I suffered sexual abuse at the hands of a relative who lived with my family. Even my husband's most tender touch could unexpectedly stir a ghost from the past, causing me to stiffen and cry. He had been blessed with an idyllic childhood and felt unequipped to deal with my increasing complexity. The tension between us grew densely acidic, eroding our bonds, and finally demoralizing my husband to the point that he concluded he was the ultimate victim of my abuse. Once, in a gesture of reconciliation, he paid a fence company to finish my project. The following week he called my father to say he wanted to return my hand in marriage.

Recognizing the seriousness of my situation, I sought professional help and got lucky with the selection of a gifted therapist to whom my opening line was, "I'm here to save my marriage." The rhythm of my weekly truth sessions was tragically interrupted by a telephone call—my mother had been hospitalized with pancreatic cancer. I spent three and a half weeks at her bedside, watching her die with astounding swiftness. Having wanted desperately to be a grandmother, the first words she said to me when I walked into her hospital room were, "If you have a baby now, I'll kill you!"

This death ripped to the quick of my soul. My mother often confided that she loved me too much and knew it was my burden. Perhaps the same could be said of this daughter's love for her. As an artist beyond her time, capable of energizing anything she touched, I admired her. She would rise at 5:00 a.m. to create pieces that were whole by the time everyone else was just getting out of bed. Her implicit youthfulness and striking looks often led others to mistake us for sisters. Beneath it all, however, she suffered from the profound unhappiness that often affects those who are too smart, too demanding, too visionary for their times. Instant accidental death would have been kinder for her than the weeks in which she lay thinking about everything that had been—and would not be—her life.

During the time my mother was ill, my husband called me in the evenings to discuss "our problems." He pressed for us to go to marriage counseling. My brain seemed too full already, so I refused, but suggested he go to individual counseling. Instead, feeling that I alone was the source of our trouble, he more naturally turned to his family for support. When my mother died, they were so protective of him, they did not even send a sympathy card until several weeks later when it became an issue between us. The month following the funeral, his family completed the circling of their wagons and whisked him away on vacation. When he returned, he stayed with friends for several weeks and then asked me to move out of our house. I complied. It was easy. Life was timeless and empty.

I was adrift in my grief. I took my dog and one carload of things and moved into my best friend's house, a lesbian co-op. Therapy sessions continued and were supplemented by a weekly group session with other abused/confused women.

My mother-in-law spent a day with me on neutral turf. "When did you kids start having sexual problems?" "Oh, honey, please give him a divorce. He's sooo unhappy. Set him free." She spent much of the day telling me about her first divorce and the deep depression she experienced in her present marriage until she was able to "gain perspective." She promised that we would always remain good friends, and even expressed an interest in working to have my sculpture shown at her local museum. I haven't heard from her since.

My husband asked his sister to visit for a week to pack up many of my belongings and store them in the attic of our house. One box was labeled, "Robin: Current Things" and contained three women's poetry books, an old letter from my mother, and a Christmas card from my first lover. The "sister I never had" is another figure from my married world who has never contacted me again.

Earth's gravity must have tripled during those months because everything I did required incredible effort. I quit my high-pressure job and spent many hours in my friend's closet crying—an ironic isle of solitude in a gay house.

I consented to an uncontested divorce, though my husband asked me to be the one to go on record as initiating the procedure. The litany progressed, often notarized by the seal of a mutual friend: Complaint for Absolute Divorce, Voluntary Separation Agreement, Consent Order, Property Settlement Agreement, Judgment of Divorce... Lawyers assumed control of dismantling our eight-year relationship.

Initially I said I wanted nothing more than what I came into the relationship with—to the dismay of my lawyer and everyone around me. His lawyer, the sister of yet another mutual friend, undertook his case with her customary efficient vengefulness, despite the cooperative nature of our divorce. Somehow, that rude and forceful woman managed to push every one of my buttons, and I came alive. I decided I wanted to return to my house. I realized it was the closest thing I had to a spiritual center. When I stated that need to my husband, his reply was, "I see you are feeling better now." At that moment, I resolved to no longer subordinate my feelings or needs out of a guilty sense that I was paying my dues for being different!

The journey back was clogged by many legal obstacles. Economic recession depleted any equity in our house, so there was no clear-cut buy out formula. I gave my husband possessions worth three times the home's value for the right to keep it, and I still had to pay thousands in legal fees just to retitle the existing mortgage. Initially the bank that held the loan denied the request because of my meager artist's income (even though at the time of purchase my salary was higher than my future husband's and my solid credit and employment history were the strength in winning the mortgage approval). In order to placate the fears of the bank's lawyer, I asked a friend to join me on the mortgage, and thus, today I only own half of the house.

In wholeheartedly throwing myself into the marriage, I thought it demonstrated deeper commitment to take my husband's name. I also added him to my credit cards. Later, in the process of trying to recover my maiden name, several of my longstanding credit card companies required that I close the former joint accounts and reapply for new status. The subsequent applications—from one who always paid her monthly balance in full—were rejected on the grounds of insufficient credit history!

A year later, I attended my last therapy session. I summed up my experience to the group by thanking everyone for a genuine bargain: Some people seek therapy to resolve domineering mothers; others seek help because they can't let go of their parents; others to confront sexual orientation/gender identity; some people need help with pressures of the work world; many people need divorce counseling; others seek bereavement therapy; and last—but certainly not least—to resolve the aftermath of abuse. I processed all of it for one modest weekly price! I came away with a profound understanding of how fluid sexuality can be when it is exposed to the atmospheric pressure of our society.

Today, almost four years since the divorce, I derive great strength from the gay community. My chosen family is tightly knit. We have marched on Washington; been emotionally overwhelmed in Yankee Stadium with 35,000 fellow spectators at the closing ceremonies of the Gay Games; and vacationed in Provincetown where even the heterosexuals forget to stare at everyday displays of affection between couples of all description.

Today I feel a personal imperative to remind my community of the threat to our existence by radical forces who feed on the tendency to deny ourselves in the very way I did to my family, friends, and—worst of all—myself. I have learned that I must embrace who I am in order to break through my emotional barriers and thus be blessed with the reward of more intimate relationships with others. This is not to say that the ride from lesbian life to wedded life and back again is altogether smooth flying now. Invisible currents still send me into occasional nose-dives which sometimes leave bruises on myself and those who love me, but together we are always learning new ways to read the winds.

Violence vs. Abandonment

PAULINE B. BART

You are a fragmentation bomb that burst
within me
I will spend the rest of my life picking
out shrapnel.

(First two lines of a poem for my first woman lover)

When I was an adolescent my mother gave me Radclyffe Hall's *The Well of Loneliness* along with other scandalous books to read and told me that Eve Le Gallienne was a lesbian. It was my sense that she disapproved of lesbians, but I had little idea why. I had crushes only on my male teachers who adored me. My female teachers for the most part thought I asked too many questions.

I was married at 19. Before being married, I never ate ground beef outside the house because it might be spoiled and my parents always took the "chill" out of my milk. But they had moved to Santa Barbara, California where the culture and lack thereof bewildered me. I had come from Brooklyn, New York, was attending Hunter College (much harder than my graduate school education), and had politics for breakfast, lunch and dinner. I was also not under sexual pressure, at least from my then boyfriend. I had never been in a bar in my life.

I was stunned by California culture shock including the anti-semitism (how can you tell I'm Jewish, I would ask?), the drinking and the sexual pressure, as well as having little in common with the students at UCSB although doing well academically (4.0 average). Then my N.Y. boyfriend accepted all my non-negotiable demands and came out to California to marry me. Shortly before the marriage I was aware it was a mistake because the culture shock had worn off, but I had read in all the marriage and family books in the library that such trepidations were normal, so I was married. The family doctor was called to give me a shot to calm me down because I was "hysterical" on my wedding day. My husband spent much of our honeymoon buying gadgets for his new camera, a wedding present from his aunt, because he preferred it to crystal.

I moved to Los Angeles, played house in a new apartment, had an illegal abortion from which I almost died, attended undergraduate and graduate school while my husband flunked out of graduate school in chemistry. It was only later that I realized the significance of the fact that it was much easier for me to study for and take my M.A. exams because he was out of town, so I didn't have to keep stopping to have coffee with him, making it of course. He was smart enough but not well disciplined.

So I did the only logical thing. I quit after my master's and became pregnant. It was bad enough I was one degree ahead of him. Two degrees would certainly be castrating. I wrote "The Lament of the Castrating Female" shortly thereafter, when the record "Songs of Couch and Consultation" came out. We worried about those things in the Freudian hegemonic fifties (which is why the revalidation of psychoanalysis by women academics and critics in the eighties and nineties makes my blood run cold). I was happy when pregnant because it was the first time in years I was doing what was expected of me, but the bubble broke after I had the baby. While my husband was the one who wanted the child and gooed and cooed at other babies while I was totally uninterested, he resented the loss of my goods and services. He said "Don't think you're so great just because you can nurse a baby," and "Why don't you make cakes anymore?" I remembered that when I met him at the airport and told him I was pregnant, knowing it was because I was "late" and having thrown up the last day of my M.A. exam, he ignored it and continued talking about his parents.

I missed the validation I received as a graduate student and realized, as my mother's shrink had told me shortly after my marriage, that I had nothing in common with my husband. I was a terrible housekeeper, cluttering up a room as I walked through it, although I could cook and garden, because I could read cookbooks and gardening books. I had cooked only when my girlfriend and I would invent dishes such as grape juice and rice krispies omelettes or make fudge.

It was downhill from then on. I couldn't make the transition from superior graduate student whom everyone loved to what I called the loneliness of the long distance mother, isolated in one of those lower middle class suburban tract houses. With no one intellectual to talk to, my intellectual activity consisted of counting interactions on my block to learn the patterns. The variables were propinquity and ethnicity. I also let in bible salesmen just to hear the sound of an adult voice. In Culver City, California where I lived, without a car you were trapped.

I was so hungry for intellectual contact of any kind that I volunteered for a radiation study at UCLA Medical School. They injected chemicals and then radium tracers into me and interviewed me about the effects. I don't remember whether they told me about the possible danger but my husband did. I was so desperate I didn't care.

My husband was an obsessive compulsive chemist and couldn't understand why I, naturally and ideologically a permissive mother, couldn't keep the house clean. My shrink who had been my child psych teacher in whose class I did better than any graduate student he had ever had, (and I was a sociologist, not a psychologist) asked me, "Can't you really keep your house clean for your husband?" I couldn't, without abusing my son—locking him out of the house as the other women on my block did to their children when they had finished cleaning. They would come to my door to ask for a drink of water.

I was physically exhausted all the time, never sleeping enough and my husband made unreasonable demands, for example that I stop at a special bakery in addition to my regular market to get him water bagels instead of egg bagels.

I left my husband about a year after my second child was born (I had thought about it earlier, but I knew my mother would have a psychotic break if I did— she did when I did) and received little support from my neighbors and none from my family. I also had no way to make money and felt guilty about my husband living in a furnished room so I could have the house. When he waited all night with a pitchfork to kill me because I had a date, I felt sorry for him and took him back. He promised to go into therapy. Furthermore, as long as we were separated, I was a "bad girl" and therefore he could have better sex with me.

Shortly after the "reconciliation" I returned to UCLA, my alma mater, and obtained a teaching credential. I hated education courses and the rigidity of student teaching and lesson plans, but I knew I had to have some way to support myself, at least in part, to stay divorced. On my 31st birthday, as a birthday present to myself, I said "I am taking the children to KPFK (a listener-sponsored radio station where I had been a volunteer producer. The work had kept my sanity while I was a housewife, it was a safe place for me). I want you gone by the time I get back." He hadn't spoken to me for several days because I called him a bastard when he bought speculative stock without asking me, and I had begun getting calls to substitute teach.

Being a single mother was the hardest thing I have ever done, and they are still the group I identify with most. There was no good, all-day child care. My daughter's morning nursery school was so Freudian that the teachers wore skirts so that the children wouldn't have gender identity confusion. And I went back to UCLA for the Ph.D. program, first informally while I substitute taught. When I received a Teaching Assistantship and later a National Institute of Mental Health fellowship to study depression in middle aged women and maternal role loss ("Portnoy's Mother's Complaint"), I could attend officially. Had I any idea how difficult it was going to be to get a job, I don't think I would have gone through it. On the other hand, I am too non-conformist to be an agent of control in the public schools, and the other teachers bored me. Besides, what I did and still do best is learn and write. I teach well but not when told what to do.

I received my Ph.D. in 1967 and had a terrible time getting a job. I had two major boyfriends post-divorce while living in L.A. When my ex-husband watched my house every night and noticed the pattern of lights going on and off and then a man leaving, he called me, threatening revenge. This time I threatened to call the police. I learned and now tell other women, "Never feel sorry for your ex (he's not a human being like you) or you won't be able to go through with your divorce if he doesn't want you to."

My first job was temporary at USC in L.A. My second was in the Department of Sociology at Berkeley, where I arrived with Eldridge Cleaver, left with Cambodia, and learned to distinguish tear gas from pepper fog. I was a Lecturer. They hadn't hired a woman in a tenure line position in the "radical" Berkeley sociology department for fifty years. The women's movement was starting. I taught the first undergraduate and graduate courses on women, had another male lover from Holland (who later had to return there) and was in two CR groups, one of older women and one with my graduate students. I knew there were lesbians in the world, but feminist books dealing with the topic had not yet emerged. When a woman approached me at the Women's Center and asked me if I were a lesbian I was taken aback.

When I took a tenure line position in the Midwest in a Medical School, for the first time there were hardly any men interested in me. I was a '60s hippie academic, and they were staid Midwesterners. My next CR group, an Association for Women in Psychology group, was half lesbian. (See "How a Nice Jewish Girl Like Me Could" in *Nice Jewish Girls: A Lesbian Anthology*, ed. Evelyn Torton Beck, for the intervening variables, also known as the details.) The woman I became involved with had just arrived from New York for a post-doc in community psychology in my Department. The feminist psychologists in New York told her to look me up. She was so interested in talking to me that she didn't start home before Friday sundown even though she was an observant Jew. She told me she was angry because people kept trying to fix her up with men and she was lesbian. I said she could pass them on to me, since the few men who were interested in me were really creeps. She started auditing my classes, and we spent more and more time together. She had the kind of analytic mind I look for in all my lovers: she had a degree in Talmud as well as a Ph.D. in Psychology. One afternoon in my office I felt sexual tension between us and we decided to see if it would work. Sometime later (I don't remember how long—she says it seemed like forever because I was afraid my daughter would wake up) I went to her apartment and I lost my heterosexual virginity. I still remember the building she lived in at the time and think about it every time I pass it. I told her how easy making love with a woman was. And she sagely replied, "If it weren't so easy there wouldn't have to be so many taboos about it."

What I appreciated most about living with a woman was the help she gave me with childrearing, and responsibility she took for a substantial part of the shopping. Remember, I had been a single mother for ten years. I didn't have to buy paper towels or toilet paper for a year after she left me. She liked my daughter (my son was away at college) because she missed her younger sister. People remarked about how much better I looked and how much calmer I was. Yes, the sex was terrific. But having food in the house and the intellectual companionship were more important. My male lovers would buy anything I asked them to, would occasionally cook, drive my kids to school or lessons, etc., but it was my responsibility to ask them and remind them.

She left me. We made a few attempts to become lovers again, but she always left. Her leaving me was the worst thing that ever happened to me except for my children's serious illnesses. I still am not over it, and it has been almost twenty years. I still dream about her—last week most recently. We maintained a close friendship for a long time, on and off, depending on whether she felt suffocated (exactly at the point I felt comfortable). I wrote wonderful poetry for her and about her. I also wrote important feminist articles because I was happy in the relationship and cannot write academically when I am depressed and angry.

My female lovers have been my muses, though two out of three were too butch to get naches (vicarious pleasure, usually from children, Yiddish) from. I remember her shouting "I will not be Alice B. Toklas!" (A male lover had similarly said "I refuse to be a psychiatric nurse.") Poet Barbara Ruth once said I am intellectually butch and emotionally femme. I would be better off if it were the other way around. I had always written poetry, but not until I became involved with a woman did I write serious poetry.

My second major lover and I used to cook together, which I enjoyed greatly. She did lots of caretaking. I would never have been able to write the grant which resulted in my study of how women avoided rape when attacked were it not for her. When she went to law school, I realized how much I liked lawyers, and that the feeling was mutual. In fact, since my first lover had a degree in Talmud as well as Psychology, all three of the really significant women with whom I was involved were/are lawyers, and my women's group in Chicago is made up of women law professors and friends. They are one of the few groups from which I have not resigned in disgust. They are, as far as I know, mainly straight but have superb, radical feminist politics.

My second lover was also very helpful and good to my children and my mother. She helped me produce a wedding reception for my daughter, whose wedding I refused to attend because her in-laws left my name off the wedding invitation. My outreach definition of patriarchy is that "If you're not attached to a man, you're not invited to your son's bar mitzvah, and your name is left off your daughter's wedding invitation." My mother figured out that we were lovers just by watching how she treated me, as well as seeing the poster "A Woman Without a Man is Like a Fish Without a Bicycle." The woman with whom I was involved also had been voluntarily downwardly mobile and had learned auto mechanics: she taught it for Women's Studies at the University of Michigan. Not only could she fix everything, which was important because by then I had a condo, but she taught me how to tune a car and about how the engine worked. She also fixed the cars of feminists driving across the country whose cars broke down in or around Chicago. It was with her that I constructed my lesbian identity, because she lived in Ann Arbor originally, and there I was known as her lover and interacted with her circle of friends. Gayle Rubin was a graduate student in Ann Arbor. Ironically, given my current anti-pornography politics, that people would say "Isn't it nice that Pauline is lovers with Marlene so now Gayle Rubin has someone to talk to." And we did, but that was before the sex wars and Gayle becoming a major pro-pornography and sadomasochism theorist.

The third great love of my life is a lawyer, but this time we didn't live together long: although we still love and see each other and write and talk with each other though she lives 1,500 miles away. But I distinctly remember one night she said she was coming over for dinner and I was concerned because I didn't have much food in the house. Needless to say, she had noticed it and brought the food over. I still remember—chicken breasts, broccoli and wild rice. She was in roles (butch or stud) and at first had lesbian but not feminist politics, which I had trouble dealing with (see "My Brief Career as a Femme—Lesbian Ethics"). Her self presentation was supercompetent, and since she was an upper upper-class WASP, I learned survival skills that I needed in a WASP-dominated society which my immigrant Jewish parents hadn't taught me, and which I didn't need before I moved to the Midwest. These women made me feel safe. They protected me from the slings and arrows of outrageous fortune. I don't have any skin, and these women formed a protective barrier in a way that the men I have known have not. They are both competent and nurturant. It is rare to get such a combination in a man. But I don't know if I would have come out were it not for the move to the Midwest and the women's movement, although some of my Berkeley students were lesbian and we discussed fantasies about women.

My third woman lover was much more concerned as was the lesbian community with my daughter's pregnancy and childbirth than my ex-husband and all the other male relatives were, except my son, whom I socialized female.

A major difference between relations with women and with men is physical violence. My husband knocked me down once and threatened me with violence. Two out of three of the men I lived with after divorce raped me and one gave me a black eye. Only one of the women in my life, and she was not significant, unlike the ones I've spoken of above, was physically violent. My threat of ending the relationship brought out the violence, as the battery literature suggests is true for men.

However, on the average, the women I loved hurt me psychologically much more than the men. First, when a man was violent, he apologized. But when a woman left me with no notice or reason, she had all kinds of psychobabble justifications and felt righteous, such as needing "space," that is, if she bothered with any reasons at all. Indeed when my first woman lover left, the women's group I was in, the Chicago Association for Women in Psychology, supported her, and when she returned to me shortly after leaving, they encouraged her to leave me again.

One difficulty with relationships with women is that we do not have a feminist vocabulary of motives to explain their behavior. We can say, "what do you expect from a man?", but there is no feminist equivalent. One has to retreat to the old stereotypes about women being women's worst enemy. I refuse to do that. As I once said at NWSA, I have learned to my sorrow that everything men do women do, but the differences are still statistically significant.

I once asked the most brilliant woman I know why my relationships with men lasted much longer than my relationships with women. She said that men were more tolerant of my dependency needs than women were. Another friend of mine said that when people decided to become lesbian, they knew they were on their own and had to make it themselves. They tried to be independent and invulnerable. My obvious vulnerability displeased them (see Sarah Hoagland's article in *Sinister Wisdom and Lesbian Ethics* about lesbians who "use" their vulnerability. She is talking about me. I don't use it—I am). There is a great deal of what I call Amazon mishigass* among lesbians. I think that this book is supposed to celebrate lesbian relationships and denigrate marriage. My marriage was pre-women's movement; I was a housewife, and I had two small children. How much of it I hated because my husband bored me, how much because he rejected my (technically "our") son and how much because of the situation, I don't know. I liked all my male lovers better than my husband. After all, all my lovers are very intelligent, and if they didn't know already, they quickly learned what I liked sexually. They were all hippies—even the academics. And I did not get involved with physical scientists again because I had had too many conversations about epoxy resins and realized that even though I knew I *should* be literate in physical science, I could take it only in small doses.

I didn't feel like breaking in another man sexually when I came to Chicago. And you don't have to break in a woman sexually, at least I don't. A disadvantage if you are a movement lesbian as I was/am is your ex-lovers show up at the same events you go to. It is very painful. This is not a problem with men.

I like domesticity but don't know about marriage to either sex. I've had lovers who wanted monogamy and then were non-monogamous. I've had lovers who were always non-monogamous but were monogamous with me. It's no big deal for me since I know no one can really replace me, and people will do what they want, whatever their formal arrangements. So I don't think that getting married guarantees anything except wedding presents. I can't stand commercial sports mania, so the probability of finding a woman not interested in our secular religion is greater than finding such a man. In fact, I always root for the opposing team because I hate Chicago sports mania so much.

The phrase "lesbian life" has different meanings now than it once did when feminism was the dominant ideology of lesbians. There are now strip shows in lesbian bars, back rooms where women can have anonymous sex, and bonding with gay men. Until recently there was little concern for men giving AIDS to women—only of people with AIDS already. The heart of the women's pro-pornography movement is lesbian. Sadomasochism and leather reminiscent of Nazis is de rigueur. If that's what lesbian life is, I don't want it. I feel like a dinosaur. I think that as more lesbians have babies, the hard edge will soften. But then they won't have time to hang out with me. It is no accident that lesbian and gay parents were a large part of the group supporting not letting NAMBLA (The National Association of Man Boy Love) march.

In sum, I hated my married life. It is true that men, in my experience, are more physically violent than women. But at this point I can't celebrate lesbian life either.

* Craziness, irrationality, or (slang) *unreal*.

Minnie Bruce Pratt, today and with her young sons.

The Laughing Place

MINNIE BRUCE PRATT

There was the time I got mad and hired a detective,
I told the oldest boy one night he asked for more
stories.   The cluttered supper table rattled and shook
like a car in low gear as he teetered back his chair:

It was spring after the fall I left your father,
and you, in the old brick house with the weedy yard.
He was after me, threats like boots and knives:
Sign the papers or never see your children again.
I was rabbit-scared foolish as if I'd slipped the pen
and, lolloping toward the bushes, heard the man's hands
about to snatch me by my hind legs up and skin me alive.

All spring I was in a sorry crouch, shank-shaking,
waiting.   Maybe he'd get tired of whack, whack
at such stupid red-eyed game.   I went and came
back for nervous visits, sprung free a bit by quick
tizzies of wind investigating the leaves that proved

summer.   Then one day your brother, smooth-cheeked
innocent, crow-eyed, told me about the strange woman
sleeping cozy overnight like a plump feather pillow
in his father's bed.   At first I was just aggravated,

and then, then, I got light-headed, hot-fingered mad at
this young Mr. Buck, laying down the law, do-as-I-say-
not-as-I-do two-faced deceitful man out to lambast
me for doing what I please, doing as he does but with a
different woman. That's how I got hissing mad as a cat

and called the detective up out of the yellow phonebook
into the snackbar red vinyl booth, a little slick-haired
weasel-worded gold-toothed man, *yes ma'm, no ma'm,*
in his lime polyester suit, green as slime, his promise
of a trail, a furtive gleam at the lit, lidded windows
of the house I later imagined him snoozing in front of,
easy in his rusty Chevy as a mole deep in his hole,
asleep in an earth of dirt, and not a speck of evidence,
mud or rock, to throw, nothing out of him for my money,

except the idea of slinking in dark moonlight to pounce.

So that's what I did, with my lover, in her car.   Sneaked
up the street to lurk and look for any pointed proof
I could use, mean as claws.   We snouted, hooted, prowled
around the house, sniffed, flitted, plotted, but rooted
out only this: a bit of courage in my heart, canny,
cunning, that I could outsmart threat.   Which I did.

I went to the hmmph-hmmphing lawyer and said, *Listen,
I have a story,* told until he slowly picked the phone
up and called the man off me with *Careful, stones, stones
and people in glass houses.*   I'd thought I needed hard
evidence, a rock in the hand.   I'd thought the house
was brick.   I'd thought I did not know how to fight,
and all the years after I've believed I did nothing
but tremble there for him to steal, kill, eat my life.

Now, telling you this, I've remembered: Those nights
I slipped around, playing the detective, making my escape.

Then the boy and I at the kitchen table both began to grin.

Finding La Femme

TERRY HAMILTON

I am the eldest of six children and attended Catholic grade school in the 1950's. The first six years, my classmates, like me, were all African American. My neighborhood was on the west side of Chicago and segregated. My street was rows of family-owned two-flat buildings that were neatly kept. Everybody knew everybody else. Parents were just as likely to discipline their neighbor's child as their own. It was like living in a small town within the city.

My dad was a Republican precinct captain and block club president. He worked three jobs: as a security guard, a mechanic on the Northwestern Railroad, and a janitor at Chicago City Hall. My mom worked at the post office. She was a Democrat, an election judge, a tax preparer, and informal legal consultant. When people in the neighborhood got letters from lawyers or college financial aid forms or insurance papers, they brought them to my mom. She would read and explain them and advise people what they should do. She would also go to court with them to explain what was happening. She did not charge for most of these services, but people were always sending gifts of food or clothes to our house or buying whatever raffle tickets, candy or cookies she was selling for the Catholic school fundraisers.

Then we moved and I transferred to a different Catholic grade school. This school was integrated. My classmates were working-class immigrants from Italy, Puerto Rico, Poland, Czechoslovakia, Russia, China, Jamaica, Ireland, and Mexico. My high school was integrated with the same working-class immigrants, and I had many white and black friends.

When my sisters were in their early teens, I watched them go boy crazy. I felt none of the feelings they described. I liked the company of men and boys because they talked about interesting things: politics, religion, philosophy— plans and dreams for making their mark on the world. In fact, one of my fondest memories is marching with Dr. Martin Luther King for housing rights when I was 16 years old.

But the girls around me seemed *only* concerned with boys—how cute this one was, who was dating whom, who had a crush on so-and-so; they went on and on about hair, make-up, and fashion. None of this was of the slightest interest to me. But let an athletic, tomboyish girl walk into the room, and I suddenly got animated. Who is she? I'd want to know. I had all the feelings my sisters described when they saw a cute boy. I'd blush, my knees would get weak, I'd grin and say silly things, I'd get clumsy and drop things or trip over my own feet.

My sisters would gossip endlessly. I personally could not see the point. I was sublimely bored with the comings and goings of my neighbors, schoolmates, and relatives. (Years later when I finally found a lesbian community, I realized I was keen to hear all the details of so-and-so's break-up; who was found in bed with whom when her lover got back early from vacation; how so-and-so met a woman while on a dig in Africa, etc. I found that I could spend hours on the phone minutely sifting through friends' and acquaintances' relationship problems. Woman-to-woman relationships captured my imagination.)

When I got to college, there was pressure to have only black friends. I would walk into the cafeteria and see a few tables of black students in a sea of white tables. I might speak to a few whites but invariably I would sit with the black students. I was rushed by a black sorority and urged to sit-in during black students' protests, but I told my friends I had to be at work—"I can't afford to sit in!"—because I was also starting my family.

I was married at 18 and gave birth to my first son, John, when I was 19 years old. Fifteen months later, Frank was born. All the pressure to marry had come from my family. My parents wanted me to go to college, but when I hadn't had a date my entire junior year of high school, they panicked. They thought I was going to become too well educated and unmarriageable, so they fixed me up with my cousin for the junior prom. When some of my girlfriends saw me at the dance with my cousin, they decided to get me a blind date for my senior prom; this was my first real date. I met my future husband a few months later in the neighborhood. He looked like Michelangelo's David dipped in chocolate, with beautiful, rippling muscles he'd developed growing up on a farm. He'd been on a world tour singing bass with a group called The Radiants, opening for The Supremes. He'd had the experience of women throwing long-stemmed roses and even pairs of their panties on stage, throwing themselves at him at the stage door. I thought he was the most sophisticated man I'd ever met, and I loved joking and teasing with him. Then he told me I was the most beautiful woman he'd ever met in all his travels! Well, that man could talk me into anything with his deep voice.

So there I was, going to college with two babies. I'd get up at 5 a.m., take the kids to Montessori preschool, attend classes, go to work, pick up the kids, make dinner, and study—sometimes until 2 a.m. My husband said I could go to school as long as nothing else suffered. He was seven years older than me and working. When Frank was three years old, I lied about being unmarried so that I could get a tubal ligation without my husband's signature on the informed consent form. The year before my sterilization, I'd had an abortion. My husband eventually found out about these choices and left me. I had enormous support from my parents during my early years as a mother.

My parents had been together 50 years. I was raised to marry "'til death do us part," and to be a good, self-sacrificing mother. Although I went to college, my belief system always put being a good wife and mother number one. I was celibate for three years until I met my second husband. Paul was 13 years older than me and white. We met at an ecumenical conference for lay people interested in doing community organizing in the inner cities.

For Paul, it was love at first sight. I was only slightly interested, but became more interested when he took his clothes off. (He disproved the myth that only African American men are well hung.) After a whirlwind courtship, he asked me to marry him. We had to wait until my divorce was final. The marriage lasted three years. During that time, I tutored Paul so he could pass his G.E.D. We enrolled in college at Southern Illinois University. I was making A's and Paul was making C's. Paul was very angry about my out-performing him. We had moved from Chicago to Carbondale, Illinois. After many trips to the employment office, Paul secured a job as a taxi driver. I waited a year and then went down to the employment office, and I got a job as assistant manager of a team of insurance salesmen. Paul was very angry and threatened my boss and the counselor who placed me. We broke up soon after that when he began a series of affairs. I was celibate and did not date for two years.

I finished my training and became a computer programmer. I had two brief affairs with women that lasted nine months each. Then I had a relationship with a woman that lasted two years. I was celibate for eight years and then in a relationship with a woman for eight years. My parents' reaction to all this was mixed. My Dad was totally accepting of me as he had always been, but Mom took it personally. She was sure she had done something wrong. After she began quoting the Bible to me, we didn't talk for a year. Eventually, when she met some of my professional lesbian friends, she realized I wasn't throwing away all the ambitions and middle-class goals she'd set for me. We even ended up going on vacation to Hawaii once with my lover and her mother, but the story of that trip is a novel in itself.

When I started my coming out journey, I had read separatist lesbian literature. I had two male children under the age of six. Just as I tried to protect them from racism, I sought to protect them from separatists' ranting and raving and exclusion. So I never took them to the lesbian coffeehouse, or the Michigan Womyn's Music Festival or even to parties held in individual lesbians' homes. I talked to many lesbians who had very consciously decided not to have children, who felt that children would impede their personal development. There was a definite anti-child, particularly anti-male child, bias in the lesbian women's community in Chicago at the time.

Yet, I talked about my children when I was in lesbian support groups. On first dates I introduced my sons. I watched closely how my date interacted with my children. If she ignored them, there was no second date.

I came out to my boys when they were six and seven years old. Generally speaking, I kept my nightlife somewhat separate from my life as a parent. The world I inhabited as a lesbian was the world of butch/femme.

Observances of a Femme

The experience of being "the other," a lesbian femme playing to a butch, I find exhilarating, unnerving at times, but always interesting and exciting. Stroking a butch ego is a much more delicate operation than stroking a male ego. The right tone has to be struck between admiration, flattery, and out-and-out lying. Sarcasm—even gentle teasing—may be too much for fragile butch egos. Your voice, as a femme, may be the only one cheering your butch champion on to greater feats. With men, I was never flirtatious. I didn't see the point.

Being in the presence of butch women elicits all my southern charm and womanliness. I enjoy the gallantry, the little attentions, the eye contact, the blushing, the shuffling of feet. I feel moved to cook up a storm, serve and urge additional helpings. I am the consumate hostess—geisha—attentive to their every sigh and shift in mood.

In my socialization as a woman, I had been trained to defer, to serve, to please, to placate, to soothe, to listen, to be patient, long-suffering, and tolerant. In my relationships with men I was all those things, and in my relationships with women I was all those things. My character and my habits did not change because I was relating to women.

Although I experimented with jeans, workshirts, and boots (the dyke uniform), I found that I was most comfortable in skirts, silk, satin, and ruffles. When I'm aware of being noticed by a butch, suddenly, my hair, my nails, my clothes become so important. Color, cut, and feel of the fabric take on new significance.

In conversations with men at parties, I ask leading questions and get them to talk about themselves and then half-listen with a fake interested face I perfected in college lecture halls. But at parties with women, I ask similar questions, and while they're talking, I stare deeply into their eyes, compliment their jewelry and clothes. Years later, I can recount exactly where we met, what she was wearing, what music was playing, and what things she told me that she had never told anyone in her life.

I love double entendres and word play. I love coming on to women subtly and outrageously. If she's not offended, then she's greatly flattered. If she's taken aback or completely bowled over, so much the better. I love to talk about sex—what turns her on, what turns me on. "Do you like to give or receive a massage? Do you like oral sex? Cream in your coffee?" (Very important to know for the morning after.)

I had great orgasms with men, but after a while I wondered, "Is this all there is?" I always felt there was something missing. I could get more satisfaction from talking all night with a good girlfriend than fucking all night with a boyfriend.

Men would accuse me of being frigid or extremely cold-hearted when they would be hot for my body. I became more and more disinterested in sex. I always said I preferred intellectual discourse to intercourse.

After my first sexual encounter with a woman, I found what I'd been missing. Men had gone down on me but it was only a prelude to fucking. They never did it long enough or seemed to be enjoying themselves. They tended to overwhelm me with their urgency to get my pants off and their penis into my vagina. It was so boring. Women would go down on me forever, never stopping to ask stupid questions. (Did you come yet?) Women were not goal-oriented to the big O. Pleasure for pleasure's sake was the order of the day. Lovemaking would go on all day, in many ways, before any genital contact. In the pool, the sauna, the steam room; massages, facials, foot rubs, back rubs, and long slow kisses would go on for hours!

I was never jealous when my husband paid a compliment to another woman or wanted to dance or spend time with other women at a party. When my butch partner tried the same things, all hell broke loose, and I surprised myself at the depth and ferocity of my feelings. I changed from a sweet, gentle girl to a roaring tiger. Later, looking back at my behavior, I am embarrassed. Luckily, my butch lover took it lightly. She felt valued and appreciated. She never did it again in my presence.

With men, I was cool, indifferent—I could take them or leave them. With women I am intensely passionate. I love, I hate, I have dear friends and sworn enemies. I cannot even feign indifference with women. With men, I seldom fought because I felt there were few things worth fighting over. With women, I have intense arguments, bickering, long-running battles and feuds. I'm supersensitive and more ready to confront a woman. I get loud. I've even gotten physical. I'm totally engaged with women. With men, I held back. No matter how much I loved them, there was a part of me they could not touch. With women, I'm totally open, honest, raw, vulnerable, intimate.

When I was with Sarah, my lesbian butch lover for those eight years, she reserved the right to make all the decisions in our relationship such as when and where we would vacation, how we would spend our money, and who our friends would be. In hindsight, two years after the breakup, I can see a lot that I didn't see then.

Sarah looked a lot like my mom. Their personalities were very much alike: mercurial, hot, dramatic, given to temper tantrums, unexpected explosions, illogical demands, fits of despair and rages. It took Sarah a long time to make a decision. She was insecure and ambivalent. It was five years into the relationship that she announced she was ready to marry me. At that point I no longer wanted to marry her.

Nine months into the relationship, the power struggles began in earnest. It was never a fair fight. As with my mother, I desperately wanted Sarah's love and approval. I felt like I would die without her. The more I conceded, the more she demanded.

This was totally familiar. My mother was overbearing, controlling, very demanding. My strategy of escaping my mom's intrusions was to retreat into my head, my books, my fantasies. I learned early to listen closely and parrot back her own words and opinions. I could never win. I gave up early and wore the facade of the obedient, dutiful child. It required less energy. I wanted to leave behind all the yelling and broken glasses.

The first two years of our relationship were quite stormy as we argued over literally everything. But gradually peace reigned as I conceded to every demand. Sarah soon realized that I'd do almost anything to avoid a scene in public. In private, I never raised my voice. She frequently interrupted me when I was talking, and I would shut up and listen to her. If I didn't agree with her, I kept my opinions to myself. In the last three years of the relationship, she stopped calling me by my name and simply referred to me as "babe." The few times Sarah got physical with me she found out that I was stronger. The few times I got really angry, she quickly became placating and appeasing. Looking back, I'm sure I could have won more fights, if I didn't have a defeated attitude at the beginning.

But I have to admit part of why I backed down was because I wanted to retreat from the world of corporate backstabbing, political infighting, sexism, and racism. My ten-year career as a data processing consultant had taken a heavy toll on my physical and mental health. Sarah wanting me to stay home dovetailed with my own unvoiced desire to retreat.

Sarah earned twice as much as I had, so I was well-kept. She took me to see my first Broadway play and Las Vegas show; and on my first trips to Hawaii, Santa Fe, and San Francisco.

My father gave me my first car, my second husband gave me my second car and Sarah gave me my third.

It was really a great fit. I showed love by cooking, cleaning and deferring to Sarah, and she felt loved by being served and deferred to.

Eventually, I left my lesbian butch partner and developed some healthy boundaries through self-help channels. Everyday I grow in self-esteem and self-assertion. At 47, I am like a teenager: experimenting, trying new things, testing myself. I'm changing careers, studying for the ministry. I've moved from California to Hawaii and back again. I've lived alone for the first time in my life. My youngest child is in his early 20's and independent. One of my peak experiences has been meeting a lesbian zen master monk. I'm planning to work with young people in South Central L.A. on their self-esteem and career skills through a buddhist-sponsored outreach program. It's really great to be able to be out as a lesbian, interacting with spiritual people, and working in the African American community all at the same time.

It's Not a Matter of Choice

Nanay Gabriel

I grew up in a small but bustling town south of Manila in the Philippines. I come from a family of 13 children where 11 survived—seven girls and four boys. Being the seventh kid, I've always thought there must be something special about being in the middle—but exactly what that is, I don't know. Maybe it's the reason I'm different from everybody else in my family.

Just like any other town in the Philippines, my hometown is heavily Catholic. Almost everybody I grew up with, largely children of prominent and middle-class families, went to a school run by the Good Shepherd Sisters. Weird as it may seem, I seriously think my Catholic educational upbringing was a major factor in my being a liberal—and eventually, a radical—thinker and mover. It is probably because the nuns in this school were all highly educated and therefore enjoyed intellectual challenges. They encouraged me and their other students to think, discuss, analyze, and debate issues. Their ideas may not always have been politically correct, but they certainly gave me the tools to use my brain in a more enlightened manner. Towards my third year in high school, I was convinced I wanted to be a nun. Years later I realized that much of my attraction to the convent was because of my heavy-duty attractions to some of my religious teachers.

It was difficult to depart from my sheltered Catholic school, but I had to have a university or college degree if I wanted to enter the convent of my choice. At that time I was very much committed to becoming a missionary. I wanted to go to Africa, a foolish idea really, when you consider how much work also needed to be done in my country. I was accepted to a university acclaimed for its academic excellence and at the same time feared (by my Catholic advisors) because of its known liberal atmosphere that supposedly encouraged atheism and communism.

My stint in the university ran smack in the middle of the First Quarter Storm—1969-1972—a very exciting period in Philippine history where the student movement literally kicked up a storm against feudalism, capitalism, and imperialism. I was swept up by this storm and proud to be involved, though as a result, my lofty ideal of becoming a nun was soon swept under.

The First Quarter Storm culminated in the declaration of martial law by President Marcos in September, 1972. I really didn't want to leave my country but under martial law you are either for the dictatorship or you aren't. Since I was strongly opposed and I refused to shut my mouth, I was in very real danger of getting caught, tortured and/or killed just like the thousands arrested immediately after martial law was declared. Because I was young, none of this really scared me personally. But at one point my underground political activities were in danger of being exposed and I had to go into hiding. It was then that I became very scared for my parents.

The military is known to arrest parents or members of families of activists to get those they cannot find. Out of my fear, I agreed to go to Canada where two of my sisters and a brother had become permanent residents. I had a lot of feelings about leaving—guilt for abandoning my comrades, excitement to be going abroad, and fear that something might happen to my family when I was so far away. Somewhere in the back of my head I vowed to return to the Philippines as soon as my parents got settled in Canada with my other siblings.

But it took four years before we managed to get my parents out. By the time they joined us in Canada I was already deeply involved in Philippine solidarity work there and I knew that this work was as valuable as the actual struggle going on in the Philippines. My vow to return was never fulfilled.

A few years before moving to Canada I had one lesbian relationship. This woman was the very first person who ever kissed me on the lips. The kiss sent electrical currents all the way to my groin and to the tips of my toes. It was awesome. *And* it made me very confused. We were so in love yet we knew instinctively that we could not let anybody know. The hiding was very painful. I came out of that relationship swearing to myself that I was never ever going to get involved with a woman again.

It was many years later, as I was building political support for the struggle in the country I left behind, that I met Gloria. Circumstances being very unpredictable sometimes, my relationship with Gloria was somehow partly responsible for my getting married. Don't get me wrong, Gloria and I had a beautiful relationship and we were very much in love. And unlike my experience in the Philippines, we had friends we could share our relationship with. I was really very happy with her. But two years into our relationship, our problems started nagging us. In the middle of all these troubles, she turned around and slept with an ex-boyfriend who happened to be in town. Then she claimed that our problem stemmed from our being too monogamous!

I was devastated. My chest cavity felt as if all the moisture had been drained out and it seemed to creak every time I took a breath. Boy did it hurt.

Gloria's inability to resolve our differences simply fed into my homophobia. It stirred up a deep-seated belief that there was no future in being with a woman. At the same time it stirred up insecurity: why had I never been attracted to men (as I was supposed to be) and why had no man ever pursued me? Maybe I really was so unattractive and undesirable that nobody wanted me—

including Gloria. That was when I decided that if Gloria could get involved with men, so could I.

Unfortunately, or fortunately, I met Arthur. A Canadian, he is a foot taller than me. He is an incredibly wonderful guy, and since I had to prove that I could attract men too, I got involved with him. It was not hard at all. He was smitten the moment he saw me making a political presentation. He was in love with me and open to a lot of things I was doing and wanted to do. He knew I had been involved with Gloria and just assumed I was bisexual. He was even supportive of my desire to continue a (non-sexual) friendship with Gloria.

Arthur appeared in my life when I needed a lot of emotional, personal and political support. My relationship with Gloria was falling apart, and so were my political activities (because in my emotional state, I could not sustain anything). In the midst of my turmoil, I did not have too many people to turn to for support. For one thing, I did not know how to get emotional support. For another, my main conflict has always been between my personal and political lives. They seem to contradict each other.

Two years into the relationship Arthur needed me to make a decision. In a lot of ways he gave me an ultimatum. Either we live together or we split apart. I didn't think I was ready for living together, but neither was I ready for splitting apart. He was my only solid emotional support, how could I give him up?

Living together might have been a much better option, but I knew my family would be very upset if I did that, and I really did not want to hurt my mother. So I said, well, if we're deciding to live together, then we might just as well get married. It's just a piece of paper anyway. But I was kidding myself. It wasn't just for my family. I, too, believed I just couldn't live with a man— I had to be married. I thought that if a guy had this much access to me and my body, then he had better be responsible and be accountable to me in a tangible way. And being married seemed to be the only way.

One of the biggest surprises in my life was finding out how that piece of paper was actually a ticket to an incredible amount of privilege and acceptance. I didn't need to fight anymore. I was legitimate. It was so amazing how everything fell into place. I no longer needed to make excuses about where I was spending my weekends or evenings. I could cuddle up close to my husband whenever and almost wherever I wanted to. Anything was possible and everything was acceptable! I really didn't think much of the privilege of marriage until I saw it happen to me.

I experienced a very comforting feeling being married to Arthur. I felt loved and cared for. I no longer had to carry the whole world on my shoulders. I had somebody to share my anxiousness about changing the injustice in this world. He also had an income which I, as a woman, could never imagine having.

While I tried to just settle down and be content about my marriage, I actually couldn't settle down. On one level I was happy with my husband, but on another level, I missed my women friends. Being with a straight man, I mixed with straight couples. A lot of them were wonderful people. They were all involved in political work — solidarity work — primarily with Latin American and South African struggles and the Canadian labor unions. These people didn't just talk politics, they acted. Arthur never really consciously stopped me from seeing or being with my women friends. However, while Arthur could take me to all his social activities, I really could not take him to mine, because most women's gatherings did not want to include men.

Two years after Arthur and I got married I was in serious trouble. My unsettled feelings never got resolved. They became worse. I didn't know what to do. I felt very unsatisfied—and it wasn't the sex, because we actually had a very good sexual relationship. I felt like I needed something else. I felt like I needed to escape.

Politically, I wasn't being effective. Finally a friend of mine suggested that I come to San Francisco and attend a political school for Marxist-Leninists for three months. She figured that being away from my husband and family, I would be able to sort out my brains a little better.

With much trepidation and a lot of pain, I went to San Francisco with the idea that I would take this class, and then go back to my husband in Vancouver. But the three months turned into nine months and the nine months into two years. Within a month of my arrival in San Francisco, I had an affair with a woman.

Arthur and I still tried to maintain a relationship during that period. He would either come down to visit or spend his holidays with me, or I would go to Vancouver to spend time with him. But the longer I stayed in San Francisco, the more I realized that I couldn't go back. Deep down, I knew I couldn't. I just did not have the guts to tell Arthur to his face.

Coming to terms with my lesbian identity was a very difficult and painful process. If being a lesbian was a choice, I probably would not choose to be one. You have to realize that what I left behind in Vancouver was a very stable setting — one that a lot women are probably wishing for. I was married to a very nice man. Arthur was in love with me and was willing to do anything to make me happy. He was conscious of sharing household chores and responsibilities. He had a high-paying job. We had a beautiful home we were in the middle of remodelling. What more could a woman want? I loved him. Unfortunately, I was not in love with him.

It was three years after I moved to San Francisco that I got a divorce. All through those years, Arthur kept hoping I would come back. He said that what saddened him most was that the divorce papers very symbolically ended our relationship. While it was only a piece of paper and it shouldn't have changed how we felt toward each other, it did.

In 1985 I met Ann, my partner of ten years. An American white woman, she is tall, handsome and beautiful. I met her through my political work—this time in struggle against women's oppression and in solidarity with women of Central

America. I thought it would be another short affair, but somehow loving Ann is different. Our love for each other just seems to keep growing. We go through our ups and downs like any couple, I guess. The difference is, we manage to get through our downs to transcend into another layer of loving. And the more layers we go through, the more profound our loving becomes. The honeymoon never really ends. We are very happy with each other and we intend to have a big celebration to mark our ten years together. Right now we're also talking about having babies. I'm in the process of trying to get pregnant—a little late, considering I'm 45, but I can only hope it works.

As a Filipina, I'm aware that I'm not white and that English is my second language. I understand it very well. I read, write, speak, think in English, but I know that no matter how good I am at it, it's still my second language. And like any non-white immigrant woman or person in this country, I feel I always have to be careful. Being a lesbian and a Filipina means I fall in that catch-all term "lesbian of color." As an immigrant lesbian I find that lesbians born in this country have no patience for bridging the gaps in our differences or learning about our similarities. While I can say that of the lesbian community, I believe it is but a reflection of the general American society. While there are a few who try to understand and learn about other countries and other cultures, I think a majority of Americans are very provincial, if not insular.

I try to understand the issues of lesbians, particularly lesbians of color in this country, as some of them try to understand the idiosyncracies of my culture. I know I am subjected to as much racism as any person of color in this country. However, I did not grow up in a culture of constant racist attacks (subtle or outright), so I can't speak for those who have. I can support them in their search and struggle for justice, as I hope that they can at least understand our differences and commonalities.

As for the Filipino community in general, I stay away. I know the community thinks homosexuals are an abomination and a gay son or a lesbian daughter is an embarrassment to the family. That's where my internalized homophobia comes in. I don't seek the community out. Right now, I have only one close Filipina lesbian friend who grew up in the Philippines like I did and I know a few other Filipina lesbians who grew up here.

It is not important to me that I go out there and look for my Filipino community. It's more important to me to be among people who, one way or another, are a little more liberal about my being a Filipina lesbian. It's sad, I'm still not out to my family. I think they probably know, but it's not something we talk about. They have met Ann and they like her a lot. They know we've been together for a long time. As to how they interpret that, I don't know. I haven't stepped out there and said, "Hey, she's my partner." I think they accept her as long as I don't talk about it. Maybe one day I will tell my Mom, but really I don't know.

Shirley Knight-López, 1994, 1957.

"Haciendo un lugar seguro para todos"

SHIRLEY KNIGHT-LÓPEZ

My mother was a farmer's daughter raised in California's Central Valley. She dropped out of high school in her senior year to help support the family. I feel like crying when I hear her tell this story—it was so painful to her. My dad graduated from Astascadero High

School and worked on local farms as a laborer. He had the potential to be a great engineer but it never occurred to him that he might go on to higher education. We lived in the tiny bicultural town of Santa Margarita when I was born on January 28, 1940. It was during the war, and my father was very discouraged when he couldn't get into the armed forces because of his poor eyesight. Both my mom's parents and my dad's parents lived in our town—I was surrounded by a lot of love. My father's mother used to hold me on her lap in the yard and teach me the Spanish names of the animals we saw: *perro, gallina, gallo.* The soft accents of my *tías* and *tíos* have remained with me all my life.

But the major part of my time was spent with my mother's parents, whose yard abutted ours. My grandfather was the local lawman. It was the fulfillment of his lifelong dream when they moved to a farm outside of town. Although I was just three years old, they took me with them. That farm was my life. I followed my grandfather around all day long. I just knew that I would be a farmer like him and someday it would be *my* farm. When we lost it in a lawsuit in 1949, it was the death-knell for my grandfather. He died soon after we moved back into town.

My grandfather's death was the beginning of a new and different life for me. My grandmother had to go to work on the Carrizo Plains as a live-in harvest cook and couldn't take me with her. I lived in several different situations but finally moved in with my mother and younger sister in San Luis Obispo, where I began junior high school. My parents had divorced but remained friends. Soon after, my grandmother contracted a fatal nervous disease and died a terrible and lingering death—though her friends all said she "died of a broken heart."

My mother remarried and moved to Southern California. My sister and I joined her as I started the eighth grade. We eventually settled in Anaheim, where I attended high school. I was a very lonely, confused teenager. I knew that I was "different," but I didn't know why. I was a Christian and very aware of all the warnings about sex, so I was careful how I carried my books, how I crossed my legs while sitting, and in my relationships with both boys and girls. I felt if I ignored what I thought of as my tendencies, I would somehow turn out okay. I was terribly shy, and afraid to form any kind of close friendship with girls. When I was seventeen, I married the first boy who asked me, thinking that marriage and children would "fix" me. I was anxious to prove that I could be a biblical (read *submissive*) Christian wife and mother.

What a mistake! For thirteen years I struggled to be the perfect housewife and mother. But the man I married was a possessive, overbearing dictator whose inability to provide for his family eventually drove me into the workplace. There I discovered that, although my home life was a continual frustration, in the semiconductor industry I could be a successful and respected individual. At home my position was that of intercessor between my four children and their often abusive dad. I was constantly trying to feed their intellects with books, field trips, and philosophical discussions; it seemed he was more often *anti*-intellectual, proud of his southern poverty origins. We were in continual conflict. Disagreement over the Vietnam War was the near-fatal blow.

In the middle of this mess, a loving woman with whom I worked held a mirror to my eyes and I realized what I had denied all my life: I was a lesbian. She wanted to help me make a new start, to give my children the boost they needed for security and peace. How I underestimated my ex-husband. The day I moved out, he stole the children and obtained a court order to prevent me from locating or seeing them. He divorced me and succeeded in turning my children against me for years. I also lost the house (which I had gone to work to buy) and nearly all my possessions. It was a nightmare from which it took me years to recover.

I decided to make a new life for myself, one that would contribute to society and give me back a little of the self-worth that I had almost completely lost during the time of my divorce. I went to De Anza College and UC Santa Cruz, and obtained a bilingual teaching credential. While earning the credential, I reclaimed my own Latino heritage. I worked hard to get it back. While my grandmother spoke Spanish, my father and his brothers were forced to speak English in school. Since my Anglo mother raised me, there was really very little Latino culture left for me. I tried to get some of it back, to learn the language and be as culturally sensitive and responsible as I could be while I was teaching in Spanish. I went to work for the Pájaro Valley Unified School District, and I've been there fourteen years, teaching bilingual language arts and science. It's not just a job, but a potential for great enrichment.

When I came out in 1970, I had no idea what it really meant to be a lesbian. I only knew that, for the first time in my life, I felt true love and attraction in my mind and body. The immediate impact on my life was tragedy and loss. The damage to my self-worth was horrendous. I believed that strangers on the street could see what a wretched and perverted creature I was. The tremendous guilt that I felt for having plunged my children into the snake pit their home became without me has taken me years to work out. Eventually all of my children came back to me, and they now realize what a twisted soul their father is. But for years they were deprived of my presence when they needed me most, and I never got to see them during their precious teen years. All because I came out during a time when the courts couldn't see past my sexual orientation to my worth as a loving mother and a decent human being.

I have always taken the hard road. I am known in my family as a person who makes life more difficult by choosing to fight. I started out as a youngster fighting for social justice. It became a habit. But like most lesbians of the time, I hid who I was and worked on other issues. It took me a long time before I decided I had to be more honest.

I was *forced* out of the closet in the divorce court. But my next steps were deliberate ones. After years of hiding, I came to firmly believe that until more of us are visible, we will continue to suffer the bigotry that we are now seeing in all areas of our lives. I told a few selected colleagues of my secret, and I told my principal, a sensitive and supportive man. I advocated for gay, lesbian, and questioning students in my district. As the district AIDS specialist, I trained teachers in inclusion and sensitivity. When a bigoted teacher in the district outed me in the local newspaper, it was no surprise to most of my colleagues. The surprise for me was the amount of loving support it generated in the district and at my school site. When my life partner and I decided to celebrate our commitment publicly, we invited many of my colleagues and announced it in local papers.

The next step in my coming out process was to discuss it with my students. Although a difficult one, this was a necessary step for me, because part of my dream is for adolescents to have role models to give them hope for their own lives and futures. I recognize my responsibility to be a role model for gay, lesbian, and questioning youth as well as for young women and Latinos.

I chose the class that I had the most rapport with; we had already talked about a lot of sensitive things. I said, "It's a burden in my heart that so many people are being hurt because they are gay or lesbian, especially teenagers, who fear being hated because they are gay." I then explained that I was one of many people trying to help gay youth. I asked how many students knew a loved one, family member or friend who was gay or lesbian. About a quarter of the class raised their hands. Just then, a student burst out, "They should all be killed!" I asked, "What makes you feel that way? Why are you so angry?" When he replied, "They rape kids," I responded, "Well, I am a lesbian, and I don't rape kids." You could hear the class gasping. It was just so interesting. There was a physical reaction. I then told them "I am a lesbian. I am just like everyone else. I have kids and a family. I love them and they love me. I have someone who I love and live with. I am just like you. I have the same feelings, the same dreams and hopes. And I am not the only one. There are lots of teachers, even other teachers at this school...who are gay or lesbian. In fact, maybe the person who brings your mail or the grocery person...anyone around you could be gay or lesbian, but they are afraid to let you know." I then told the class, " I am willing to answer a lot of questions about my life, but I won't answer real personal ones." The students showered me with questions. Every so often I would ask them if they wanted to continue the discussion or move onto a new topic. They replied with a resounding, "Let's keep talking!"

I could feel them warming after that first horrible shock. A couple of kids said something negative, but all in all they were very curious, positive, and respectful. They wanted to know about sex. I was ready for that because I teach about sex in this class. In the context of AIDS education I teach about the three most common ways people have sex and how much risk there is in each one. So I went on to this and said, "women can do this together and men can do this and men and women can do this" and they understood. Then someone said, "Teacher, do you do those things?" I replied, "I won't answer that. It's too personal, but now you understand what lesbians and gay men can do."

The next day, at the beginning of class as usual, I asked my students to write in their journals about the previous day, without reminding them about our discussion. Some students didn't even mention the event, while others wrote at length about it. The following is one example:

Al principio cuando me dijo, yo no podía creer eso. Yo pensaba que las lesbianas eran de otra forma. Pero ahora se que son personas normales. Maestra, muchas gracias por enseñarnos esto. La apoyo mucho con sus sentimientos. (At first when you told me I couldn't believe it because I thought lesbians were different. But now I know that they are normal. Teacher thank you for teaching us this. I support you with your feelings.)

This year I am going to come out to all my students early in the year. I am going to put it out there and see how it goes. I believe that gay, lesbian or questioning students need to hear that they are okay; otherwise, we are killing them. If they turn to drugs, alcohol, or suicide, it's on our hands. I will always work on inclusiveness in the curriculum. Teachers who don't support gay youth are not mean-spirited—they are just ignorant. Once you educate teachers about this minority they just can't help but give support.

The rainbow flag on our classroom door is not a "gay" flag, but a symbol of peace and harmony among all people, gay or straight, black, white or brown, boy, girl, man or woman. And it says "Este salón es un lugar seguro para todos"—"This room is a safe place for everyone."

South Asian women who may be lesbians are compelled to submit to heterosexual marriage. A few who cannot face the prospect and feel they have no options have been known to commit suicide together, their tragedy reduced to a brief sensational item in the newspaper column devoted to sundry crimes.

—Anu, from "Sexuality, Lesbianism and South Asian Feminism," in *Between the Lines*

JoAnn Loulan when she first came out and with her son.

One of The Girls:
An Interview

WITH JoANN LOULAN

It was in the late fall that Ellen and Deborah drove through the burnished oak-studded hills of Portola Valley to JoAnn's psychotherapy office. JoAnn flung open the door, greeted us with her disarmingly femme smile, plunked into a flowery overstuffed chair and, with little prompting, began this account of her years before and after marriage.

Deborah: So, JoAnn, tell us about your adolescence. Did you date boys?

JoAnn: Yeah, I dated boys. I am one of those lesbians who didn't know I was a lesbian, didn't think I was different. I was one of the girls.

I played with dolls, I dated boys. I made out with boys. That was not a problem. But there was always something missing until I came out. But of course I didn't know until I came out, right?

So, going back to then, I was a popular girl. I dressed right. I knew how to do my hair. I wore girl's clothes and that was all right with me. I didn't fight dresses or slips. I loved dressing up.

In fact, my mother was a sort of dykey kind of straight girl who was much less "frilly" than me. I mean, she had short blonde hair, blue eyes. She always had this Marilyn Monroe figure—big breasts, a little waist, and big hips—which in those days was very in. She used to wear low-cut bodices so her cleavage would show—which was horrifying to me since I was an uptight Catholic girl. So she was very sexy at the time in the sort of male traditional sense. She didn't say anything off-color or anything, but she wore tight skirts and had very sexy energy, lots of sexy energy.

In the last two years of high school I really didn't date anybody. I was upper-middle class. I was one of the really popular kids so I could be a girl and I didn't have to date but I still fit in everywhere. So like when the dances came along, I just got some guy to go with me. I could do that. I'd say "hey, why don't we go to the dance?" And he'd say, "hey great." I would usually pick one of the cute, popular boys. Sometimes they would ask me or I would ask them, but it wasn't like a date...you know what I mean?

Ellen: You didn't get into intimacy?

JoAnn: I did have a boyfriend for the first two years of high school. We were very tight, kissing and making out and necking and all that. Fondling. But we never had sex. You see, this was Ohio in the early '60s. But after I broke up with him, I just floated through the dating scene. I was always one of the major organizers of dances and other school activities, so I had a role. I didn't have to have a real date. I remember the senior prom. I asked this guy to go to the prom and all we did was table-hop. We got our pictures taken. We goofed off, making faces. None of us thought it was odd, clearly, I was not uptight; he thought it was a riot. We'd ask other people to dance. We'd jump into people's dancing, and you know, that just wasn't done in those days. Because it was really that boy-girl formal. You went and you only danced with your date.

Deborah: What was happening with your girlfriends? Were you tight with girls? Did you have any glimmerings of attractions?

JoAnn: None. No attractions. But girls were my life.

Deborah: They were your dear friends, but it never occurred to you to be sexual?

JoAnn: It never came into my mind, but I wonder how much of that is because of my Catholicism. Because I never thought to masturbate in my whole life until I was in my early 20's. You know, I learned about masturbation in sex lectures after college. I was like "Masturbation? What's that?" So sex with girls never occurred to me. But we certainly spent all our time together—me and my girlfriends. We'd ride home on the bus together. We'd hang out if we lived near each other—although we lived in the country so it wasn't as easy, especially on school days. But then we'd be on the phone all night long.

Ellen: So it was a crowd of girls? It wasn't one particular friend?

JoAnn: Yeah, I always had about four best girlfriends who I'd talk to in sequence on the phone. I'd tell everything to all four of them and then hang up and do my homework and go to bed. We'd spend the night at each other's houses, we'd have slumber parties. I never played doctor or practised kissing. The only thing I did do was with my girlfriend, Linda. Linda's father got *Playboy*—which was quite scandalous—so Linda and I, we would sneak his *Playboy* and sit under her vanity table that had a little curtain around it and look at the *Playboy* pictures. I remember that very distinctly.

Deborah: So what happened after high school?

JoAnn: Around the time I went to college, I had started dating a boy from home. Then I went away to Northwestern, outside of Chicago, and he went to school in southern Ohio, so we really weren't around each other much. He wanted me to have sex with him, but I wouldn't, so he broke up with me after a few months. But when I first went to college I was going steady with him. As

I look back on it, it was a wonderful excuse. I didn't have to date. Everybody kept saying to me, "Oh, come on, you've got to break up with him and go on a date here." It was perfect. I wonder how many lesbians did that?

Deborah: So having this out-of-town boyfriend was a protection for you?

JoAnn: Right. In those days people weren't so mobile. I'd never been on a plane. We didn't fly back and forth like kids do today. We didn't drive back and forth at the drop of a hat in the midwest. So I didn't see him until Thanksgiving. He broke up with me then and I sort of pretended I still had him when I went back to college. Not so much from a broken heart. I really see it as protection. And that it answered all the questions.

Deborah: What an interesting parallel to marriage. Marriage as protection.

JoAnn: Isn't that the truth? Eventually I started dating lots of boys. Lots of boys were asking me out. But I wouldn't have sex with anybody.

Deborah: And what is your sense? Was it some combination of your Catholicism and the times, or...

JoAnn: Well, now when I look back, I don't think I wanted to have sex then, although I later had sex with boys and liked it. A lot of it was Catholicism. A lot of it was the little town I grew up in. I thought if I had sex, everybody would be able to tell, and the boys would spread it all over. I didn't think it was right to not be a virgin when you got married.

I got involved with a boy when we were in college, and I did think I was going to marry him. His name was Stevie. He was Jewish. And he had a mother who he said would go absolutely berserk if she found out about me, because I wasn't Jewish. He never even told her about me. He went to Europe to medical school, so I went to Europe when I graduated college, and we toured for several months. We lived together and did all that. Then we came back on the plane together. His family lived in New York. I was going to change planes in New York and go on to Ohio. I had a five-hour layover. Our plan was that he was going to go home, get rid of his stuff, come back and wait with me—he didn't live that far from the airport. He never came back.

Oooh, and I spent an hour searching for him when I came out of customs. We had just been in separate but parallel lines—he just vanished. His parents were waiting for him; he was going to introduce me. We had a wedding planned; he was going to tell them... I instinctively knew what had happened. I went screaming around the waiting room. I'm sure people thought I was totally insane. I left all my bags, all the gifts I'd brought home from Europe. I just left them at Kennedy Airport. God only knows why they weren't stolen. I'm screaming through the airport, "Stevie, where are you, you fuckin' mama's boy. I know you're in here, you fucking baby, Stevie! You're afraid to introduce me to your parents because they're gonna know I'm a shiksa." I had gone literally insane.

Deborah: So Stevie was the man you almost married. How about the man you *did* marry?

JoAnn: I was done with college, I had done my requisite trip to Europe, I'd come back home. My parents' marriage was falling apart; they were getting divorced. I couldn't wait to get out of town. I didn't want to go back to Bath, Ohio. I soon figured that out. It was an internal mandate. There was a voice in my head screaming "Get out of town." I was in a panic. Partly because I'd been dumped. I was more mad than anything. And interestingly, in terms of the prospect of getting married, I was very relieved. I thought, "Great! I don't have to do that. I'm out of here." My mother was much more disappointed than I was because Stevie was going to be a doctor. He was going to be rich.

So I went back to my college town because I had created friendships there. I had surrogate parents there who were ten years older than me who I'd lived with in my last semester of college. I went back and lived with them again. Even though they were very groovy, very hip—we all smoked dope together—they were really invested in me getting married.

So I met the boy next door who was staying with his brother for the summer. His brother and soon-to-be sister-in-law had gone to Northwestern with me. He and I became lovers and lived together for a year. This was the first time I had formally done that and told my parents. We were hippies and had this wedding in a park with a "minister" who had sent in ten dollars for a license. It was all quite '60s and cool. Our parents and my old friends from Ohio were a little stumped, but we had a blast. We moved to California, opened a clothing store, and I made close friends with lots of women. I joined a N.O.W. consciousness-raising group. Everyone in that group eventually got divorced or came out or both.

My husband had affairs the whole time we were married, and I didn't know it until after our separation. We separated mostly due to his immaturity and, as I know now, his marijuana addiction. That's how I was able to get out of the marriage.

Deborah: What was your marriage like? How did you get along with your husband?

JoAnn: We actually got along quite well for the year we lived together and much of our three-and-a-half-year marriage. He and I had a lot of laughs. He was three years younger than me but much more infantilized than that. Very wealthy, he'd gone to rich boarding schools, dropped out of college because he was a hippie. But, you know, dropped out of college with a fully-equipped Volkswagen van, and never wanted for money. He was always mommy's darling. He wanted to give me a big diamond when we got married, but I said "no" (JoAnn makes gagging sounds), well, because of South Africa, diamonds were very bad karma. I never took on any of the trappings of that wealthy family. I never thought of his family as one I could be attached to, though I did get close to some of the kids, and especially to one sister-in-law, who, by the way, has come out, too. So now our ex-mother-in-law feels vindicated because both the divorces were from lesbians.

Deborah: Why do you think you got married?

JoAnn: Well, see now, back to my surrogate parents. In those days, by that time, you could certainly live together. But they really started pressuring me. I kept saying "I just want to live with him," and they kept saying, "You know, to make a real commitment you have to get married."

Deborah: Do you have a relationship with your ex-husband?

JoAnn: No. No contact. Of course, he'd done me wrong kind of thing, you know what I mean?

Ellen: What happened after your marriage ended?

JoAnn: I dated men occasionally after that, but I never really had any relationships. Then I got into graduate school. During graduate school, I took a women's studies class. I'd never been in women's studies. It absolutely blew my mind out. Absolutely. I was, like, undone. And I absolutely decided to be a lesbian before I'd had any...

Up until this time I'd had just one sexual romp with a woman friend of mine for about an hour and had gotten very excited about maybe being bisexual. I was definitely a feminist by this point, certainly, but I had no concept of being lesbian. Then I took another graduate course in human sexuality. One part was an all-day class taught by Tee Corinne and Pat Califia. It was incredible to hear about lesbians in a graphic, sexual way. That was it with me and men. I never dated men again. But I had also never really had sex with a lesbian or done any of that. Then, at the end of the women's studies class, we had a party at my house. I had a three-way with two other women in my class. Neither of them were lesbians. All three of us are today. (JoAnn chuckles.) That was really a trip.

Ellen: How was coming out?

JoAnn: I didn't feel bad about a thing. I was in celebration. I have been in celebration from the second I figured it out until today. I was so lucky because I owned an import store—I could dress however I chose. Of course, every lesbian had to dress the same way back then. I had to cut off my hair and get rid of all my dresses. I had to wear jeans and T-shirts and flannel shirts and everything. Interestingly, at the store I sold dresses.

Deborah: What would have been different if you had stayed in Bath, Ohio? Would you have come out?

JoAnn: I have had that discussion so many times and I think probably not, unless something had happened where I was suddenly in some situation with a very aggressive lesbian. That's the only possibility I can think of. If some lesbian had come on to me—I'm very impressionable, which I see as a positive trait—come on to me very strongly and made a sexual pass at me, I think I may have figured it out. But I don't know where those lesbians would be in Bath, Ohio. Although one of my sixth-grade teachers was obviously a faggot, and my high school English teacher was clearly one, too, and the women who ran the dog kennel had to be dykes.

Deborah: Had you ever heard of lesbians when you were in Ohio?

JoAnn: Hardly. When my mother and father got divorced, my mother took an apartment. I was out of college. My mother lived next-door to two of what she called "those kind of women." I asked her, "What kind of women?" And she said, "Well, you see, they're together. They are in the same apartment together." And I said, "I've shared an apartment with some girls." And she said, "No, no, no, no, JoAnn. They are, well, they're lesbians." I had never heard the word.

And then, of course, I found out Johnny C.'s mom had left his dad. Well, I never knew why. Clearly, when I look back, this woman is a #10 butch dyke. Later on when I was out of college, I learned she'd run off with a woman in Florida. When her rich husband choked her off at the purse strings, she came home. Of course, back in those days, she didn't think she could make it on her own. Once we were at a party celebrating something and she came up to me and said, "See what John, Sr. gave me to come back?" It was this huge, giant diamond pinky ring, which was a complete man's ring. I look back on it...(We all break into laughter.)

Deborah: What do you see as the trade-offs for you? When you tell the story, it seems it was clearly wonderful to come out, but do you now see trade-offs?

JoAnn: I see trade-offs now when I go back and compare how my heterosexual counterparts—meaning the kids that were brought up in my same class in my same time period—are faring. When I see their economic stability, the lives they have seem settled, decided, clear. They don't have to work with their children's homophobia. There's the whole societal stress factor. My relationships aren't regarded as anything in particular. You know, when my lover and I of five years broke up, my son was just five. She and I hadn't had the baby together but she came into his life at six months. My brother was completely unconcerned about our relationship ending. No one in my family except my close cousin ever asked me about what happened. No one ever said a thing to me about it. Not even my aunt and the people I've remained in relationship with.

Another trade-off I see is around basic rights. I am one who believes that lesbians ought to have the legal right to get married and we ought to fight for it.

I've seen a lot of biological moms keep kids from staying in non-bio moms' lives when they break up. I see that as one of the travesties of homophobia in our community that I have issue with. The child loses and the non-adoptive or non-bio mom—the non-legal status mom—has to fight for every single inch she gets. And the bio moms, in all the vitriol and negativity of the breakups, or simply because of the conditioning of the culture, have the power and sometimes keep it. So as a mom, I think kids ought to have the rights that marriage affords, and the non-legal status mom ought to have legal status. Some of the perks of heterosexuality are these rights, not to mention the other benefits—you know, tax benefits, insurance benefits. We deserve to have all those benefits. I believe in the institution, as it's mandated in our culture, the privilege of the institution that affords children legal parents, inheritance rights, ownership rights.

Deborah: You mentioned acceptance. I'm thinking of the social and psychological ways that marriage provides a validation. That it gives a couple support from the outside, that it helps the people in the relationship take their commitment seriously.

JoAnn: Yes. My friend went to her cousin's daughter's wedding recently. There were 700 people in the church, and they did this little ritual after the couple was married. The minister was there with his arms around the couple and said to the congregation: "Who here will support this union?" 700 people in unison said "I will." What an incredible mandate.

And of course it has its drawbacks because a legally married couple has a hard time getting out if they want to get out, but the support is unbelievable. They get a washer and a dryer and the family helps them out if they get in trouble and just on and on. Even if you don't like the spouse and you're from the other family, you still support the union, which is interesting. The union has a whole life of its own.

Ellen: And then there are the effects on the kids. Anything different from the typical Mom/Dad nuclear family is suspect. So any families outside of this marriage "norm," like single parents or lesbian parents make kids feel weird.

JoAnn: Oh, yeah! As a lesbian, I don't let them intimidate me; I don't feel left out because I have my own scene as a lesbian. In the several years that Gardner's been in school, I've dated and haven't had a lover live in except for a few months. That living in time was hard on my son—my lesbianism was more visible then—but we talked about it out loud and he survived it. It is difficult, especially with children, to keep standing up to the norm and fighting. I am always coming out to teachers, administrators, parents. Then I have to make sure my lovers have gotten respect from my son, his peers and the community. Also, if you don't have a long-term relationship with one person, it is even more awkward. Having one "love of your life" is the norm. Thus, as a lesbian with varied relationships, with no long-term partner, people in heterosexual community don't know how to act towards my lovers. In lesbian culture, we tend to put ourselves down for that. I feel it's just part of our creativity, part of our cultural standards. We aren't willing to stay in relationships that aren't fulfilling and intimate. Lesbian relationships, I think, demand a kind of closeness that heterosexual people find with their same-sex friends, not usually from their sexual partners. We want both functions met in our lover relationships which makes the pressure intense.

In my neighborhood in California—if you can believe it, even in the '90s—the women don't work outside the home; there's this whole enclave of women whose husbands support them totally. They are completely financially dependent. I have no idea what these women would do if they got a choice.

There is a group of moms I connect with. We send our kids off on the school bus and then we sometimes spend an hour in the morning walking around our neighborhood talking about stuff. All of these women have difficulty with their husbands. They tell me everything. It's very interesting. There's one woman who has two sons and then, of course, a husband. One day she says to me, "Can I just sit in your house for a while? I hate men." Isn't that interesting? Most of these women feel stuck. In fact, that particular woman was going to get divorced a couple of years ago and she said, "I can't afford to get divorced. I have not worked for ten years. I am a school teacher. Where am I going to get a job?"

Deborah: Just for the hell of it, what would you see as the difference between being a wife in a heterosexual marriage and then in a lesbian "marriage."

JoAnn: For one thing, as a lesbian I don't feel any concerns about the power differential whatsoever. I absolutely hold my own, powerwise. I don't think I feel any fear about leaving a relationship except the feelings, you know. There's the dilemma of loving this woman and how to disengage. I don't feel any stricture. I mean, definitely, when I was married I had to think about how I was going to get divorced; it was such a big legal hassle.

There's that freedom in lesbianism in that I'm not seen as a role. I am not a wife. So, therefore, I don't have to "do anything." I don't have to cook, I don't have to clean. I don't have to be the one to take care of the kids. You know, my son is 12. I have had partners who have participated at different levels with my son. Every single lesbian household has a new and creative way of doing it. It's like an endless sea of combinations which offers lesbians a most amazing freedom and joy and, at the same time, the most tremendous pressure and anxiety because we have no rules. Straight married couples don't have to figure out the rules. And we have to figure them out every god-damned day.

Deborah: What's exciting is also stressful.

JoAnn: Very stressful. I think it's one of the biggest reasons our relationships collapse. Lesbians get into mourning about the fact that our relationships don't last as long as heterosexuals'. We all have the obvious reasons why they don't. But what I'm seeing is that we often have lifelong polyfidelous relationships. (Not all of us, of course. There are certainly lovers that I never want to see again, but...) I often say lesbians wouldn't have this problem if we didn't define every live-in lover as a committed lifelong partner. I think lesbians move in together as a way of dating. If we saw this as dating, we wouldn't be in such distress when we moved apart.

My first lover and I...I just talked to her this morning. We have been intimate friends for 19 years. We are absolutely connected up, absolutely tight, absolutely the sweetest hearts ever, and will forever be that way. Barring some unforeseen huge thing, I can't imagine what would ever tear us apart. She has a lover of many years with whom I am also quite close. We are going to have a lifelong love relationship in which we will support each other as much as any married couple and maybe more so. We're not sexual—which a lot of heterosexual marriages aren't either. They just feel forced to live under the same roof and maintain what I call the cottage industry of raising the children.

Deborah: So, JoAnn, since you've written so much and spoken so much about lesbian sex, this interview wouldn't be complete if we didn't ask you about sex. How do you compare sex as a wife with sex as a lesbian?

JoAnn: Sex? (JoAnn smiles broadly.) I actually always had good sex with men. I enjoyed it. I was orgasmic. I had fun. I was very careful not to choose aggressive or pushy men. I chose not necessarily wimps, but close to it. Sex with men was not very creative in my mind. A lot of statistics show that lesbians who have been with men sexually have more creative or varied sex lives than lesbians who've only been with other women. That's not my experience at all. I certainly had just fine sex with men, but with women my sex has always been much more fulfilling, much more deep, much more touching. I've certainly been able to have casual sex as a lesbian and, you know, have never regretted it, have never had a bad experience, although I'm sure there are lesbians who have. I just haven't. My sex life as a lesbian has been much more exciting and varied and just gets more so as I get older and have been out longer. It has definitely been true for me that my sex life has been much better, ten times better, because I have my heart and my soul available for being connected up.

I don't have any answers as to how to stand up to the expectations of the majority culture and the needs of our lesbian selves. I only know my life as a heterosexual woman cannot compare in any way to my life as a lesbian. I feel full, excited, and real now. I feel I have no limits to being who I am.

I love lesbians. I love the lesbian culture. Lesbians are my heroes, my family, my lovers, my friends.

Janell Moon with her son, 1970 and today.

New Year

Janell Moon

my son motions me to him
my lover wraps herself around me
they say "stay"

I remember walking
before them unsteady
on new ground
remember how he seemed like
an injured bird
when I first loved a woman
who lingered in dark edges
of her own

now time's gift gives us
this morning of the new year
with the smell of strong coffee
drifting through the house
fortune cookies left
on the blue lace tablecloth
scatter midnight's good
wishes all around.

I give him a patchwork quilt
made with pieces of our lives
give her kisses, keep her promises

he puts chocolates on my pillow
for after my nap
asks her to teach him how to drive a car
she reads his French book
he gives her his favorite Monkee record
and wears her flannel shirt

he gives us yeses
we give him a silver box
for treasures

I give her roses
she gives me lockets of love
they give me a family back
flowers in the heart

Arie Schwartz on her first honeymoon and today, left, with her partner.

Going Our Way

ARIE SCHWARTZ

The Beginning

When I heard she'd moved into my New Jersey neighborhood, I wasn't interested. If anything, I was irritated. Not just another family, the third Schwartz family in a four-block area. More confusion for the post office, telephone company, and delivery services. More aggravation for me.

A friend of mine met the new Schwartzes. "The wife is very nice," she said, offering to introduce us. A Welcome Wagon dropout, I replied, "Give her my number. If she calls, I'll invite her for coffee." But she didn't, and I forgot about it.

A few months later the same friend, aware I was a feminist, said, "You really ought to meet Jill Schwartz. She went to a N.O.W. meeting." A N.O.W. meeting? Without me? NOW I was interested. Could she be another suburban housewife whose conversation didn't focus on how well the new drapes matched the sofa pattern or how her husband liked his dinner cooked? I called and invited her over.

Our first conversation lasted a lifetime. We discussed the women's movement, role models for children, stereotypes in politics and the arts, our feelings about womanhood in the '70s. Jill was in the throes of a new self-awareness; I was impressed with her insights. We were so much alike, it was déja vu. She was me five years earlier.

She hardly mentioned her husband during our four-hour dialogue but often spoke with glowing devotion of a friend she'd left behind in Chicago. Odd, I thought, that she should talk so little of the spouse and so much of the friend. Very odd. I, myself, a reluctant born-again heterosexual, had deserted the lesbian ranks ten years earlier to marry and start a family. This was, after all, a time when gay was hardly a household word, and even gay women choked on the "L" word; a time when shame, not pride, was the feeling associated with many people's homosexual orientation.

Nonetheless, I was immediately smitten with Jill and could barely contain my desire. In a matter of weeks we became best friends. She confessed to an "involvement" with her Chicago friend; I confessed I wanted more than friendship. But it wasn't that easy. (It never is.) In short order, Jill had gone from faithful but unhappy wife, to falling in love with a woman (her first lesbian relationship), to being pursued by a lustful gadfly—me. It was more than she could handle, and she told me so. I recognized she had feelings for me that went beyond friendship, feelings she could not openly acknowledge, but I also recognized the emotional roller coaster she was on. Taking the highroad, I backed off. Ironically, doing so precipitated a fear on her part of losing me, ultimately adding a sexual dimension to our already enormous emotional attachment. A few months later, she terminated the Chicago connection. And so began a very intense love affair, now in its 18th year. Things got hot in our households, too.

The Affair

Unbeknownst to us, Jill's husband had intercepted love letters from Chicago, and was listening in on our phone calls. He confronted us about our affair. It wasn't your everyday confrontation; he wanted a piece of the action, suggesting a ménage à trois. When we demurred, he threatened to inform the neighborhood and our families. Nice guy.

Jill was between a rock and a hard place, wanting to leave her husband but having few marketable job skills and three small children, including a severely retarded daughter. One evening, following an argument in which he tried to physically harm her, I told Jill to pack up the kids and move into my house. It was early in our relationship; rational was not the operative word. They came, staying with my husband, son and me for three months. Each night I left my husband's bed and went to Jill's. Lust is powerful, obliterating logic and common sense. My husband knew what was going on; even today, I marvel at his restraint. Eventually, Bill exploded. He never used the word "lesbian," but let me know, in no uncertain terms, my lover could no longer take refuge in our home. Reluctantly, Jill returned to Bob, promising to end our affair. He insisted they sell their house and leave the neighborhood. They purchased a townhouse 20 miles away. At that point, a hundred miles wouldn't have kept us apart.

We planned to continue our relationship surreptitiously, save money from our household allowances and my part-time job, and leave our husbands in ten years when our sons were in college and Susan was old enough for placement in a residential facility.

After a few months, ten years seemed like forever. Jill's marriage was filled with animosity; mine, while not as tense, had only one common thread—our love for our six-year-old son. I made plans; I returned to my former full-time job, informing Bill I wanted a separation. We set up a schedule; he would leave at the end of the school year so Greg would have the summer months to begin adjusting to the change in our lives.

Jill's husband, acknowledging their marriage was over, began dating. He found a girlfriend, moved in with her and agreed to pay temporary child support until a permanent amount was negotiated. Jill found work near home and an after-school sitter for the children, a woman who grew to love Susan and watched her for almost ten years.

The Divorce

Our separations and divorces were as different as night and day. Initially, to avoid heated arguments, Bill and I communicated through letters, working out terms of our settlement. These were drawn into a formal agreement, later incorporated into our no-fault divorce. We were in no hurry to divorce because of the benefits of filing a joint tax return. By the time we officially divorced in 1981, five years after my relationship with Jill began, Bill and I were amicable enough to sit together in the courtroom. Bill is a pretty nice guy; once he accepted the end of our marriage, his primary concern was to not lose his relationship with his son, and he didn't. Except for holidays, neither of us ever invoked the visitation clause of our divorce. He saw Greg often, including overnight visits and vacations together. Together, we went to school events and visitors' days at camp.

Jill's husband refused a no-fault divorce, using our relationship as a wedge in their negotiations. Jill sued for divorce in 1977 on grounds of mental cruelty, requesting custody and child support. Bob countersued, charging mental cruelty and adultery. I was named as co-respondent. The shocker was that he asked for custody of the children, the same children he'd barely bothered with when they lived together. On the advice of his attorney, he began playing the dedicated, concerned father. Privately he told Jill that, because of what she had done to him, he would rather take the children and pay a full-time housekeeper to watch them than give her custody. Jill was devastated. The possible loss of her children was something she couldn't deal with. Bob knew this; he counted on it.

We mounted a precedent-setting case. Doing all the research and legwork ourselves to save legal fees, we found state-of-the-art witnesses, psychologists and sociologists who had studied and written about lesbian families. They were prepared to testify that two lesbians can provide a warm, loving home for their children without raising them, heaven forbid, to become homosexual. We were examined, tested and evaluated by a prominent New York City psychologist who would testify that our lifestyle and sexual preference were not likely to affect our children's psyches. The presiding judge ordered all of us—including the children—interviewed by a Social Services investigator. The report was to be submitted to the court with a recommendation regarding custody of the children. Jill had straight friends of longstanding prepared to testify to her stability as a parent and her husband's prior indifference to his children.

On the morning of the trial, the judge called the attorneys into chambers. He informed them the Social Services report strongly favored Jill retaining custody of the children. The judge had also contacted Lambda Legal Defense and the Gay Activists Alliance in New York for their input. By no means was the judge liberal; he was seeking a legal precedent for awarding custody to homo-sexual parents. There was none in New Jersey or New York at that time. He directed the parties to try to negotiate a settlement.

For the next two days, Jill's attorney demonstrated his worth or, in this case, worthlessness...spinelessness also comes to mind. He advised and pushed her to accept all child support as "unallocated sums," making the payments tax deductible for Bob and taxable for Jill. He also allowed Bob to claim the children as his dependents. Bob insisted on a clause in the divorce agreement saying in the event his sons wished to pursue higher education, he would not pay for them to attend a private university. So, if they were accepted to Harvard or Yale they could only attend if their mother could pay for it; state university was what he'd pay for. Some of this came up at the last minute in the courtroom. Adding insult to injury, Bob, who had requested Wednesday night visitations with his children, in addition to every other weekend, told the judge he might not wish to exercise that privilege. This from the man who lived two blocks away and had filed suit requesting custody.

Whenever Jill disagreed or objected, her lawyer addressed her through clenched teeth while snapping pencils in half with his hands. Where was I while this was happening? Right there. It was not one of my shining moments. Why did we allow this to happen? Keep in mind this was the '70s. The stress and pressure lawyers and judges exerted on women in divorce matters, lesbians in particular, was unimaginable. The essential atmosphere in the courtroom was hostility toward Jill and myself; the unspoken message: "You're lucky to keep your children. Don't push us." In the end, Jill lost virtually everything but the kids.

When the divorce was final, we were so upset we could barely function. The legal system, with its preponderance of male judges and lawyers, was clearly stacked against women. It's just beginning to change.

Together At Last

By agreement, we sold the houses we owned with our husbands and purchased a small townhouse near the one Jill had owned with her husband. Her kids had been shuffled around too much in the past three years; she wanted to stay put for a while. It made sense.

The new house had only three bedrooms. We gave the boys the master bedroom, which was big enough for all their furniture with an area left for play. Susan got one of the small bedrooms, we took the other. For months, if I got up at night, I walked into a wall.

An adjustment period began. There were problems to work out; much healing was needed.

As housewives, before we lived together, we'd had abundant free time. The radical changes brought about by full-time jobs and the mental drain of the divorce put tremendous strain on all of us. We had not foreseen how different life would be. I left an eight-room colonial, housing three persons, for a six-room townhouse with six people. I was accustomed to ample space, both physical and mental. There was nowhere I could go to be alone, to clear my head and regain my perspective. Even little things were upsetting. To my chagrin, Jill had apparently failed Dishwasher Loading 101 and Basic Towel Folding; I had a Ph.D. in both. You don't notice these things at the beginning, in what I call the "Period of Denial." When you finally stop jumping into bed at every opportunity, reality sets in. We argued about everything. I insisted, she resisted.

There were confrontations over who showered first in the morning, how much time was spent in the bathroom by whom, the boys' choice of clothing, who left an empty cereal box out, who couldn't find his homework. The last thing we wanted was to send our kids to school with anger reverberating in their ears. In fact, that's what they got much of the time.

Once we lived together, my focus changed from Jill to my son. I felt he needed more attention. He was in a new house, new neighborhood, new school. Greg thought he was gaining two brothers and a sister. It didn't work out that way. Before we lived together, the boys were good friends. Now, Ricky and Michael stayed closer together, often excluding Greg from their activities. I was aware they blamed me for the breakup of their household. They couldn't take out their resentment on me, so they transferred it to Greg. I'd like to say I was mature and handled it well. In truth, I gave them a hard time for treating Greg poorly. It was not textbook behavior, but probably common in step-parent/step-children situations, gay or straight.

Jill was smothering me. Early on, she was so insecure, I couldn't go to the bathroom alone. She resented the time I gave Greg. Actually, I think resentment was the key element in our house for the first year. Everyone resented everyone else. It was far from the "happily ever after" we'd imagined before her divorce.

We set aside family time with the kids. We had family meetings in the form of open seminars, where anyone could bring up anything. Unlike the Brady Bunch, our kids viewed these meetings as a penance to be endured. We played board games and cards, read stories, rented movies. We took them to museums, parks, concerts, and the theatre, trying to ingrain in them our middle-class values. During part of the summer, all the kids went to camp. Jill and I usually took our vacation then, although the quiet at home was vacation enough for me.

Some children never fully recover from the shock of their parents divorcing. Jill's ex was old-fashioned and traditional. He didn't cook, clean, feed, bathe or play with his children. He rarely bothered with them before the divorce. He was more taken with his ability to impregnate his wife than with parenting his offspring. He attributed his son's cleft lip and his daughter's Down's Syndrome to an imperfection in Jill, never acknowledging that *together* they were genetically mismatched. Not that he didn't love his children. I believe he did—at least the boys. But he didn't understand parenting, and didn't try.

After the divorce, Bob became "Mr. Nice Guy" to his kids. It's not hard when you see them two days every two weeks. Following his contractual obligation, he took them every other weekend from 8 p.m. Friday night until 8 p.m. Sunday night. In between he never called, although we encouraged the boys to phone him. They invited him to school functions and Little League games; he rarely came. After weekend visitations, Ricky and Michael came home wound tighter than alarm clocks. They were cranky, moody, and overtired. They'd had too much freedom and too little supervision. Sunday nights were upsetting. They were dirty and disheveled, and often returned wearing the same clothing they'd left in Friday night. Little Susan looked like a ragamuffin; the boys were too young to care for her and their father and new stepmother gave her minimal attention. Susan, thankfully, couldn't understand the divorce and its ramifications.

With Greg, we had different problems. He returned upset at having to leave his father. Greg suffered from childhood migraines. After a while, I could predict that every other Monday he would have a migraine headache. In addition, the weekend separation was cause for conflict between Jill's boys and Greg over who had done more or had a better time. A jealousy factor crept into their relationship because Bill didn't restrict his visits to every other weekend. He called regularly, often took Greg out during the week, came to school events and Little League. He visited Greg at summer camp and took him on separate vacations. Because Jill's ex was untrustworthy and difficult, she projected these faults onto Bill. For years, she refused to allow him past the entrance hall of our home, much to my chagrin.

Things improved enormously when Jill's ex-husband died unexpectedly (no, I did not take out a contract on him). We no longer had to worry about timely support payments or disputed expenses which he refused to reimburse. Jill got a monthly Social Security check for the children, the benefits were non-taxable, and she could now claim the children as her dependents on her tax return. The "Doting Dad" left none of his sizable estate to his children. NOTHING. His second wife became a wealthy widow. On behalf of the children, Jill received the proceeds of a small insurance policy Bob was required to keep as part of the divorce settlement. The money wasn't enough to put even one child through college. Thankfully, scholarships and student loans were available.

Coming Out

I had come out in my late teens and lived a lesbian life for several years before marrying. Mostly, I married to have children. For lesbian couples, artificial insemination was not then the common practice it is today. In my heart I knew my marriage was a façade. The first clue was my ongoing attraction to other women. But until I met Jill, I had no compelling reason to end my marriage. With her, I was struck by lightning.

A short while after Jill and I became lovers, my parents separated after 45 years of marriage. My mother, in her 60's, was going through a rough time. She felt alone and humiliated. Right around that time my sister, who had come out a few years earlier, decided to reveal her sexual orientation to Mom. She thought it important for Mom to understand her lifestyle and accept her live-in lover as her spouse. I thought it a less than propitious time to come out to Mom. Nonetheless, she did. Shortly after, my mother and I had the following conversation:

Mom: "What do you think about Sandy and her 'friend'?"

Me: "Whatever makes her happy is what Sandy should do."

Mom: "I thought you'd say that. You've always been very liberal."

Then she looked at me. I could see the light dawn. "You're that way, too, aren't you?"

"Yes, Mom, I am."

Here's my mother, a 66-year-old "till death-do-us-part" woman whose husband has left her, with one divorced and one about-to-be-divorced daughter (all firsts in our family) whom she now learns are lesbians (more firsts). I thought she'd go into the kitchen and put her head in the oven.

Eighteen years later, Mom handles our relationship well. She can barely say "gay," still chokes on the "L" word and refers to our friends as "your people." But we're far more open with her than we could have been years ago.

Our children, and my sister's, are now adults. They're comfortable with our relationship because they grew up with it. Jill and I are close with all of them. When our grandniece was born, our nephew and his wife flew to Florida to show off the newborn. We doted on the baby like two old biddies, argued over whose turn it was to hold her, like two little kids. Our nephew and his wife treat us lovingly, their two eccentric aunts.

Jill has a large family. Early on, we told her sister who, in turn, related the news to Jill's mother, brother, a lesbian cousin, and probably a few dozen other people. Jill's mother reacted with anger. She all but accused me of casting an evil spell over her innocent daughter, then told Jill to choose between us, which she did; they didn't speak for a year. When her mother finally accepted our relationship, she worked hard at coming to terms with it. Jill and her Mom are close now. Her mother is extremely nice to me, and I have genuine affection for her.

Overall, our relationship is subtly acknowledged by Jill's family. I am generally recognized and treated as her spouse. Still, when her brother was married four years ago, my son and I were invited to the wedding but not asked to stand beside Jill when the groom's family was photographed.

When we were first together, we had no gay friends. Through N.O.W., we learned of gay and lesbian organizations and conferences, and began attending. Some of the groups were formed by radical lesbian feminists, whose philosophy and politics differed from ours. Males were excluded from their agenda; we did not want to exclude half the population from our lives, not only because of our sons, but because we like men. We just happen to love women.

We felt a need for lesbian friends, especially women with children. We joined a lesbian rap group and occasionally went to gay bars, mostly because Jill wanted to see what they were like. Several of our friends were lesbians with children. Sharing experiences with them gave us reassurance that our problems were not insurmountable and our kids were okay. These friendships were much needed; eighty percent of our waking hours were spent in business or community environments pretending to be heterosexual in the company of straights.

Eventually, all of our straight friends knew of our relationship; some were told, others surmised and asked. We knew the real test of friendship lay in their willingness to accept us as we were rather than what we thought they wanted us to be. That worked pretty well. We lost only one friendship to the truth.

We did not come out to the neighbors. We told them we were two divorced women with children sharing a home. We acted like friends, because we were. When we argued, if the shouting got loud, I'd rush around the house closing windows so the neighbors wouldn't hear. At work, and away from home, we fabricated tales: "I live with my sister," or (a favorite), "We're the original Kate and Allie." Because of their limited access to your personal life, co-workers, acquaintances, even relatives know only what you choose to tell them. Not neighbors. They see you every day, without your makeup, your mask and your armor. For the most part, our neighbors were nice. If we were the subject of lesbian jokes or unkind remarks, it was without our knowledge. We assumed our respectable straight front was working. For a long time we had no idea the neighbors knew all about us.

One Halloween, we came home to find "Lezzie" scrawled in soap on one of our cars. Angry and upset, in the safety of our home, we chastised the ignorant, bigoted parents who had ingrained this homophobia into their children. Our boys, now teenagers, told us over the years they'd been teased a number of times by chums and schoolmates about our lesbianism. When we asked why they hadn't told us, they replied, "There isn't anything you could have done. We had to handle it ourselves." They were right. We'd had many conversations with them about the inequities of life and people who are narrow-minded and unkind. We said difficult situations would arise and they'd have to deal with them. They did, and we're proud of them.

With our children all having the same last name, and attending the same schools, there was considerable confusion among the teaching staff about who belonged to whom. All three boys were in the school district's program for gifted and talented students. Their teachers marveled at them. We hope they thought the "lezzies" were doing something right.

A straight couple and their daughter lived a few doors away from us. Occasionally, we socialized, mostly on summer evenings when we sat outside talking. I don't think we were in each other's homes more than twice in eight years. When the husband, in his early 40's, died suddenly of a heart attack, Jill went to pay a sympathy call on the wife. While they were talking, she took Jill's hand and said, "Walter always stood up for you girls." We were touched. Walter, we hardly knew you. Thanks.

Money and Work

Once things fell into place in our personal relationship, we wanted more: to be totally in charge of our lives. While working our regular jobs, we opened a small weekend business in a flea market. After a few years of learning retail, we were ready to make the leap into a full-time business. We left our regular jobs and opened a store. This was one of the scariest times in our lives. Also, one of the most exciting. We knew we were taking a risk, but what is life about if not taking risks? Besides, it wasn't the first time we'd thrown caution to the wind.

We had our business for ten years. The shopping center in which it was located was sold to a new owner, a poor businessman who ran it into the ground. Business fell off, the economy turned sour. Ultimately, we were forced to close our store; losing just about everything. We were depressed, feeling cheated and angry.

We were also between a rock and a hard place: two middle-aged, educated women, with plenty of life experience, asking ourselves what we wanted to be when we grew up—again.

We decided to move to Florida. New environment, new start, new hope.

Today

The children are grown and on their own. Life is different. In our new South Florida setting, there is a large, active gay and lesbian community. We've undergone some very positive changes. I began writing, and discovered both a style and an audience. Jill and I finally emerged from the closet, tentatively at first, then completely. We don't introduce ourselves saying, "Hi, we're Jill and Arie, and we're lesbians," but when people ask about our relationship, we're forthright. Being open and out has increased our self-esteem immeasurably. We came to realize it wasn't other people's homophobia we feared, but our own. You have to like who you are before other people can.

Our children turned out well, not unlike others emerging into adulthood from non-traditional homes. They're no different from their friends who have two straight parents. Our children, making their own choices, are all heterosexual and accepting of other lifestyles. We are concerned about one, though - we think he may be a closet Republican!

Although we have no finances to fall back on, life is good. What we have with each other is more important than money or possessions. People often say to us, "You two have figured it all out." Not really. We still fight. In fact, I think we thrive on a good argument. There's no finite amount of garbage a relationship can't tolerate. The world is far from perfect, and so are we. What we have figured out is to not draw an imaginary line and say, "Once you cross over, we're done." The line moves constantly, sometimes all the way to the wall with our backs against it.

We acknowledge each other's faults and attributes. We say we're sorry to each other; we think that's important. We pretty much don't stand on ceremony. And, WE DON'T KEEP SCORE. When we take stock of the good and bad times we've had, the positive ones always outweigh the negative. Every relationship gets bad after a while. If you hang around, it gets good again. For me, it's worth everything to have those good times with Jill.

Our sex life is active. We've heard people speak of *lesbian bed death*, which supposedly occurs to couples after a few years. The term must be the mythical invention of a single lesbian; from speaking to others in long-term relationships, we know we are not an anomaly. *Lesbian bed death* is not an issue in our relationship; brain death will probably come first.

If you were to ask me what Jill's most endearing qualities are, I would choose words like generous, intelligent, good-natured, warmhearted, witty. She is a wonderful spouse and devoted parent.

We've been through a great deal in eighteen years; times when we barely coped; times when the stress of merging our lives and families made me wonder if we would survive. Jill has endured more heartache and tribulation than anyone should have to. I have dealt with severe bouts of depression throughout my life, much as my father did.

The reality of losing our business and everything we owned was, at first, devastating. But we survived. We have our family, our friends, each other. I have the love and devotion of a woman I would die for—still, after all these years. Somehow, we'll get through the "what if's" of tomorrow and the next day. We've got a special love, something few are blessed with. I feel so very, very lucky.

Contributors' Notes

BLAKE C. AARENS "I am the granddaughter of Dicy and the daughter of Cobia. I am a lesbian of African descent whose best friend on the planet is her blond, blue-eyed, Jewish ex-husband. I am a survivor of childhood sexual abuse who writes award-winning erotic fiction. I am a working artist in search of her tribe. My fiction has been published in *Open Wide, Aché: A Journal for Lesbians of African Descent, Herotica 2 & 3*, and one of my *Aché* stories appears in *The Best American Erotica for 1993.*"

PAULINE B. BART is a professor of sociology and will be teaching at the University of California at Los Angeles after retiring from the University of Illinois at Chicago. She has written about depressed middle-aged women in "Portnoy's Mother's Complaint," a feminist illegal abortion collective in "Seizing the Means of Reproduction," and women who were attacked and avoided rape in "Stopping Rape: Successful Survival Strategies," as well as other articles, has co-authored the *Student Sociologists' Handbook* and edited, with Eileen Moran, *Violence Against Women: The Bloody Footprints* an award-winning book. She received the first Feminist Activism Award from Sociologists for Women in Society, henceforth to be called the Pauline B. Bart Feminist Activism award.

ELLEN BASS has published several volumes of poetry including *For Earthly Survival* and *Our Stunning Harvest*. She is also co-author of *The Courage to Heal*. She lives with her partner of 12 years, Janet, and their two children.

CHRISTINE BERRIER has published stories in *Afterglow: More Stories of Lesbian Desire* and *Common Lives/Lesbian Lives*. She is pursuing a Ph.D. in English with a concentration in women, gender and literature at the University of Texas at Austin.

KATHLEEN BOATWRIGHT uses her conventional appearance, her status as a mother of four, her Christian roots, her knowledge of scriptures, and her disarming personal warmth to wage a gentle battle for reform in the church she loves—and to change the hearts and minds of individuals within the church.

ELTEASER "TINA" J. BUTTRY is a volunteer counselor and group facilitator at the Gay and Lesbian Service Center and a freelance writer living in the San Fernando Valley.

MARGARETHE CAMMERMEYER, a Colonel in the U.S. Army, earned a Bronze Star for duty in Vietnam, and served as Chief Nurse of the Washington State National Guard, marking a long and distinguished military career. Her goal to become Chief Nurse of the entire National Guard was abruptly ended in 1992 by her discharge based on sexual orientation. Colonel Cammermeyer made a decision to challenge the official policy on homosexuality and earned a recent victory in Federal District Court. *Serving in Silence*—a book and film telling her story—has been recently released. Colonel Cammermeyer lives in Seattle, Washington with her family.

PATSY CHU wishes to remain anonymous.

GALE (SKY) EDEAWO is a freelance writer and poet who writes mostly for and about women. She has been writing since 1972 and has been published in the U.S. as well as abroad. She is former poetry editor of *The Cauldron*, a women's periodical, and is presently contributing editor and columnist for *The Dyke Review Quarterly*.

ROBIN FINLEY, a native of Anchorage, Alaska, has lived throughout the U.S. and Canada. Currently, she resides on the Chesapeake Bay. She divides her time between working as an artist and supporting herself as an editor.

MARGE FRANTZ has taught American studies, women's studies, and history at the University of California, Santa Cruz, for twenty years. She's now retired but continues to teach a course or two every year. Before UCSC, she did civil rights work, labor organizing and was a senior editor at the Institute of Industrial Relations, University of California, Berkeley.

NANAY GABRIEL is a pseudonym.

TERRY HAMILTON is an African American lesbian writer, activist, mother, community organizer. "Under my pen name, Terry Love, I contributed to *There's Something I've Been Meaning to Tell You* and *Parents Matter*."

DR. ZANDRA JOHNSON-ROLÓN is a chiropractor with a private practice in Santa Cruz, California. She is politically active, serving on the national board of LLEGO (Latina Lesbian and Gay Organization). She and her partner, Deborah Johnson, have appeared in *Making History* and *Ceremonies of the Heart*. She notes with irony: "Even though I've been married to a woman for 13 years, my brief marriage to a man will always be considered more legitimate. When I die, society will probably consider me single."

JOANNA KADI is a writer. Her first book, *Food For Our Grandmothers: Writings by Arab-American and Arab Canadian Feminists*, was published in October, 1994 by South End Press. She burned her wedding pictures the evening before her commitment ceremony with her lover, Jan.

SHIRLEY KNIGHT-LÓPEZ was born in central California in 1940. She is the mother of four grown children, teaches at E.A. Hall Middle School in Watsonville, California, and is the AIDS Specialist for the Pájaro Valley Unified School District. In 1993, she made a life commitment to Judith Rickard.

SHARON KNOX-MANLEY was born in Brunswick, Maine, attended parochial and regular schools, married at age 17, and by 25 had four beautiful children.

"Lately, with my partner, Pam, I have organized women's softball and basketball leagues for our small town. I also volunteer in women's crisis support services."

ANN D. KWONG is the eldest daughter of Chinese immigrants. She grew up in the midwest and currently lives on the east coast with her lover/spouse. She shares parenting responsibilities of her daughter with her former husband in a joint custody arrangement. She has been active in Asian Lesbians of the East Coast, the Asian Pacific Lesbian and Bisexual Network, and the Metropolitan Community Church of New York.

ZANNIE KYD is a professor at a midwestern university. Since her second coming out she has spent many happy hours catching up on all things lesbian: music, novels, separatism, festivals, philosophy, potlucks, politics, marches, symbols, spirituality, female friendships. She lives in loving and joyful relationship with her partner.

JOAN LARKIN is the author of two collections of poetry, *Housework* and *A Long Sound* (and a play in poems, *Currents in a Cold River*, about AIDS.) She co-edited the anthologies *Amazon Poetry* and *Lesbian Poetry* with Elly Bulkin, and *Gay and Lesbian Poetry in Our Time* with Carl Morse. She lives in western Massachusetts.

STELLA LOPEZ-ARMIJO is a hard-working, rowdy and religious woman. Born into a large Mexican-American family, she grew up in Albuquerque, New Mexico and San Leandro and Oakland, California. At 18, Stella joined another family by going to work in a close-knit factory. She married a man from the factory at 21 and had four children. At 32 she was divorced; at 34 she entered the gay life; and at 42 she became a grandmother. Stella met Ina in 1980. Stella is now 60 and has been with Ina for 15 years.

JOANN LOULAN is a mother, lesbian, and psychotherapist in private practice in Portola Valley, California. She is the author of *Lesbian Sex, Lesbian Passion, The Lesbian Erotic Dance*, and the coauthor of *Period*. She presents lectures and workshops throughout the United States and Canada on issues of lesbian sex, health, and self-esteem.

BETTYE MARVEL was born in 1936 in a small southern Indiana town. She graduated high school in 1954, and got married (heterosexual) in 1957. She married (lesbian) in 1992. "I am a homebody and enjoy puttering with mechanical things. I enjoy writing, walking, bike riding, and playing sports. My partner, Chris, and I love our life and our families. We look forward to each new day together as we go gaily forward."

JANELL MOON is in private practice as a hypnotherapist in San Francisco and a workshop instructor at the College of Marin. She is cofounder of a San Francisco art and writing salon, *Sunday's Child*. Her poetry has appeared in *Beyond*

Definition: An Anthology of Gay and Lesbian San Francisco Writings by manic d'press, *Bound by Diversity* by Sebastian Press, and *Out From Under* by Alyson Press. Her chapbook, *Woman with a Cleaver*, is available in San Francisco bookstores.

MARJORY NELSON is a 66-year-old fat white lesbian living in San Francisco whose writings about her life appear in many anthologies including *Shadow on a Tightrope: Writings of Fat Women, Women of the 14th Moon, Sexual Harassment: Women Speak Out*, and *Long Time Passing*. She has also had articles in *Broomstick, Sojourner, Sinister Wisdom, Common Lives/Lesbian Lives*, and *Womanspirit*. She is part of the San Francisco Women's Building History Project.

ESTHER O'DONALD lives with her wife, Mary Ann (they both refer to themselves as wives, thank you!), their cats, dogs, goats, and one house rabbit in a quiet rural community south of Missoula, Montana where they operate a thriving pet-sitting business. They are happily "out," working for gay rights and the repeal of Montana's deviate sexual conduct law. Life is good.

EKUA OMOSUPE is southern born and raised. She is mother of three children and a grandmother of two. Ekua lives in Santa Cruz, California and teaches at Cabrillo College in Aptos. She is part owner of an ethnic jewelry and crafts business, MAKUA Productions. Ekua is presently writing a dissertation: "The Politics of Constructing Black Lesbian Identities in the U.S."

SHARON 'JOH' PALOMA "I was born in Ft. Worth, Texas on March 12, 1944. I'm a woman who celebrates being a lesbian. I want to help future generations of lesbians by being 'out and visible' in my daily living. I've left the fast lane of Respiratory Therapy and made the decision to work a simple job and live a simple life. I'm married to my best friend, and our life is full and happy here in Ashland, Oregon. This story is lovingly dedicated to Harriett, who taught me the true meaning of courage. I'll always love you."

JUANA MARIA GONZALEZ PAZ is a New York born Puerto Rican lesbian and former welfare mother, with a special interest in lesbian feminist community-based education and lesbian land. Currently living on a commune in Luisa, Virginia, she is the author of a book on lesbian of color land and offers workshops called Womyn, Values and Community.

MINNIE BRUCE PRATT is the author of *S/he*, stories of gender boundary crossing, published by Firebrand this year. Her other books include *Crime Against Nature*, the 1989 Lamont Poetry Selection of the American Academy of Poets, *Rebellion: Essays 1981–1992* and *We Say We Love Each Other*. She lives in Jersey City, New Jersey.

MARGARET RANDALL lives and writes in Albuquerque, New Mexico. Among her books are *This is About Incest, Dancing With the Doe, Gathering Rage: The*

Failure of Twentieth Century Revolutions to Develop a Feminist Agenda, Sandino's Daughters Revisited, and *Our Voices, Our Lives: Stories of Women from Central America and the Caribbean.* For the past several years she has been working on a book about women and money, which Routledge will bring out in 1996.

MARDI RICHMOND spends her work-time writing, editing and teaching; her play-time boogie boarding, taking long walks, and planting flowers. She is once again married, this time to a woman, and is definitely living happily ever after.

ROBIN TERESA SANTOS, a second-generation Portuguese-American, was born in Oakland, California. She grew up in a family with a strong narrative tradition; as a child her favorite pastime was to sit beneath her grandmother's grape arbor and listen to stories about the old country. Robin is currently working on a novel about the experiences of a Peace Corps volunteer in Nicaragua in the early 1970's. She says: "In writing this retrospective narrative, I've struggled with the very things I wanted to write about: fear, self-denial and containment. These *fantasmas antigos* became obstacles to telling the story, which like those obstacles to coming out, I eventually overcame."

ARIE SCHWARTZ is a freelance writer living in south Florida with her life partner. They have been together since 1976. Her syndicated columns "View From the Other Side" and "Women's Wit and Wisdom," appear regularly in lesbian and gay publications throughout the country. Her feature stories and essays have been published in numerous newspapers and magazines including *Ten Percent, Christopher Street, Windy City Times, The Fountain,* the *Philadelphia Gay News, Class, TWN,* and the *Sun Sentinel.*

JACSUN J. SHAH a Houston resident, is an M.F.A. graduate student in the creative writing program at the University of Houston and teaches creative writing to elementary school students through Writers In The Schools. She shares a home with a feminist activist and two Persian cats.

ELLEN SYMONS "I am a white, anti-racist dyke in my early thirties, living in Ottawa. Between paid work, selling environmentally safe menstrual products with my lover, and hanging out at women's dances, I tell myself the stories about lesbians I wish I'd read before I got married."

KAREN TAKATA "is not my real name. While talking recently to my father, I mentioned this project and my piece. He requested, out of consideration to my mother who is still struggling to accept her lesbian daughter, that I use a fictitious name. I was born in San Francisco and have lived in California all my life. At one time passionate about painting, my time is now devoted to parenting. Over the years, I have had help along the way from people I never really thanked: my good friends Pilar, Sharon, Beth; Robin, who always listened and rarely gave advice; my sister and brother; my former husband and his mother; my children and of course, Laurie. Thank you."

REVA TALLEYGRONE is the pen name of a writer who grew up in the Pacific Northwest where she teaches English at a community college. She lives with her companion and is the mother of two grown sons. Reva has published in *Portland Review*, *Northwest Magazine*, and *Calyx*, and is working on a collection of stories.

KAY WARDWELL "I'm in a Ph.D. program at the University of New Mexico, studying noncanonical literature. My favorite things to do include backpacking and kayaking. I am teaching at a college in the Southwest and have a novel in progress."

JOANNE WAROBICK "I was 27 when I came out, working as an R.N. in oncology. In the ten years since, I have survived a major earthquake, five years of chronic immune illness and a diagnosis of cancer. I'm becoming a lucky vagabond, a visionary artist and a lover, each day a crossroads of darkness and light."

MORGAN GRAYCE WILLOW has published under both this and her former, patriarchal name which was Nancy Weber. She has a chapbook entitled *Spinnerets*. Her work has appeared in *Hurricane Alice*, *Sinister Wisdom*, *The Evergreen Chronicles*, *Moving Out*, and others. She has three collections in manuscript currently seeking homes

TRISTAN WONG wishes to remain anonymous.

Further Reading

This wide-ranging list of books helped inform our work. We came to the task of editing with many of the unconscious assumptions of white women. On our quest for understanding, we gratefully, although sometimes awkwardly, grew in our ability to approach a larger vision of society.

Alarcón, Norma; Castillo, Ana; Moraga, Cherríe. *The Sexuality of Latinas.* Berkeley: Third Woman Press, 1991.

Albrecht, Lisa and Brewer, Rose M. *Bridges of Power: Women's Multicultural Alliances.* Philadelphia: New Society Publishers, 1990

Alpert, Harriet. *We Are Everywhere.* Freedom, CA: The Crossing Press, 1988.

Anzalduá, Gloria. *Borderlands: The New Mestiza = La Frontera.* San Francisco: Spinsters/Aunt Lute, 1987.

Brant, Beth. *Gathering of Spirit.* Ithaca, NY: Firebrand,1988.

Cade, Cathy. *A Lesbian Photo Album: the Lives of Seven Lesbian Feminists.* Waterwoman Books, 1987.

Cassingham, Barbee and O'Neil, Sally. *And Then I Met This Woman.* Mother Courage Press, 1993.

Chung, C., Kim, A., Lemeshewsky, A.K. *Between the Lines.* Dancing Bird Press, 1987.

Faderman, Lillian. *Odd Girls and Twilight Lovers: A History of Lesbian Life in Twentieth-Century America.* New York: Penguin, 1991.

Grahn, Judy. *Another Mother Tongue: Gay Words, Gay Worlds.* Boston: Beacon Press, 1984.

Gunn Allen, Paula. *The Sacred Hoop.* Boston: Beacon Press, 1992.

Johnson, Sonia. *Going Out of Our Minds: The Metaphysics of Liberation.* Freedom, CA: The Crossing Press, 1987.

Joseph, Gloria I. and Lewis, Jill. *Common Differences: Conflicts in Black and White Feminist Perspectives.* Garden City, NY: Anchor Books, 1981.

Lewin, Ellen. *Lesbian Mothers: Accounts of Gender in American Culture.* Ithaca, NY,: Cornell University Press, 1993.

Lim-Hing, Sharon. *The Very Inside. An Anthology of Writing by Asian and Pacific Islander Lesbian and Bisexual Women.* Toronto: Sister Vision Press, 1994.

Lorde, Audre. *Sister Outsider.* Freedom, CA: The Crossing Press, 1984.

Lorde, Audre. *A Burst of Light.* Ithaca, NY: Firebrand Books, 1988.

Lorde, Audre. *Zami: A New Spelling of My Name.* Watertown, MA: Persephone Press, 1982.

Marcus, Eric. *Making History: The Struggle for Gay and Lesbian Equal Rights, 1945-1990*. New York: Harper Collins, 1992.

Moraga, Cherríe and Anzaldúa, Gloria. *This Bridge Called My Back: Writings by Radical Women of Color*. Kitchen Table Press, 1983.

Morris, Jenny. *Alone Together: Voices of Single Mothers*. London: The Women's Press, 1992.

Pollack, Sandra and Vaughn, Jeanne. *Politics of the Heart: A Lesbian Parenting Anthology*. Ithaca, NY: Firebrand, 1987.

Rafkin, Louise. *Different Daughters: A Book by Mothers of Lesbians*. Pittsburgh: Cleis Press, 1987.

Rafkin, Louise. *Different Mothers: Sons and Daughters of Lesbians Talk About their Lives*. Pittsburgh: Cleis Press 1990.

Rich, Adrienne. *What is Found There. Notebooks on Poetry and Politics*. New York: Norton, 1993.

Rich, Adrienne. *Of Woman Born: Motherhood as Experience and Institution*. New York: W. W. Norton & Co., 1986.

Sange, Barbara; Warshaw, Joyce and Smith, Adrienne J. *Lesbians at Midlife: The Creative Transition*. Minneapolis: Spinsters Book Company, 1991.

Segrest, Mab. *Memoirs of a Race Traitor*. Boston: South End Press, 1994

Silvera, Makeda. *Piece of My Heart: A Lesbian of Colour Anthology*. Toronto: Sister Vision Press, 1992.

Sinister Wisdom Issue #52, Allies. Berkeley, CA: Sinister Wisdom, Inc., Spring/Summer 1994.

Smith, Barbara. *Home Girls: A Black Feminist Anthology*. New York: Kitchen Table: Women of Color Press, 1983.

Trujillo, Carla. *Chicana Lesbians; The Girls Our Mothers Warned Us About*. Berkeley: Third Woman Press, 1991.

Wiesen Cook, Blanche. *Eleanor Roosevelt, Volume One, 1884-1933*. New York: Morrow, 1992.

Note: For insight into the forces behind U.S. homophobia in the twentieth century: Summers, Anthony. *Official and Confidential: The Secret Life of J. Edgar Hoover*. New York: G.P. Putnam's Sons, 1993.

About the Editors

DEBORAH ABBOTT was born in 1953 in a small adobe house in a neighborhood of girls. She grew up with one sister, no brothers, a Dominant (read: confident and assertive) Mother, a Passive (read: kind and gentle) Father, and a Lesbian Aunt. When she was 22 she got pregnant; she married a very nice man, had two sons, and then one day—much to her astonishment—fell into bed with her best friend whom she had adored for years. She instantly realized she was a lesbian. For the past 13 years she has co-parented her sons with her ex-husband (who is still a very nice man). One week she lives in a world of reggae rhythms, adolescent boys and much laundry; the next week in the company of wonderful women friends, her lover, many books, and hardly any dishes. She is a licensed psychotherapist in private practice; and a published writer whose stories, poems, and essays have been widely anthologized. She lives in Santa Cruz, California.

ELLEN FARMER works as a senior editor at the University of California, Santa Cruz. She publishes poetry and gives readings in the San Francisco and Monterey Bay Areas. "When Deborah asked me to work on this book, attending the April '93 March on Washington was just a twinkle in my partner's eye. I was sort of out to a few people, but my transition from suburban married woman with kids to lesbian mom had gone mostly unnoticed except for the kind support of my lesbian moms' group and a few young dyke housemates. Now I've spoken with over 200 women on similar paths, and I feel strong in my conviction that we find the source of our personal power by acknowledging our own truths. Like so many of the authors in this volume, I had to unravel the knots of conventional wisdom and learn to live with a sometimes paralyzing fear of the unknown until my new and unique life as a lesbian took shape. I hope this book is useful."